4/12

3-77.

Emergency Verse

Poetry in Defence of the Welfare State

Selected and edited
with Forewords and Afterword
by **Alan Morrison**

featuring a dialectic
by **Norman Jope**

Patron
Caroline Lucas MP

First published as an e-book in 2010
First print publication 2011
by *Caparison*
imprint of
the Recusant
www.therecusant.org.uk

Printed in Armo Pro by
MPG Books Group,
Bodmin and King's Lynn

Cover design © Caparison 2010/2011
All illustrations © to the designated artists
Editing and design: Alan Morrison
Proofing and editorial assistance: Matilda Persson

ISBN 978-0-9567544-0-0

Contents

Poems in the Defence of the Welfare State

Invitation for the Government to Join the Fair Society:
An Alternative Budget and Response to the Spending Review

Emergency Verse is a literary campaign in defence of the Welfare State and the National Health Service and against the coalition Government's 'emergency' Budget, which it perceives as a return to the draconian politics of Thatcherism. *Emergency Verse* is as well a petition of 112 poets calling on this government to comprehensively amend its 'emergency' Budget to lift the burden of paying back the deficit *off* the narrowest shoulders and onto the broadest. *Emergency Verse* asks the Government, for the sake of our social democracy, to do the following:

Cancel or significantly lower the planned £18 Billion cuts from the welfare budget; reverse the move to tie benefit rates to the Consumer Price Index and reinstate their alignment with the Retail Price Index;
Significantly amend plans for mandatory assessments for all those on Incapacity Benefit and Disability Living Allowance by ensuring that those with mental health problems are not unfairly discriminated against through plans to scrap almost half of the already paltry 41 mental health descriptors in a new 'simplified test';
Cancel plans to restrict council house tenancies to five year terms;
Cancel plans to raise social housing rents to 80% of market value and to cap Housing Benefit (without first reintroducing rent controls), in order to avoid a massive increase in homelessness and social ghettoization;
Cancel plans to further privatise the National Health Service;
Reverse plans to cavalierly cut over 600,000 public sector jobs.

Emergency Verse also argues that the Prime Minister's announcement of a plan to empower private and unaccountable credit-checking agencies such as Experian with powers to rifle through benefit claimants' credit accounts in a cynical scrutiny of their spending patterns, via the incentivising of 'bounties', and all the accompanying scaremongering propaganda propagated by his government, constitute an unambiguous victimisation of the poor, unemployed, sick and vulnerable of our society, and an abuse of their human rights, therefore a breach of the Human Rights Act 1998; as well as a breach of the Disability Discrimination Act 1995, the Mental Health Act 2007 and, as the Government's own

Home Secretary and Equalities Minister has pointed out, a possible breach of the Equality Act of 2010 in its targeting of 'women, the disabled and the old'.

In light of responsibility for the recession and its consequences being that of the City speculators who have been let off scot free with a paltry £2 Billion levy, *Emergency Verse* petitions this government to repay the deficit by enacting the following alternative budgetary policies:

Introduce a Robin Hood Tax on all culpable City speculators, banks and affiliated agencies in order to raise £20 Billion to help fill the deficit and save the Welfare State from barbaric cuts, a percentage of this be allocated to the welfare system in order to increase its provisions for an increase in unemployment;
An abolition of all City and banking bonuses and a cap on all City salaries;
A re-introduction of rent controls, incorporating a universal reduction in rent rates so they do not exceed recently capped housing benefits;
A significant reduction in the newly implemented MP Attendance Allowance and a freeze of MP salaries for the next five years as the Government proposes for workers in the Public Sector; the public says that £60,000 per annum is more than enough for an MP to live on;
Coalition MPs with second jobs and second homes to donate these to those about to be made unemployed and/or homeless by their cuts, by way of a good will gesture on behalf of their 'Big Society';
Introduction of Mansion and Land Taxes, and a raising of Inheritance Tax so that 'unearned income' is taxed at a rate equal to, if not higher than, 'earned income';
A new drive to clampdown on tax-avoidance and a public enquiry into the moral authority of the Chancellor to impose the Budget cuts on the people while he himself is allegedly avoiding paying a portion of his tax contribution to the nation;
In order to truly 'make work pay', introduce a living wage and provide decent jobs for all according to their skills and abilities. McJobs do not qualify; EV believes no one should have inappropriate labour imposed on them: a job unsuited to a person's talents and temperament is seriously injurious to their mental health in the longer term.

Emergency Verse petitions the Government to enact this 'alternative' Budget in the name of *true* 'fairness'.

In spite of the Chancellor's protestations, the 2010 coalition emergency budget was neither unavoidable nor fair. Instead it was a massively failed opportunity to shift the economy onto a fairer, greener pathway. Devastating public spending cuts are not an economic inevitability — they are an ideological choice. So I warmly welcome *Emergency Verse* and the campaign to bring together various voices in defence of our Welfare State and our public services.

Caroline Lucas MP
Patron

Emergency Foreword:
Autumn Harvest: Bonfire of the Benefits:
A Response to the October 'Cleansing' Review

The views expressed herein are exclusively those of the writer and do not claim to speak on behalf of the other 111 contributors to this anthology whom, though in support of the broad principles of this campaign, have varying individual opinions, the expressions of which are confined to their poetry contributions.

20th October 2010 is a second date, after 22nd June's 'emergency' Budget, to go down as one of the most ethically and politically despicable in our downturning national history. For today, an ironically sunlit one after recent bleak skies, has surprised only in the Con-Dem government's indefatigable propensity for top-down ruthlessness in its attempts to rebalance the country's books and reimburse 'the deficit' with the lifeblood of the sick, poor and unemployed, and half a million public sector workers. *Anything* to avoid tackling the true culprits of this recession: the City speculators; or the parasitic multi-millionaire tax-avoiders who contribute precious little from their own gratuitous fortunes (either inherited, or amassed on the backs of others' exploited labour) to the economic lifeblood of this country — a number of whom, by the most grotesque irony, are leading lights in a Cabinet which is asking *us*, the people, to surrender the foundations of our social democracy so that their own vested interests can be perpetuated at all our expense. They then further insult us by stating that this is all 'fair' and 'progressive'. It is with breathtaking temerity that this doctrinaire government, without full electoral mandate, is seeking to fill up a financial black hole created by the crimes of the City speculators in the *private* banking sector by making the *public* sector pay, through the loss of half a million jobs. But most relevant to this particular campaign, which I spearheaded back in July 2010 as a response to the then savage prospect of £11-13 Billion cuts from our Welfare State, is George Osborne's cavalier announcement in the October Spending Review that a further £7 Billion is to be added to that already monstrous figure, now making the total an almost incomprehensible *£18* Billion

(£7 Billion per year for the next four years). All this in addition to: a universal capping of total household benefits; a Malthusian capping of Housing Benefit without any attempt at reintroducing rent controls to bring private rates down accordingly (government apparatchiks labouring under the absurd notion that somehow rising rates in Housing Benefit over the years have themselves inflated private rental rates, when it is blindingly obvious that it has been exactly the opposite: escalating private rents pushing up HB levels); an abolition of indefinite council housing tenancies; and most disgraceful of all, a slashing of social housing and imposition of near-market level rents on the tenants. At every single turn the 'emergency' Budget and Spending Review hammer the poorest in society, seemingly in order to appease *the Daily Mail* and *News of the World* readers of our ever right-shifting society. It is October's unexpected extra bombshell regarding our hunted Welfare State that has prompted me to pen this extra preamble to my original Foreword and Afterword, the gloomy predictions of which are tragically beginning to come true.

The latest vicissitude is the final slipping of Iain Duncan Smith's 'compassionate' Tory mask to that of a latter-day boot camp Baden-Powell announcing that the long-term unemployed (who *ipso facto* demonstrate a distinct lack of 'work ethic') will be expected to do 30 hours manual labour per week for four weeks in order to get them back in the working 'mindset'. This further intensifies what is rapidly becoming a tacit criminalising of unemployment; mandatory community service echoing punitive probationary measures for ex-prisoners. Visions of claimant chain-gangs in tabards digging at the roadsides now seem much less the stuff of dystopian fantasy; and it is not difficult to imagine IDS mumbling something about 'keeping the buggers busy' in private. Not so much *Work Makes You Free* as *Make You Work For Free*; tapping in once again to the *Daily Mail* 'scrounge culture' mythmaking, the twisted utilitarian logic that to *make work pay* means to make you *pay* to work. The usual implication of imposed labour or mandatory community service is that the protagonist is reimbursing society for his or her criminal wrongdoing — since when has unemployment been categorised as a crime? Would it not be more in the spirit of the law to have the bankers and speculators, rather than their victims, forced to do community manual labour and to put a bit back into the society they have stolen from?

Instead of creating a working culture in the fairest and most obvious way, by raising pay to a living wage, the Tories seriously expect us to swallow the contemptible and pessimistic drivel that the only way to make work appealing is to cap and cut benefits so that unemployment is simply too painful and impoverishing to bear. This is a satanic sociology; a sweatshop politic. In the knowledge that unemployment is set to soar, and that there will be pitifully few new jobs to soak up the rising numbers of unemployed, IDS et al have no doubt cooked up this workfare clause in order to both get claimants contributing to national productivity on pain of destitution, and to massage the tensing muscles of malcontents that could ultimately threaten the Coalition's longevity. Ingenious — but with just one flaw: *we are not going to put up with this*. To use politicians' favourite mantra, such a proposal is simply 'unacceptable'. Such punishing and ethically expedient methodology is tantamount to a fiscal fascism. At least the Labour Party is speaking out against these new proposals — albeit ones inspired by the groundwork done by New Labour's bouncer double-act, Purnell and McNulty, under Gordon Brown's puritanical premiership — led most prominently by the UK's heroically outspoken social conscience of the Cloth, Archbishop of Canterbury Rowan Williams; along with a phalanx of social charities and pressure groups. Nevertheless, this week the unemployed have been further battered mentally and literally by IDS's latest punitive tub-thump at the despatch-box — *and* at the tail-end of a week in which our ever-remote PM Cameron has put his own mobile salon on the public payroll, including his personal photographer, who is no doubt there to help airbrush out the hoof-marks from his policies. To behave in this manner is not only tactlessly frivolous, but is also, at a time of austerity and accompanying rhetoric, and the imminent axing of 500,000 legitimate public sector jobs, an insult to the public. The Prime Minister clearly takes his inspiration from the Emperor Nero School of Priorities.

Cameron was clearly a salesman in a former life: he is currently selling to us the new oxymoronic concept of '*mandatory* voluntarism', which is in essence a new form of social conscription, which will force the many long-term unemployed of a so-called democracy into entirely undemocratic slave labour. And that this work is emphatically manual-based betrays the punitive attitude of those about to administer it; those who, of course, have never got their hands dirty in their lives, nor had to struggle on benefits; nor, in fact, ever had to 'stand on their own two feet' outside of gratuitous inheritances and seat-warmed top-jobs. The only way for a government to carry the public with them through such horrendous policies as this administration intends, is to show them it does not include in its Cabinet a bunch of multi-millionaire tax-avoiding hypocrites. Here then we hit on the second gaping flaw in this government's strategem (and a further thumbs down for Andy Coulson's credibility as head of communications at No. 10).

The Poetry's Not For Turning

The vital transubstantiation of *Emergency Verse* from electronic to the tangible print version you are currently holding is the result of the generosity and dedication of its contributors. The deluge of passionate email feedback I received following the distribution of the original e-book version showed the sheer momentum forming behind the campaign. Scores of contributors were pressing home the point to me that *EV* needed to be a print entity, and so the next step was to work out how to fund this. Even though the e-book has sold steadily since it was first advertised — and largely thanks to the journalistic intervention of Gordon James in a *Guardian Society* piece in August, which triggered wider coverage through various media outlets as diverse as *the Morning Star* and Reuters — it was clear that at £2.99 a time, this was unlikely to ever get anywhere near to funding a full print production. It was on crucial advice from contributor Alan Corkish, who suggested my appealing to all contributors for small donations towards a book production (via an affordable printing deal tipped by Alan), that the tide turned in alchemising *EV* into a tangible print entity. As soon as I contacted all (then) 107 contributors to the e-book (now 112), I was flooded with donation pledges, many considerably exceeding the initial appeal for £5 per head. Not wishing to single out any donors above others, since each contributes according to his/her means, one particular intervention significantly pushed the book project forward: £400 from Children's Laureate and *EV* contributor Michael Rosen, which meant that the original plan to simply publish a copy per contributor was upped to the far more substantial prospect of producing twice that amount. Among other generous contributions, I also recently received $300 (£174) from contributor Prakash Kona. 200 copies has meant that each contributor secures a book, while 90 copies can be distributed to the media, targeted government departments (most particularly the offices of the Tresaury and the Department for Work and Pensions) and the remainder, it is hoped, sold. Any revenue coming back from sales will be put towards further promotion of the campaign. *EV* comes under the banner of Poets in Defence of the Welfare State (PDWS), an ongoing literary campaign which will continue to oppose the Con-Dem Government's war on the poor and vulnerable in our society as long as it is waged. Meanwhile, *the Recusant* will continue to ensure an ongoing online presence for the cause.

Now to the pressing — and highly *de*pressing — issues relating to the nature of the October Spending Review, and other recent political developments. As argued in both my Foreword and Afterword, there has always been an ethically convincing case for some element of means-testing in relation to welfare benefits: the reason being, essentially, that if the Welfare State is to achieve its ultimate goal of levelling society in terms of income and opportunity, stringent adherence to the principle of *universality* — one which in terms of the NHS *is* justified, since health is a universal issue, whereas poverty, so far, is not, even if it always has the potential to be — in the long-term means, and has meant, that while basic state provision has cushioned the last few generations from pre-1945 slum-level poverty (though not entirely by any means), the self-defeating political cynicism of dishing out benefits to the better off in society via such top-ups as universal child benefit and tax credits has, rather than levelling the social classes, simply pushed them all up a couple of rungs while keeping their defining frontiers firmly in place. Ironically, then, the principle of *universality*, originally conceived as a political means to avoid any middle-class prejudices against, or ghettoization of, the Welfare State, has not only failed to avoid such invisible but implicit cultural apartheid — negatively promulgated by successive governments' active demonization of those on benefits — but has also arguably perpetuated the very circumstances that necessitated its creation in the first place: deep and widespread social inequality. Therefore, it can be argued that means-testing, made fairly and as un-intrusively as is possible, is the only common sense and socially just way to assess benefit eligibility. What we have instead is a far more arbitrary tick-box system that equates to an adulterated form of *universality*: based not on real-term household income and outgoings, but on theoretical, uniformed estimates.

Through the usual expediency, this government rushed through a chimerical cap, somewhere between universality and means-testing, whereby any family with one adult earning more than £40,000 a year would lose their entitlement to child benefit. The obvious unfairness of this criteria was reflected in an immediate near-universal backlash: the net result of the change will mean that a family with only one adult in work but on or above £40,000 per year will lose their child benefits, while a family with two adults earning up to £39,000 each a year (nearly double the other household), would retain it. Thus, by avoiding the implementation of full means-testing by measuring eligibility against total household income, but opting instead for a more abstract estimate based on the salary of a household's highest earner, the Government has managed to offend *both* means-testing *and* universal camps in one move. But the fallout from this nonsensical policy has not been entirely helpful from a left-wing point of view: our largely right-wing media immediately leapt in defence of the 'squeezed middle', while the newly elected leader of the Labour Party, Ed Miliband, squandered his first PMQs by immediately rallying to this constituency, having initially muttered a worryingly glib offer of support for government proposals to 'reform' (or rather, blitz) Incapacity and DLA benefits. This then allowed the Prime Minister, ever the pettifog, to swerve the debate off course and onto Labour's continuing ideological identity crisis: that the Opposition, traditionally the party of the poorer in society, appeared to be arguing, rather bizarrely, *against* the government's measures to protect lower-waged taxpayers from continuing to subsidise benefits for the better off (a typically opportunistic *touché* moment for Cameron). While the true crux of Miliband's criticism was on the blatantly unfair application of this cap, his choice to prioritise the matter over the far more devastating caps to Housing Benefit, hinted at the lingering spirit of New Labour Middle Englandism. Equally bizarrely, this glaring own goal for Miliband unfathomably inspired the liberal media (i.e. *the Guardian* and *the Independent)* to a unanimous cheer for what they perceived to be a triumphant despatch-box debut for the new Labour leader. Aside from some well-placed quips that appeared to temporarily wrong foot David Cameron, Ed Miliband's maiden joust at the despatch-box was an ideologically fudged opportunity; frittered away on a political opportunism to once again champion the 'squeezed middle' instead of the 'squashed bottom of the heap'. This was all the more disappointing a performance for coming so soon after a refreshingly social-democratic victory speech at the Labour conference, in which he spoke out against the Iraq war, and talked of reconnecting with the traditional Labour heartlands who he recognised had come to feel alienated from the movement of which they had once been a core part. Hopefully this lapse was down to teething problems, and the promise of a Labour renaissance *will* bear fruit — not be abruptly truncated by a loss of nerve and a rightward lunge back to the comfort zone of vacuous centrism. But Miliband's absence from the Union demonstrations at Westminster recently does not bode particularly well for those of us hoping for a wholly unified left-of-centre ideological opposition to the cuts; it also seemed a slightly tactless rain-check from a leader largely thrust into his position on the backs of the party's Praetorian Guard. Labour must now focus its guns on the neo-Thatcherite government it is in official Opposition to, and stop wasting ammunition on fruitless counter-offensives to quell red-top accusations of dangerous 'leftward' lurches; anyone who understands what *left-wing* actually means knows how absurd and spurious the red-top trope of 'Red Ed' is (if only it *were* a representative description).

Enclosures and Clearances

Ed Miliband would do best to take note of commendably vocal backbenchers such as Michael Meacher, John McDonnell, and the indefatigably 'no-nonsense' John Mann who recently gave a lugubrious Osborne a true Socratic grilling at a recent treasury select committee. Another notable left-winger in Labour is of course John Cruddas, who recently wrote an exceptional diatribe against the Malthusian tradition both his party and the Tories have inherited, with some irony, from reforming liberals, such as William Beveridge, and Fabian intellectuals such as Sidney and Beatrice Webb; in the extract below, Cruddas saliently and powerfully summarises the fundamental disenfranchisement of the common people over the last two hundred years, and more poignantly, reminds us how industrial capitalism itself *created* the 'social problem' we know as *unemployment* (whose inventors now continually seek to stigmatise and near-criminalise):

...the English working class was defined by three acts of dispossession. First, people were dispossessed of their land and livelihood. In 1801, the enclosing of land was standardised in the first General Enclosure Act. The Industrial Revolution turned common people into shiftless migrants. Second, there was the political dispossession of the labouring class. The enclosures forced the people off their land, and the Reform Act of 1832 excluded the landless from the franchise. Finally, people were dispossessed of their own labour. The Poor Law Amendment Act 1834 established a competitive market in labour. The poor were divided between helpless paupers confined to the workhouse and a new category — the unemployed. Labour was turned into a commodity, and capitalism emerged. ...

This government's £18bn benefit cuts will leave the poor to pick up the tab for the economic crisis, while its housing strategy amounts to a modern enclosure movement. This clearance, together with the hasty redrawing of electoral boundaries and moves to discourage electoral registration, signal the political disenfranchisement of the poor. To complete the job, the poor are being dehumanised and redefined as a "social residuum" — a feckless mob undeserving of our sympathy.

['Osborne's modern-day clearances', John Cruddas, *the New Statesman*, 28/10/10]

Ed Miliband needs to guard vigilantly against any protracted New Labourish retrenchment. His child benefit offensive achieved little except to help keep the more apocalyptic announcement of Housing Benefit caps off the front pages for that week. Labour's continued championing of the 'squeezed middle' and *universality* also debatably (though indirectly) gave Osborne more elbow-room to cavalierly increase the overall welfare cuts by another £7 Billion to a now psychopathic *£18 Billion,* as flippantly as passing the port. Had Ed Miliband chosen to argue against the broader assault on the Welfare State rather than cherry pick at only those cuts that will affect the middle classes, at least he would not have been inadvertant party to the self-centred consensus that has now assisted in further punishing the poorest and most vulnerable benefit recipients. And all in the spirit of *universality*! Do Labour really want to be known, particularly at a time of austerity, for defending the right of a multi-millionaire baronet to claim child benefit? All welfare recipients, whether comfortably off or destitute, have to suffer the same axe across the board; a cut on the better off is then swiftly backed up by further cuts to the poorest. This, one can reasonably argue, is yet further evidence of the self-defeating and regressive effects of *universality*; but unfortunately for us, both the Con-Dems *and* Labour are stubbornly in favour of a principle oddly incongruous, even quixotic, in such a deeply unequal society as ours; and in spite of the devastation it is about to indirectly inflict on those who are financially defenceless. So, yet again, those who desperately need every penny of their already meagre benefits in order to survive have to take impoverishing cuts in order that the middle classes can continue to get their pocket money for tolerating the Welfare State's existence. Better Labour is in indefinite opposition, but as a genuinely fair and progressive parliamentary hammer on the coalition of cuts, than a whimpering poodle to the establishment in hope of an ideologically impotent bone at the next general election. We can only hope that Ed Miliband, still finding his feet as leader, will eventually come out unequivocally on the side of the Unions, the students and the common people against this new Falangist quagmire of politics *against* the people. If he fails to, then his party might as well merge with the coalition itself, till we have a permanent National Government dictatorship in the interests of the rich and capitalist classes, and have done with any pretence of democracy altogether. At least then we will all know clearly where we stand (or don't, as the case may be). It is however hopeful that on his third outing at PMQs, Ed Miliband took on David Cameron over the proposed Housing Benefit caps, which is undoubtedly — along with social housing cuts and rent hikes — the most insidious proposal yet from this Malthusian regime of a government. Nevertheless, apparently we are still *all in this together*. Well, as the cuts hit, such vacuous and hypocritical spin will start to fall on deaf ears. If we are to start living in a fiscal-fascist state (I mean, a 'Big Society'), we might at least be spared the sophistry that tries to patronise us into thinking we still have some semblance of social democracy. The October Spending Review spelt out once and for all that social democracy in this country is well and truly on the path to extinction.

Bail Outs, Bonuses and Benefits for Baronets

The second and final issue I wish to mention here is that of the palpable lack of any significant measures taken against the culprits of the banking crisis, the City speculators, and the marked absence of any significant clampdown (as has been paid lip service recently by some Ministers) on wealthy 'tax-avoiders'. Here the Falangist credentials of this ultra-capitalist administration come to the fore beyond any scope of political camouflage: one simply has to look at the figures, which show that while the Welfare State, about to be besieged by a further half a million new claimants, is to have its budget axed by £18 Billion, the City banks are only to be levied £2 Billion by way of their contribution to an economic mess *they* created (apparently the country still needs their 'talents'). Not only that, but via a cut in corporation tax on the side, Chancellor Osborne has effectively cancelled that levy out. This all in effect means then that it is overwhelmingly the poorest 10% in society who are being punished for the recession, while the richest 10% are allowed to continue avoiding tax, and the City banks continue to make profits and award themselves bonuses on the back of our double bail-out. But for *the Daily Mail* constituencies, this is all apparently par for the course in free market capitalism, while the real scourge of our society are its victims: the unemployed families milking exorbitant housing benefits from the saintly tax-payers. All these cuts, and the scurrilous memes propagated by the government in order to justify them, we are expected to agree are 'fair and progressive' and putting the burden on the 'broadest shoulders'. It is indeed also ironic that the only possible morsel of argument this atrocious government has that its budget is in any way 'progressive' is by incorporating the tax hikes brought in by the previous oh-so odious Labour government, who, we are told on a daily basis, 'created this economic mess' that the poor Con-Dems 'inherited'. Curiously enough though, when it suits the Con-Dems to wave the flag of progressiveness, they are quite happy to have inherited these particular tax measures, mix it into their overall spending review, and then use it to balance out what is via their own measures otherwise entirely and unacceptably regressive. The Con-Dems of course use a similar tactic regarding the IFS, citing their appraisals when they back up their claims to being progressive, and debunking them as flawed when they demonstrate that they are in fact being unambiguously regressive; which is most of the time. Their Stalinism does not even spare the Office for Budget Responsibility's appraisals if they err on the side of any criticism — even though it is an agency the Government created.

It is germane here to mention the recent broadcast of a by turns fascinating, by turns infuriating to the point of minor infarction Channel 4 *Dispatches* programme, which exposed the systematic tax avoidance of the very high profile multi-millionaire ministers currently telling the rest of us to accept the sacrifice of our benefits, jobs, pensions and public services. Osborne himself, architect of the Hell-fare State, is one of these multi-millionaire ministers, himself an heir to a baronetcy and inheritor of vast wealth and property who, while bashing the unemployed — able or disabled — as uniformly workshy is, without any justification of material necessity whatsoever (being already richer than most of us could comprehend), 'avoiding' contributing some of his own portion of tax to the very nation he is imposing savage cuts on. Such financially duplicitous behaviour on the Chancellor's part regarding his own domestic exchequer strips him of any political credibility. It is only a matter of time before the metaphorical scaffold is installed outside Westminster, and obscenely self-interested aristocrats as Osborne dragged into the sharp air of public accountability. *We're all in this together*? Well, we the public are all in it together, while the politicians, the propertied and the rich are in quite another place altogether — call it a private tax haven.

It is frankly a disgrace that at the beginning of the 21st century our country, supposedly a social democracy, has at its head two highly privileged products of the private education system and landed aristocracy, forcing those who have nothing to spare to pay for the crimes of the City, while they routinely continue avoiding paying taxes on their gratuitous earnings and inherited estates. Such a fiscal apartheid can only eventually lead to one thing: democratic entropy, and then chronic social unrest. It will begin with the burgeoning resistance to the cuts, principally and justifiably through the Unions — that is, until this regressively un-democratic government begins tinkering, as it already hints, with the already punitive anti-Union laws in order to further inhibit strike action — marches, protests and demonstrations of various political and social pressure groups; but wil in the long run, if the Con-Dems do not come-to and moderate the most vicious and socially devastating of their budgetary cuts, develop into wider discontents; even violence. In short, a return to the style of the Poll Tax riots of 1990 is now very probably on the cards.

In the meantime, it is all of our duty on the progressive left of this political conflict to muster all our means to protest and speak out against the oncoming storm about to let rip on our public sector and Welfare State. This current coalition government is, without doubt, the greatest threat to our common progressive national purpose and social democracy that we have yet faced; even more potentially devastating than the tyranny of Thatcherism, the scars of which have not even in themselves healed for the majority of this country (the North in particular). And Ed Miliband and the role of Labour in all this? Quite simply, the Opposition has to build an ideological alternative to the regressive right-wing regime currently entrenching itself in a fixed-term rule until 2015; the Opposition must strike at the heart of the Coalition's hypocrisy by continually arguing for the City to bear the largest part of the burden to repay the deficit, and additionally, for increased taxes on the rich and for an expedited clampdown on wealthy tax-avoiders and non-Doms. In the latter regard, Labour must keep up the pressure in particular on those members of the Cabinet who themselves are duplicitously avoiding tax while preaching the *we're all in this together* sophistry at the same time. Ed Miliband must have the courage of his convictions and once and for all break with New Labour's fence-sitting championing of Middle England alone, and take on the far more crucial and challenging debate as to the working and lower classes — particularly those currently on benefit, the unemployed, sick and disabled — who will be taking the brunt of the austerity cuts.

Most importantly of all, Miliband's Labour must have the courage to counter the right-wing anti-welfare consensus propagated by a pernicious reactionary media, bypass such regressive forces and swerve the national political dialectic back to its original focus on the true culprits behind the recession: the speculators and bankers. Crucial to this will be the realignment of Labour firmly at the side of the Unions in the current Coalition of Resistance against the government cuts; a direct communication to all classes in society, from the unemployed up to the professional middle classes, that the Unions represent all of our rights and not any vested interests (in contrast to the blatant vested interests represented by the establishment propping Con-Dems) and that without them, we would all be well and truly at the mercy of the doctrinaire whims of this neo-Thatcherite government, in thrall to Murdoch and the markets. Now more than ever, a new dialogue between Labour, the Unions and the ordinary citizens, all of whom are to be hit at varying degrees by the oncoming cuts, is absolutely imperative if we are to finally break the Thatcherite market-driven autocracy we currently live in and rescue our social democracy from a dark age of social apartheid and public sector meltdown.

On the poetry front, PDWS, through publications such as *Emergency Verse*, will, it is hoped, encourage other sections of the literary community to start speaking out against the ongoing assault on our Welfare State. So far some have spoken out against the oncoming cuts from the already depleted Arts arena, which is of course another crucial issue to champion, but it is hoped even wider cultural and social dialectic from the literary community outside its own vocational constituency will emerge in time. The literary and arts communities have as much duty to speak out against the broader social injustices of the Budget and Spending Review as they have in defence of the Arts; and it is hoped more groups will join us at the vanguard of artistic resistance to this grossly regressive and ruthless government. If that latter description sounds like partisan hyperbole, one only has to watch the footage of rows of government back-benchers roaring in celebration and waving their order papers at the conclusion of the Chancellor's viciously punishing Spending Review on 20th October; a truly disgraceful sight which, as Alan Johnson pertinently noted to the House — with intuitively choreographed prehensile gesture — was a manifest breaking of cover by the Tory rank-and-file in their shameless ideological quest to shrink the state down to near non-existence, devastating the Welfare State in the process. After the rape of our economy by the City speculators and the subsequent bank bail outs imposed on us under an ineffective New Labour, this malicious and arch-Thatcherite government is truly the very last thing the country either needs or deserves.

The Spending Review has, tragically, served not only to confirm the gut-sinking dread of the ideologically-driven social carnage that the 'emergency' Budget so ominously promised; it has even surpassed many of our wildest predictions back in August at the inception of this campaign. Our multi-millionaire, allegedly tax-avoiding, aristocrat Chancellor spilt from his green book all the bile and malice stored up in Tory chests over the past thirteen years towards what they irrationally perceive to be a monolithic Soviet-style state. But far worse than this libertarian prestidigitation was pulled out from that dog-eared red suitcase and unleashed in the Spending Review: a deadly and heartless contempt for those in poverty who remain reliant on the state for their survival, and a vicious drive to herd the poorest and most vulnerable in our society into sociological and literal ghettos outside the self-centred confines of the 'Big Society' — apparently not 'Big' enough to incorporate the poor. For all New Labour's failings — and they are legion — I think now many of us would rather still have *them* in power, even under the lugubrious Brown, than the pack of salivating, state-hating wolves we have now (and their Lib Dem lap dogs, now justifiably labelled by many disaffected grassroots Lib Dems as 'vote thieves' for their transparent betrayal of principle — most abjectly, their broken tuition fees pledges — in return for pyrrhic power).

I cite three major tragedies in our country's recent political history: the first was the ill-timed general election of 1979, which by a narrow margin saw Margaret Thatcher embed herself at the helm of the nation to plunder and corrupt a generation; the second, the untimely death of John Smith, who would have proven a far more socially democratic Labour Prime Minister than his ideologically duplicitous replacement; and the third, that the 2010 general election had to come at a time of such dire economic crisis — because when cuts are required, the very last thing we need is a Tory administration to oversee them. What we are about to see unleashed on our nation is not only a return to Thatcherism — only partially truncated for thirteen years by New Labour — but an even more extreme version of it, that is absolutely intent on punishing the poor for being poor, the unemployed for being unemployed, and the sick for being sick. The Spending Review has announced a fiscal cull of the perceived 'dead wood' of society, a 'gamble' indeed, using human beings for chips, which, even if it succeeds in sorting out the deficit, will be socially devastating in both the short and long-term. We are expected to surrender the rudiments of our social democracy in exchange for ...*what*? A return to market-driven autocracy, greater social division and inequality, and a generation blasted for the crimes of a small banking elite. In one fell swoop, George Osborne has gone beyond any possible future revisionist justification in his bellicose and hubristic thirst for notoriety: by capping Housing Benefit and raising the single person eligibility to a ridiculous 35 years of age, raising social housing rents, abolishing long-term council house tenancies, time-limiting ESA, even docking mobility allowances for disabled people in care homes, Osborne has left no stone unturned in turning the poor up on their backs like tortoises, carrion for the private sector vultures. Already the likes of Atos, sub-contracted by the Government to 'help get the sick back into work', are bullying people with chronic, even terminal conditions onto JSA and its accompanying pressures to find jobs that do not even exist. The private sector is and always has been a profiteering exploiter of a country's economic miseries, dressed up as 'wealth creators', and there is no reason to believe that it will behave any differently now or in the future. The private sector — represented at its most vile by such parasitic agencies as absentee private landlords and City hedge-fund managers — is ever poised to come in and mop up profits from a bankrupt state; only this time, it will be mopping up those profits from a mess it largely created, through the avarice of the buy-to-let boom and hiked rents driven by the unregulated greed of the property speculators.

It is now time for we, the people of this country, to make 'tough decisions' of our own, unite together, with placard or pen, on the streets or on the page, to start the fight back against a government without mandate for its malice; one which has proved, on 20th October, that it is ethically unfit to govern, because it is ignoring the will of a vast section of its electorate in its callous pursuit, through means none of us voted for and many of us deplore, to achieve vague and ill-defined ends, largely geared towards perpetuating the ancient privileges that have helped its leading lights — Cameron, Osborne and Clegg — rise through public schools, Oxbridge and well-connected circles to be in their positions of unmerited power today. This is an administration of pin-striped puppets to Rupert Murdoch and the markets. So now we must fight, through argument, dialectic, protest and permanent opposition to force the Con-Dems to down their tools of destruction: Britain cannot remain a social democracy without a welfare state.

Alan Morrison, October 2010

Foreword

The Low-Hanging Fruit Is Ripe for the Picking

The views expressed herein are exclusively those of the writer and do not claim to speak on behalf of the other 111 contributors to this anthology whom, though in support of the broad principles of this campaign, have varying individual opinions, the expressions of which are confined to their poetry contributions.

2 June 2010 was a dark day indeed: after thirteen years of New Labour's slow-burning betrayal of its own values and of all those on the Left and on the social margins of British society who had voted them in believing that the party would finally staunch the interminable bleed of Thatcherite politics; after the bankrupting of the country by the speculators and the further insult of the bail outs and a return to the City bonus culture; after the brief oasis of hope in the sudden rise of the Liberal Democrats' popularity for a broadly left-of-centre agenda only to inexplicably dry up at the polls; after the agonising aftermath of a Hung Parliament and the faint hope then dashing of an anti-Tory Rainbow coalition; after the bartering and shabby backroom pact that resulted in the most oxymoronic 'coalition' in British history and the plunge of the gut at witnessing a Tory Prime Minister once again step through the door of No. 10 — after all these vicissitudes, any vestige of hope still left that this Con-Dem coalition would be more 'Dem' than 'Con' was blasted at the despatch-box when a pasty-faced George Osborne laid out like a litany of lashes the most viciously regressive and socially apocalyptic Budget of state cuts this country has ever faced.

The sheer horror and disbelief at realizing on that day the fact that this society had been catapulted back to unadulterated Thatcherism — a new breed of anti-state, anti-public sector, anti-welfare, ultra-capitalist dogma, but without even the meretricious trimmings and progressive window-dressing that had made the last decade intermittently endurable under New Labour — compelled me to do what I could in my own power to speak out against this fiscal holocaust of an 'emergency' budget: its utterly draconian and unjustifiable plan to slash what has now risen by a further £7 Billion to a staggering £18 Billion from the Welfare State (which can only be seen as a direct attempt to finally dismantle the greatest ever British gesture towards a fairer, more egalitarian society); the acceleration of the nastiest of New Labour policies to manipulate thousands of incapacitated people into unsuitable jobs; the cap on already shortfalling housing benefits but not on rent rates; the capping of council house tenancies to five year leases; the proposals to universally privatise the NHS; and the blatantly ideological cuts to the public sector labour force. It was clear to see that this ruthless budget of cuts was tantamount to a declaration of war on the poor, unemployed and sick of this country. If New Labour, comfortable with people getting 'filthy rich', had aided and abetted the Thatcherite curse which made self-interest 'respectable' (to paraphrase Roy Hattersley), then the dawn of the Tory-in-all-but-name 'coalition' government, through its flagship 'emergency' Budget, consolidated a new dark age in which an economic pogrom on the poor, unemployed, sick and public sector workers will be officially sanctioned as 'respectable' too. Iain Duncan Smith's smooth-talking dismantling of our welfare state will prove to be the finally nail in the coffin of our social democracy; while Michael Gove's utilitarian educational 'reforms' — given an acid-yellow twist with the Liberal Democrats' unprincipled abandonment of their now clearly opportunistic and spurious pre-election pledge to prevent any rise in university tuition fees, now set to treble with the support of the party's duplicitous Orange Book Brigade — will put a seal on any last-ditched hopes that this country will ever progress towards a true social meritocracy.

Blue Plutocracy: Against the New Falangism

As a poet, and editor of left-wing literary webzine *the Recusant*, I decided that all I could do outside of writing my own protest poems was to galvanise support among likeminded poets throughout the country (and beyond) to contribute poems or poetical statements in defence of the Welfare State and the NHS; *and* in support of a Robin Hood Tax on the Banks and the City culprits of the recession and an immediate government drive to smoke out offshore tax havens and claw back the billions of pounds milked through tax evasion (starting with their own 'non-doms'). In titular riposte to the 'emergency' Budget, the name 'Emergency Verse' instantly sprang to mind. I realised that now was not the time to write in isolated protest but to gather as many voices together as possible in order to demonstrate the scale of opposition among poets and writers to this unprecedented assault on the liberties and rights of the poor and unemployed. This was a time when numbers counted as much as depth of dialectic in order to demonstrate it was representing more than a fringe minority opinion. Fortunately, running a webzine with an average of roughly 2,000 visitors a week, including a loyal and regular readership, and a vast number of contributors, I had a good vantage point from which to begin recruiting for contributors. I also had knowledge of a number of highly useful poetry network sites, such as Jim Bennett's invaluable repository *The Poetry Kit*, from which to gather email addresses of many poets whom I was not already in contact with in some capacity. In a relatively short time, I was pleasantly surprised, not to say quietly moved, by the sheer quantity and quality of poems appearing in my inbox each day from a variety of poets and writers, established and emerging, as well as some notable sociological academics and commentators. After roughly one month (that of July) I had received and selected contributions from 111 poets and activists, an average of 2-4 poems per submission. I have not yet even stopped to count up the exact amount of individual poems included in this e-anthology, but the reader may if he or she wishes. The sheer scale of contributions to this poetry campaign has exceeded even my expectations, and goes to show definitively that British poetry does still have a radical trait to its character, even if this is all too frequently absent in its mainstream guise. We now, urgently, need to change that: to combat the 'Big Society' we need a 'Big Poetry' in opposition to it.

Although I am politically minded, I am not a natural 'activist' in the classic placard-carrying sense; but I suppose I might be described as an 'activist of letters', and felt that now was the time to put that directly into practice by attempting to organise a direly needed Rainbow Opposition of the literary Left via a creatively charged 'campaign in verse', as opposed to the proverbial multi-signatured petition letter (though that is not to disparage the purpose of such). Audacious though it sounds, part of this campaign's ambition is to show that, to circum-paraphrase the famously left-wing W.H. Auden: poetry *can* make things happen. While this project obviously pales in comparison to the very literal sacrifices of young left-wing poets and men of letters of the 1930s who volunteered (ambulanceman Auden among them) to defend the Fascist-besieged Spanish Republic (in what turned out to be a poorly-equipped preamble for the Second World War), I cannot help thinking that there is something of a narrative echo of that ideological crusade in the wider national cause (as represented by the Coalition of Resistance against the cuts, of which *Emergency Verse* is but one small part). After all, things are beginning to smell potently of top-down class war — on the poor and the unemployed, the sick and disabled, schoolchildren and women, and most fundamentally, on our very social democratic principles in general (back towards the more selective Classical model of 'democracy', which excluded women, children and 'slaves' (the unemployed) from its political privileges — what we need now is another Solon to bring in a *seisachtheia* ('shaking off of burdens'/debts) — that, together with a coalition cobbled together frantically after only four days of negotiation, more to appease 'the markets' than the needs of the British people, it does not seem entirely hyperbolic to draw up at least a paper parallel with the Falangist coup against the social-democratic Republic of Thirties Spain. With two millionaire aristocrats in charge of our country and its economy, supported by the world's biggest media mogul, it is rather difficult not to see this latest ultra-capitalist putsch as anything other than a reactionary retrenchment of an ultra-capitalist administration on behalf of the vested interests of its own landed and propertied classes, and against the interests and liberties of the common people. In short, an attempt to plunge an already muddy British 'democracy' even deeper into the Kafka-esque shadows of Murdoch-sponsored oligarchy, fronted by Conradian puppet politicians.

If anything has finally and emphatically put seal to the faint pre-election hope of a true root-and-branch reform of our politics to heal the deeply damaging sense of an Us and Them paradigm between the electorate and the political classes — as inflamed by the MPs' expenses scandal — then it is this opportunistic coalition and its Budget against the most abjectly affected victims of what is, basically, a crisis of capitalist authority. In return for rolling over on our backs and letting the political class kick us in the guts once again, we are being offered distractive carrots such as Alternative Vote referendums and the right to recall MPs; little pats on the head for we establishment pets. In the meantime, the scaffolding of dystopia stacks up ever higher around us all, to blot out the sun of accountability before we notice. The classic Tory tactic of divide and rule comes back into play to split any sense of collective resistance to its dogma by pitting private against public sector worker, doctor against patient, and taxpayer against claimant. Most disturbing of all is that so far the polls indicate that most of the population is swallowing it. But then, the cuts have yet to really pinch. And they will pinch, and will keep pinching thereafter, until we wake up to the injustice of a mass punishment inflicted on us for crimes of which we ourselves are the victims. We are expected to demonstrate thrift, humility, empathy and forgiveness towards the behaviour of the banks and City speculators; and yet we are also expected to expect no such concessions to be made to *us*; rather, quite the opposite, to take it on the chin for the next five years at least, while our entire social fabric is torn up into bits and thrown on the bonfire in front of us. This is not fair, nor reasonable, nor is it any solution whatsoever to the endemic problem with our society, which is, in short, that it is maintained on the insidious con-trick of unregulated capitalism, an economic dogma that only benefits a minority, and that is as productive of poverty as it is of wealth. Social inequality is the grease that turns the cogs of capitalism. Wherever there is extreme wealth, there is always extreme poverty, and frequently in close proximity; and wherever there is that stark parochial contrast, there is also chronic social instability. This hard fact to capitalism was most iconically articulated by Karl Marx: 'in proportion as capital accumulates, the lot of the labourer, be his payment high or low, must grow worse'. It's a tribute to Marx's vision and our lack of it that his observation of over a century ago is tragically incontrovertible today.

Whenever I visit Sweden, I feel as if I am entering into the very civilised social democracy that my own country should be and indeed probably would have been now had its more egalitarian pre-1979 values not been savagely abraded by Thatcherism in the 1980s. With its even sense of redistribution, superior public and health services funded by altruistically high progressive taxes, its un-begrudging and non-punitive benefit system (which, depending on how long one has worked, operates on a sliding scale, after which it lowers to a standard means-tested minimum comparable to the standard levels available in the British system), and its sensibly stringent market regulations — Sweden frequently makes me nostalgic for the England of the late Seventies, before the monetarist bomb dropped. Returning to England after each visit is rather like entering George Bailey's nightmarish vision in Frank Capra's *It's A Wonderful Life*, as the communitarian Bedford Falls is replaced by the seedy, unfriendly, pugilistic parallel town of Pottersville, where a wholesome sense of cooperativeness has been replaced by the false values of unadulterated materialism and its baser attractions of pawn shops, night clubs and rowdy binge-bars. David Cameron may be aiming more for Bedford Falls with his 'Big Village Green Conservation Society' vision, but his policies and budget seem destined to prolong, even intensify, the soul-destroying Thatcherite Pottersville in which we currently have to survive. Further, this country's own previously perceived 'Angel' Clarence, Vince Cable, has turned out to have wings of clay after all.

Poverty is the proverbial shadow cast by capitalism. In Britain, we have become so sanitised to the reality of 'homelessness', since its rapid escalation under Thatcherism, that it is almost becoming a tacit part of British culture, as if it is somehow unavoidable, or the 'life choice' of a drug-addicted sub-culture. But it is neither unavoidable nor acceptable in any even vaguely civilised society, least of all one which still loosely identifies itself with Christianity. Yet, instead of radical measures to try and finally alleviate this devastating inter-generational diaspora — by, say, reintroducing the sanity of controls and regulation to freeze and begin lowering our country's scandalously high rental and housing prices, and by reforming an obfuscating and punitive benefits system to one of greater flexibility and means-testing — the Con-Dems opt almost psychopathically to cap already shortfalling housing benefits and council house tenures, without doing anything at all to address the other, causational side of the equation that has forced them up so high in the first place: usurious landlordism. This Cabinet of multi-millionaires rage about freak cases of people claiming exorbitant amounts in HB, when what they should be raging against is the exorbitant rents private landlords get away with charging, often for poorly maintained slum dwellings, especially in London. The solution would be to put a cap on private rents rather than the top-down approach of further punishing the poor by capping their housing benefits, which will inevitably tip many more into homelessness. More Robber Baron than Robin Hood.

It is also germane to note that it was the Tories who removed rent controls in the first place back in 1992, in the landlord-friendly Thatcherite spirit of deregulation; this reprehensible measure single-handedly enabled private landlords to rack up their rent rates to obscene levels unheard of practically anywhere else in Europe. New Labour's market-besotted regime failed to readdress this problem, instead encouraging the very profligate property grab of the buy-to-let boom (the modern day 'land grab') of the last decade that contributed to the current recession. Now the Tories can mop up from the economic mess which is as much their own inheritance as New Labour's; but deflect their own culpability by claiming they would not have borrowed during the last boom had they been in government (even though in Opposition they voiced no such opinions at the time). The seeds for the mushrooming economic inequality in this country over the past generation were sown with Thatcherism in the Eighties. Had Thatcher not sold off most of the council housing stock, there would not have been so many people forced into the private renting sector who in turn needed to claim Housing Benefit to keep up with the constantly inflating rents. So instead of trying to make a genuinely radical change to the way our society is run — where consumption outweighs production, where the accumulation of individual capital is practically unlimited — by overhauling the grossly unfair system of wealth distribution to one of long-term redistribution, the Government chooses to 'patch over' the cancer rather than commit to its surgical removal, which will have to be done eventually if this nation is to survive intact.

This government asks *us* to change our way of living, *us* being the ordinary people who have to work all our lives in wage labour because we have not inherited sufficient capital or property to enable us to do otherwise; while the privileged classes it represents are asked only to sacrifice a marginal rise in tax, and for a limited period only, while our far greater sacrifices are set for the long-term. It then has the sheer gall to appoint a billionaire retail giant with questionable tax arrangements, Philip Green, as an 'austerity tsar' to 'advise' on which parts of a public sector he has probably never had to utilise himself, to cut. It's a bit like outsourcing a corpulent feudal baron to tell the peasants that they'll have to make do with less chicken bones. On top of such insults, we are being intimidated by government brinkmanship with the oncoming stripping of the Welfare State to its most basic component parts and the selling of our National Health Service to the unaccountable private sector. In other words, we either plod on in largely unfulfilling jobs until our newly extended retirement ages, or we go under, because the 'state', such as it will be in five years' time, will now be telling us that it can't support us anymore. The truth is: the cuts have been *chosen* by this government: they have not been thumbscrewed on them by New Labour's debt legacy, but petitioned for by the very market forces that plunged the country into recession in the first place.

But it does not have to be this way. There are many truly progressive alternatives: a Robin Hood Tax; a Mansion Tax (whatever happened to that one?); a mass operation to recover billions lost through tax evasion; intra-bank transaction taxes; a raising of the inheritance tax rate (currently, earned income is taxed at a higher rate than unearned income, so try and even that one out with 'fairness'); a scrapping of Trident; an abolition of Parliamentary expenses; withdrawal of the troops from an unwinnable Afghanistan campaign — to name only a handful. Instead, the coalition *chooses* the easiest and most unconscionable option: to kick the crutches of the Welfare State clean away and cut over 600,000 public sector jobs while they're at it. Then the private sector will come in and mop up. All this in the name of 'localism' and 'people power': but these are Humpty-Dumpty euphemisms for profiteering, opportunism and zero accountability. It is abundantly clear that not only are such knee-jerk and draconian short-term cuts not necessary, they are also at risk of tipping the economy into a double-dip recession. While Labour might be accused of having not 'fixed the roof while the sun was shining', the coalition can be accused of trying to 'fix the roof while it's raining with a tramp's holey umbrella'. The Welfare State, particularly in a time where unemployment is likely to soar due to public sector cutbacks, should be the very last thing used to plug the deficit; any ethically decent government would see it as the very last resort. This government is picking it out first for the stripping.

Defending the Defenceless/ Fighting the Indefensible

*E*mergency Verse also questions whether this 'coalition' has any real legitimacy of electoral mandate to impose such regressively 'radical' restructuring of the fabric of our society, when no one actually voted for 'it'. We also challenge David Cameron to 'walk the walk', to echo Barack Obama's idiom, and become Britain's first voluntary Prime Minister in the spirit of his 'Big Society' ethos, and to donate his salary to one or a number of the charities to whom he plans to hand the Welfare State. *EV* also wants it to be a matter of open debate as to whether Mr Cameron's scare tactics against the most vulnerable in our society via his witch-hunt on Incapacity Benefit claimants is a breach of Human Rights Law; and whether his and his government's open and unapologetic contempt towards anyone who is unemployed, no matter their reasons, as *de facto* subscribers to 'institutionalised idleness', is tantamount to harassment and 'inciting hatred' against a vulnerable social minority. In short, *EV* would like to throw into contention that this nation might quite possibly have the legal right to acquire an Injunction against its government's viciously discriminative propaganda. *EV* is particularly exercised by the increasing verbal scapegoating of the unemployed, sick and disadvantaged of this society, implicit in the terminology and policies of successive governments. This anthology campaign is as much in defence of benefit claimants as it is of the Welfare State; it seeks to combat the disgusting stigmas tagged on them by politicians and the media with increasing viciousness, not to say the hypocrisy, given the parliamentary property-flipping and expenses scandals. Nevertheless, this 'pot-calling-the-kettle-black' propaganda is being gleefully revelled in by the Tories, and most noticeably by Cameron himself, from 'hug-a-hoodie' to 'bug-a-doley' in a very short space of time.

There are so many myths to dispel about the claimant culture, and, most pointedly, the loophole-ridden Kafkaesque 'passport' and 'non-passport' benefit system. One of the more controversial benefits, though for all the wrong and most specious reasons, is Incapacity Benefit. It is not as easy to acquire as politicians and the media would have us believe: it has to be sanctioned officially via a GP sick note, and, where appropriate, backed up by psychiatric documentation; sick notes have to be issued initially for periods of between three and six months over the course of twelve months or so, after which, if a claimant is deemed to still be incapacitated, they are no longer required to acquire GP sick notes. If this latter clause is deemed by some reading this as enabling claimants to languish in an indeterminately unmonitored state of worklessness on some sort of DWP loyalty card, then it is hardly the claimant's fault. But what certainly isn't the answer is to bulldoze in 'assessments' designed to pressurise the vulnerable into unsuitable employment, as arbitrarily proposed by this present government from next March onwards (initially cited for 2013, suddenly it is expedited to early 2011, just to keep the incapacitated on their toes and tarnish their already austere Christmases). IB is also the most disenfranchising of benefits: it is more of a premium than a 'benefit' since it is treated as taxable income, is expected to be declared to Inland Revenue, and is *not* what the DWP now term a 'passport benefit': unlike Income Support or JSA, IB does not entitle the recipient to free medical care or prescriptions — which, given its supposed purpose, seems rather absurd. The real reason for the 'increase' in IB and Disability Living Allowance (DLA) claims is more likely to be due to a combination of spiralling economic pressures and the continual failure of successive governments to properly address and treat the more invisible illnesses such as depression, anxiety and obsessional disorders, and the deeply complex, multi-varied symptoms of psychosis and schizophrenia; or to combat the stigmas that exacerbate them. If we really are 'all in it together' then it is more than time to end the stigmatisation of the sick and unemployed, who need support and gentle encouragement to find work again, not bribes and sanctions. But soon no doubt, with the oncoming fiscal *blitzkrieg* against the public sector, those made redundant due to ideological grudges under the subterfuge of deficit reduction, the ex-DWP frontline workers, will be in the unenviable position themselves of having to fathom out the very obfuscating Humpty-Dumpty benefits system that they have been attempting to elucidate to countless claimants over the past decade or so.

Mandatory Voluntarism: Invitation to Join Unemployment

What politicians and the media also fail to ever mention is that a large section of the unemployed have already been contributing their time and energies as volunteers within the community and the public sector. Some of this shadow army of volunteers are on benefits such as Incapacity and DLA, and, in spite of their illnesses, have a genuine sense of altruism towards their communities, and put it into practice through voluntary roles, finding in providing free service to society a flexibility and autonomy that conventional employment simply cannot offer. The inestimable value of some of the voluntary services contributed by many unemployed and incapacitated individuals more than repays 'the taxpayer' for the relatively modest amounts of benefits they receive. This poses the question, why not introduce a Volunteer's Stipend for those who are not well enough to hold down full time waged employment, but who can contribute some valuable skills and services for free if allowed flexibility and autonomy of managing their own time and application? Surely it is more than time now for us to take a long hard look at the often uncompromisingly stressful culture of the workplace, and think of ways to reform its restrictive structures and suffocating routines that pointlessly suppress the creative personality? Further, is it not time too for the apparatchiks of industrial capitalist society to finally concede that human beings are more than just work-units, that they have intellectual and creative needs as well as material ones; that, to paraphrase William Morris, only occupations that employ the hearts and minds of workers are of authentic and sustainable value? We are a society of individuals, and each individual has his or her own distinctive skills, abilities and personalities to contribute, to society; for some, the high octane 'rat race' of competitive employment simply isn't a sustainable option. All the coercion and financial bribery at a government's disposal does not change this, and in most cases, only serves to drive more and more people into nervous exhaustion, even breakdown, and in turn, temporary or short-term incapacity.

The notion of occupation as something which should employ the full personality of the worker, not simply the one or two components to it that profits industry, is an ageold one, and as I've touched on, has been discussed by such luminaries as Karl Marx, William Morris and D.H. Lawrence, among many others. This humanistic ethic, which was championed by the Arts and Crafts Movement of the nineteenth century and revived via the holisticism of the Sixties, was as early as 1970 — first year in the last decade of pre-monetarist dialectic — perceived by notable sociologists to already be in disturbing decline. In their brilliantly illuminating work, *Poverty: The Forgotten Englishmen* (Pelican, 1970/ rev. 1973), Ken Coates and Richard Silburn reignited the polemic on not only unemployment but also the neglected issue of *impoverished employment*, a spirit of dialectic which this Foreword (and its related Afterword) seeks to rekindle. The following extract from the prophetically titled chapter, 'The Decline of the Welfare State', touches a raw nerve in its exposé of the intransigently atomist attitude of right-wing economists regarding the nature of labour, still so intractably entrenched today:

Rather grudgingly they will concede that some of the welfare measures adopted after the Second World war were, at the time, appropriate, but would claim that they had only a temporary justification until capitalism could overcome the shortcomings so apparent in the thirties. Given steady economic growth, however, 'the true object of the Welfare State ...is to teach people how to do without it' [A. Peacock, 'The Welfare Society', 1961]. Whatever temporary benefits may have accrued from welfare interventions may now, it seems, flow from the workings of unimpeded market forces, and the Welfare State should be allowed to wither away as speedily as possible. [...] This particular point of view is coloured by the social and political values of a hundred years ago; it is naively convinced of the primary importance of material incentives as a stimulus to activity, and fearful of the effects of welfare policies upon their recipient's moral fibre (with particular reference to his will to work). This quite extraordinarily crude assessment of the role (or non-role) of welfare is, of course, shared only by a handful of serious commentators....

Not so today unfortunately, nor for the last thirty years. Coates and Silburn must have shuddered at the acceleration of market-driven atomism under Margaret Thatcher a decade later. She of course famously championed 'Victorian values', among them, 'self-help', which is still perceived as an inalienable virtue while altruism, through, for instance, voluntarism, seems only to be seen as a virtue among those who can afford to commit to it, who have, in a twisted sense, earned the right to volunteer; while those who volunteer but who can least afford to, which is invariably the majority of volunteers, are at best tolerated as eccentric, at worst castigated for their economically unproductive martyrdoms. But if Cameron is relying on the altruism of the wealthy to crank up voluntarism in this country, he is likely to be eternally disappointed as he and we come to be reminded of the intrinsic and demonstrable antinomianism of such classes.

The already widely active volunteering culture in this country shows that Cameron's slightly vague 'Big Society' concept with all its accompanying platitudes ('do the right thing' etc.) is already in existence, particularly in areas of the public sector where gaps in state and healthcare provision, most baldly regarding the mentally ill, are filled increasingly by a shadow culture of altruists who are putting more than their fair share back into a society that in the main cynically views them as *workshy*. (How thoroughly perverse it is that our society, one which only values economically productive labour, actively castigates those who are volunteering for the good of the community, and resents contributing paltry amounts of tax in return for their contributions via benefits, and yet praises only waged labour, which is, in spite of financial necessities, still more guided by self-interest than the former. How perverse it is that David Cameron, himself an inherited beneficiary of distinctly non-altruistic capitalist ethics, should start asserting the notion of a new volunteering society, when his own class, by very virtue of their material riches, has for centuries put prices to any contributions they have made to society, even worse, cynically exploited the labour of others to enrich themselves. How contradictory it is too of Cameron to on the one hand call for more volunteering while on the other hand politically victimizing those who are 'economically unproductive', as the modern parlance goes. He is right to emphasise the importance of volunteering, of a more altruistic and co-operative culture, but his policies are ensuring that eventually no one but the very rich will have either the time or financial flexibility to do any volunteering. Or is this country's squirreled-away aristocracy going to finally start mucking in for a change? Somehow, one doubts it.

Indeed, Cameron's actual policies, far from enabling his 'Big Society' to root and flower, are likely to seriously impede, if not entirely stall, any possibility of a co-operative society, outside of the odd rogue blue-rinsed village fete to raise money for a new lick of paint on the parish church. Additionally, the coalition seems to have a very Kitchener-like stance towards voluntarism, effectively pointing a finger saying YOUR COUNTRY NEEDS YOU (...TO LIVE ON THIN AIR); a press-ganging mentality which is hardly conducive with cultivating a genuine spirit of spontaneous communitarianism among the populace. It seems in Cameron's 'Big Society', volunteering will be mandatory, which is something of an oxymoron. It is also, ironically, nearer to Stalinism than ever New Labour managed, and quite a world away from traditional Tory libertarianism. Cameron should be more honest with us and spell out the real reason for this new drive towards a spirit of voluntarism: 'because there won't be any bally jobs for anyone!'

Cameron talks about a new society in which one asks 'what can I contribute' rather than 'what's my entitlement?' — but where are the sacrifices of *his* social class, one which is historically based upon a highly dubious notion of inherited entitlement to privilege and land-ownership, to the old school tie and Oxbridge? And since when has *his* class stopped to think, What can *we* contribute to this society? Is Cameron going to 'roll *his* sleeves up' and volunteer *himself* for his 'Big Society'? Never before has a British government set itself up with such flagrant hypocrisy and duplicity as this Con-Dem coalition; nor has one before, *including* New Labour, instigated such an instant and contradictory culture of spin, and to such a self-parodying extent. The Con-Dems have surpassed even New Labour's Humpty-Dumpty Newspeak by employing 'Old Politics' under the label of 'New Politics', and turning the definitions of certain words and phrases on their heads: *draconian* is now defined as 'fair', *avoidable* as 'unavoidable', *regressive* as 'progressive', *reactionary* as 'radical', *top down* as 'bottom up', *predictable* as 'unprecedented', *mandatory* as 'voluntary', *privatisation* as 'mutualism', *capitalism* as 'localism', *unemployment* as 'idleness', *recession* as 'deficit', *malversation* as 'talent', *embezzlement* as 'mistake' (in the cases of MPs and non-doms only), *mistake* as 'fraud' (in the case of benefit claimants), and so on.

On the local level, a recent news item in *the Brighton Argus* revealed that the city's key base for ethical community volunteering, Community Base, has had its sign on the side of its building banned by Tory Councillors — in spite of dogged Labour and Green opposition — on the spurious grounds of it being 'detrimental to surrounding conservation areas'. Anyone living locally will tell you that it has never been in any obvious way apparent that the grimy Queens Road part of Brighton was a 'conservation area', unless it is one of conserving congestion, polluted air and dirty buildings. But it has also been revealed that the Tory Councillors were actually motivated politically, resenting the fact that during the last election, the Community Base sign was adorned with a poster promoting Caroline Lucas of the Green Party. It is therefore clear that this is not only a knee-jerk malversation by said Tory Councillors, but also a blatant poke in the eye for any sincerity to the new spirit of voluntarism being promoted as a core component to the 'Big Society'. Banning the sign for a city's core community organisation is hardly conducive to promoting voluntarism. So much for localism. This is, indeed, on both national and local levels, one of the most punctually corrupt of administrations, attempting as it has to up the percentage of MPs needed to vote a government out of office: the most anti-democratic move of any British government since Thatcher shaved off half the rights of the Unions in the Eighties leaving us with the most restrictive anti-Union laws in Europe. 'Things *can* be different' said Clegg prior to the election — now we know he stopped short of the final caveat: 'They can be *even worse*'. And already, in only three months, Clegg has played his part, through an unfathomable acquiescence with Tory policies, by demonstrating this in as shamelessly capitulatory a manner as Tony Blair did when scrapping democratic socialism for the demands of the markets on accession to the Labour Party leadership back in 1994.

This 'Big Society' (or 'Little State') will be ever more dependent on charities and volunteers to take on the grubbier jobs of government (which now elucidates the Tory manifesto slogan 'Invitation to join the Government'), putting an unreasonable burden (not to say moral blackmail) on goodwill agencies to operate as a scattered 'shadow Welfare State', as we are already witnessing in the worrying growth of community food banks (one wonders at what point workhouses will be brought back). Things get more Dickensian by the week, Cameron's 'Big Society', with a bit of Clegg's 'bluish liberalism' thrown in, rapidly mutating into more of a 'Whig Society'. This 'vision' of a volunteering society is not only deeply exploitative, but profoundly contradictory coming from a party which only values economically productive labour; not to say, deeply flawed, since it is based on the assumption that there will be anyone left in the position to be able to volunteer any more once the oncoming benefit cuts force thousands out of voluntary community roles into ill-matched employment. This will in turn exacerbate mental health problems and result in further psychiatric referrals, therapies, medications — all of which will cost the State more. That is also assuming there will be any jobs left, after a massive portion of public sector workers are laid off through George

Osborne's ideologically motivated cuts: his is an 'Invitation to Join Unemployment'. In the meantime, of course, many MPs still enjoy their implausible 'second' jobs/professions and lucrative bits on the side for after-dinner speeches and corporate 'consultations'. Perhaps if the coalition MPs were prepared to sacrifice their second jobs and second homes to free up some space in their 'Big Society' for the thousands who are barely able to keep their first and only in both categories, then their austerity sophism might have more credibility.

Inevitably, the oncoming welfare cuts will have a considerably negative effect on all those incapacitated due to mental illness. Through my own volunteering as a creative writing workshop tutor in a psychiatric hospital, I notice an increasingly fast turnaround of patient entrances and exits, and re-entrances; much of this is down to the target-driven pressures the NHS is being put under by successive governments. More and more people are finding the unrelenting pressures of modern British life, whether in work, or out of it (with all the associated government-spun scapegoat motifs of 'closed curtains during the day'), taking their toll. Our society is in dire need of recharging its battery, but our new government is hell-bent on piling ever more stress onto all of our shoulders through increasing austerity, and decreasing opportunities to transcend it. Homelessness will rise, as will psychiatric referrals, and most harrowingly, suicides. The NHS will have to work harder than ever before to meet the oncoming tsunami of demands on its services; siphoning off responsibilities to the private sector will simply muddy the waters by putting profits before patients, as we have witnessed with our de-nationalised railway: from services to 'providers', from passengers to 'customers', privatisation is the repeat offender of over-charging, compromised safety and zero accountability.

Siege of the Hundred Days

The writing is on the wall and has been since 2007, with the economic crisis and the ensuing MPs' expenses scandals: the British will take so much, but will not continue to accept cut after cut without any clear signs of both fiscal and ethical green shoots. New Labour were masters of duplicitous spin but the Con-Dems are amateurs: the cracks are already showing in their rhetoric only 100 days into power: David Cameron can use the phrases 'tough but fair' and 'the right thing' as much as he wants, but he and his government are so brazenly and brutally doing the exact opposite that even the average *News of the World* reader will begin to get a bit disgruntled in time, once the cuts hit home on the domestic level. The protests in London in 2007 will seem like a picnic compared to what will inevitably come if this government does not rein in its ideological malice against any semblance of state or public sector power; because now even those who have behaviourally kept their heads down through the quiet despair of the New Labour era are starting to lose patience and to realise that we now potentially face the worst institutional assault on our collective social rights from any government in living memory, including Margaret Thatcher's (under whom, incidentally, we also had a huge deficit which the Tories seemed far more sanguine about then than their inheritors are today: and that is of course because *this* government, in spite of publicly blaming Labour for being the root of all our troubles in order to score political points, knows full well that this is a global recession with macrocosmic ramifications).

Nick Clegg and the Lib Dems, by way of a side issue, have opted for political oblivion outside of the coalition by their flagrant and unnecessary betrayal of their own values and core voters in their pact with a party situated on the opposite end of the Parliamentary scale to theirs. In many ways, a more likely coalition — but for superficial tribal rivalries — would have been between the Tories and the evermore Malthusian and Thatcherite-capitulating New Labour, than between the Tories and Lib Dems; and commentators are inclined now to think it more a matter of personality than policy, in that Cameron and Clegg, from almost indistinguishable material and educational backgrounds, simply got on better in private than either did with the notoriously 'difficult' Brown. Formerly an evangelist for greater involvement within Europe, the scrapping of Trident, the liberalisation of immigration controls, for further spending and stimulating of the economy and opposition to drastic and swift cuts for the remainder of 2010, and adamantly for the instigation of Proportional Representation, Nick Clegg has shamefully settled for a partnership of expediency with a party that is pathologically against all of his former 'sacred cow' policies. Apparently compromises have been made — but it is extremely difficult to see the evidence of this, except perhaps in the new and welcome humanistic approach to criminal and prison policy. The only sense in which the two parties of the coalition seem to complement one another is in their mutual hand-wringing at the last government during the newly established Three Minute Hate at the despatch-box after the Opposition has thrown its first question in PMQs. It can only be a matter of time before the thunder-faced Danny Alexander starts publicly flagellating himself on the front bench every time the 'unavoidable cuts' are mentioned, to an accompanying howl of 'repent all ye who overspent'.

The recent documentary about the four-day negotiation limbo after the Hung Parliament result of the Election revealed that ultimately the Lib Dems decided that the arithmetic was stacked up against them forming a Rainbow coalition with Labour and the smaller left-of-centre parties (all filmed as if we're already years down the line and it's some sort of forgive-and-forget nostalgia fest). But exactly 100 years before the 2010 'Volcano' Election, there was the famous 1910 Election, in which the then Liberal Government under the radically reformist Herbert Asquith (ideological protégé of Henry Campbell-Bannerman), was intent on reforming the Second Chamber due to the evident fact that all reforms they planned to push through were being systematically filibustered, pettifogged and basically blocked by an essentially Tory House of Lords; this ideological face off between the elected Commons and the hereditary Lords — initiated by the ailing Liberal PM Campbell-Bannerman who then passed the baton to his chosen successor Herbert Asquith — threatened to develop into an out and out split in the British establishment, and was already a figurative Class War, both on behalf of the Liberal middle classes who wished to have more political autonomy from the Second Chamber's landed classes, and for the ordinary people, for whom the Government's failure would mean the loss of the belated introduction of state payments for the unemployed (the foreshadower of the Welfare State).

A Hung Parliament resulted from the first election of 1910, and so Asquith bravely opted for a second election in the hope it would prove more decisive. It didn't: instead, an identical amount of votes resulted between the Liberal Government and its Tory Opposition. The relatively new Labour Party, then under the leadership of Arthur Henderson, was the fourth party, and, as it turned out in the second election of that year, the surprise deciders as to whether to allow in a new Tory minority government with support from the third largest Unionists, or to support the Liberals as a minority government, in spite of the arithmetic not quite being there. In 1910, the Labour Party chose an 'alliance of principle' over arithmetic. In 2010, the Lib Dem kingmakers chose an 'alliance of arithmetic' over principle, yet oddly citing the decision as one of democratic scrupulosity: they felt although the nation had voted indecisively, what it had clearly *not* done was vote for an extension to the then-New Labour government's term of office, and certainly not under the leadership of the unpopular Brown.

So the Lib Dems fell back on their obsessive-democratic disorder and decided to impale their principles on the will of a baying tabloid mob. Even now Clegg still uses this worn out, rather self-defeating line of argument to justify continuing in the coalition even if AV is not voted in, because then 'the country would have spoken'. This is hardly inspiring stuff from a political leader but is ideologically spineless: it is a way of palming off personal responsibility to the whims of a First Past the Post system which Clegg and his party are supposed to be completely against as a grossly disproportional representation of national opinion. And yet when put into a corner, he and his Orange Book apologists suddenly talk as if FPP is somehow a proportionate gauge of national opinion. But the point remains that even if the Lib Dems felt it would not be representative of the will of the people to join with Labour in order to keep the Tory party out of power, he still did not have to go into an alliance with the Tories; he could have either remained on the opposition benches, or agreed to support the more amenable policies of a minority Tory administration. By joining in a coalition with the Tories, the Lib Dems have made a pact for political oblivion by betraying their own party's heritage even more swiftly and brazenly than New Labour managed with its own: it was a Liberal, William Beveridge, who inspired the founding of the Welfare State and NHS with his now legendary 'Beveridge Report' of 1942.

Many on the Left, disillusioned with the ideological degeneration of Labour — its engineering of 'benefit-stigmatisation' via the paradigm of the 'deserving and undeserving poor' by way of one example — trusted in Clegg's 'alternative' at the time, and our trust has cost us dearly. Never before, even with Tony Blair, have we witnessed such a graphic illustration of ideological truncation in return for power as we have with Clegg: in a matter of months, he's swung from loud-hailing electoral radical to Tory prop. Clegg faces a similar legacy of party betrayal as that which dogged Labour's first Prime Minister, James Ramsay MacDonald, for forming a National Government with mostly Tory MPs during the financial crisis of the Great Depression in 1931. The only difference here is that Clegg's Liberal Democrat colleagues have yet to show the courage of their 1931 progenitors and expel their Leader in order to preserve the integrity of their party. So far, most are truly deserving of their party's colour. The much-trumpeted 'New Politics' seems every bit as corrupt as the 'Old'; the only difference is titular.

It is with some considerable temerity that the Con-Dems are now referring to Labour's economic legacy as 'criminal', when its own deeply discriminatory and draconian Budget might well be given precisely the same epithet on any objective ethical or moral basis. The only salvation left for the Lib Dems now is for left-of-centre Deputy Simon Hughes, already making noises as to a future pact with Labour being 'on the agenda', to challenge Nick Clegg for the leadership of his party and swiftly detach it from the stitched-together Frankenstein's monster of a coalition, and cross the floor to join a Rainbow Opposition of the centre-left. Better still, Hughes and the Lib Dem executive could just oust Clegg (as the Labour Party did Ramsay MacDonald back in 1931, leaving him to reign as Prime Minister over a virtual Tory government.

Not only that but it is more of an aggressive Thatcherite administration than the comparatively more compassionate One Nation/Disraelian Toryism that Cameron's party 'makeover' had led the electorate to expect (which, given the softening of right-wing policies one presumed would come with Lib Dem inclusion, is all the more nastily surprising). That Clegg recently stated that the Liberal Democrats were not, nor ever would be, a party for the disaffected Left (in spite of his cynically baiting their votes which helped him maintain sufficient seats to still be leading the third party in Parliament; though it is hoped the Greens will usurp that position in 2015) is the final insult.

The Whig Society

Cameron's much-vaunted though seldom-defined 'Big Society' looks set to turn the clock back to the days of Victorian-style self-help and deferral of social responsibility and altruism to charities. The Tories — with precious little opposition from their incumbent Lib Dems — appear set to dismantle the Welfare State and privatise the NHS out of existence. These right-wing obsessions with the free market — which has proved itself every bit as wasteful, profligate and bureaucratic as the so-called big government and bureaucratic state traditionally blamed on Labour governments — and a fanatical anti-statism betray the out-dated ideological roots of the 'Big Society': it is a quaint One Nation Tory idiomatic sampler for what will actually be another crack at the Thatcherite whip. What is dangerous about Cameron's social doctrine is its being born from ignorance of the nitty-gritty of ordinary life, one of the legion privileges of the upper classes. How can, in all reasonableness, someone of Cameron's pseudo-aristocratic, Eton-educated background possibly understand in any real empirical sense the harsh realities faced by those millions still living in relative — even in some cases, absolute — poverty in this country, anymore than an average tenant of a council estate can fathom the punctilious obscurantism behind the tradition of passing port-decanters to the left at stately dining tables? Of course no one can help the background they are born in to, but they *can* help the course they take afterwards, and Cameron hardly enhanced his chances at gaining a more comprehensive understanding of modern working-class life by joining the Tories, a party which is almost by tradition socially myopic. Accusations of 'class war' might be punctually forthcoming to such comments as these, that it is 'rude' now to refer to one's class; but one might reasonably say it is 'rude' to have a class system in the first place, and that the standard for any new class war has been pitched and raised on the high ground of contemporary Tory politics, through its transparently ideological cuts to the public sector and its deeply scarring assault on the Welfare State — for thousands on thousands, the only safety net left between hardship and destitution, between unemployment and homelessness.

This government needs to move extremely carefully in making its fiscally-driven adjustments to the fragile and crucial structure of the Welfare State. It is not something to be toyed with half-heartedly like a bored toddler's train set. It presently keeps millions from abject poverty, even if it is also correct to argue that it also maintains millions in relative poverty and is certainly in dire need of reform. *EV* cautiously welcomes proposed efforts by the seemingly well-meaning — though shelteredly silver-spooned — Iain Duncan Smith, the new Work and Pensions Secretary, to attempt simplifying an absurdly complex and frequently disenfranchising benefits system. Such propositions as those are hopeful and reasonable and could conceivably make it much easier for many to get back into employment without suffering the nonsensical stripping of all state support on signing off, thus a first month's impoverished labour until the first pay packet. However, Iain Duncan Smith's simultaneous smearing of benefit recipients as if to further fan the flames of George Osborne's frankly nasty remark about 'curtains closed during the day', with phrases such as 'institutionalised idleness', is far from helpful, not to say deeply insulting. This government's attitudinal posture that tacitly implicates all benefit claimants in a broad Rab C. Nesbitt stereotype is, along with the demonisation of the public sector, absolutely typical of Tory divide and rule methods: pit the public against the private sector, galvanise public resentment towards the largely fictive 'bedsitter capitalist' who milks his fortune of £65 quid a week off the hard-working jolly-good-egg taxpayer. This is not only deeply draconian and irresponsible of a government, but it is also intellectually pathetic.

It seems, though, that even the small and rather shoddy modicum of 'compassionate conservatism' still gasping for its share of air in an otherwise Thatcherite Cabinet is about to be scuppered on the jagged shores of Osborne's unapologetically regressive budget: as I write this, there is an internecine dispute simmering away between IDS and the Chancellor regarding the vexed welfare reform issues. Unfortunately the more compassionate IDS seems to be singing from a very different hymn-sheet to the Chancellor. It remains to be seen whether Osborne will moderate his callow classist excesses now that Home Secretary Theresa May has warned him that his budget's transparent targeting of women, the disabled and the old in society might be in breach of the Equalities Act 2010. As I write this, the Equalities and Human Rights Commission (EHRC) are threatening the Treasury with censure if it cannot meet a legal requirement to assess the impacts of cuts on the poor. The results of this welcome intervention remain to be seen.

Osborne's malicious cuts are blatantly ideological, not to mention entirely unmitigated on any moral, ethical or even electoral level: to use the purely incidental inherited government deficit as a smokescreen for an ideological *blitzkrieg* on the Welfare State and public sector is the worst form of political calumny imaginable and has only taken Osborne a mere two months to cook up. Even more scandalous of course is the Lib Dems' apparent support for these vicious cuts, even after running their election campaign specifically opposing anything even vaguely as severe as the ones now proposed, while supporting Labour's stimulus package. While it is clear that Business Secretary Vince Cable is growing noticeably ever more weary of his new role as Tory Hatchet Prop, it is far less than clear that Deputy Prime Minister Nick Clegg is tussling with his conscience to the same degree. Quite oppositely, Clegg seems now to be nothing more than a perpetual and intransigent apologist for the 'emergency' Budget, still deludingly referring to it as 'progressive', and openly barking back at independent body the Institute for Fiscal Studies, that he and his Tory colleagues 'don't accept' its expert verdict on the 'emergency' Budget, alleging it is 'selective' and 'partial'. But such intransigent allegations are likely to fall on deaf ears since the IFS's conclusion is absolutely adamant:

Our analysis shows that the overall effect of the new reforms announced in the June 2010 budget is regressive, whereas the tax and benefit reforms announced by the previous government for introduction between June 2010 and April 2014 are progressive... Low-income households of working age lose the most from the June 2010 budget reforms because of the cuts to welfare spending. [quoted in *the Guardian*, 25th August 2010].

The most damning statement of all however came from the coalition's own ranks when local government minister Bob Neill admitted to the House of Commons in June that: 'Those in greatest need ultimately bear the burden of paying off the debt.' After constantly calling their Labour opposition 'deficit deniers', the coalition apparatchiks are now demonstrating yet another new dimension of hypocrisy by openly being themselves 'regressiveness-' and 'double-dip deniers'.

Poets in Defence of the Welfare State (PDWS)

*E*mergency *Verse*'s core purpose is to defend our Welfare State, its sixty-five year history and its founding principles, from an unacceptably Thatcherite £18 Billion of cuts. And all this at the further expense of a British public that was forced to bail out the very banks and speculators who bankrupted its economy and who have got off scot-free with a paltry £2 Billion levy! This half-hearted slap on the wrists for the speculators no doubt had them, as one commentator put it, 'laughing into their champagne flutes' while the rest of us have to scrimp every penny just to survive. *EV* is more than just a titular response to the 'emergency' Budget, even though the latter hardly needs any dialectical damning since its own flagrant unfairness damns itself. [A petition in defence of the NHS is also implicit in the sub-title of this anthology, since Nye Bevan's brainchild came into existence under the umbrella of 'the Welfare State'. *EV* is unequivocally opposed to the apocalyptic proposals of the arch-Thatcherite Andrew Lansley to further spread the virus of privatisation throughout the publicly-funded NHS, which will inevitably turn our universal health care system into nothing more than a business, putting the profits of unscrupulous pharmaceutical capitalists before the needs of patients]. Any threat to the Welfare State is a direct threat to every single person in this country, unemployed or employed, who does not come from a background of sufficient inherited wealth — unlike the majority of our plutocratic Cabinet, most of whom are multi-millionaires, chiefly through capital inheritance (and, no doubt, property speculation) rather than through their own hard work — to be able to survive without any state assistance when, as inevitably will happen, they are tipped onto the scrapheap of unemployment following the oncoming storm of enormous public sector sackings. The Welfare State is the ordinary citizen's only insurance against destitution. The upper classes have their own safety nets, their own health and educational resources, their own sector; in effect, their own society.

So what right, therefore, do emissaries from the privileged elite have to come into power and tell the rest of us to tighten our already tightened belts, to surrender our public health and social services to unprincipled charlatans and profiteers, our state education system to middle-class cabals of parental privatisers, and our welfare benefit system to the snatching jaws of a penny-pinching, miserablist, Scrooge-like administration of millionaires? What right, even more fundamentally, do those such as they, who simply wish to devolve all governmental powers, localise and privatise, have to go into politics, into public service, in the first place? Marxist dialectics can instantly augment these questions by posing further and more penetrating quandaries, and should not be overlooked: is this new capitalistic pseudo-aristocratic government essentially the vanguard of a fiscal plenipotentiary to defend the interests of the capitalist elite at the peoples' great expense? Based on all evidence so far, the answer has to be unequivocally Yes. This government is naturally in thrall — as New Labour was to its own ruination — to Rupert Murdoch, the distinctly uncharismatic Citizen Kane of our times. Murdoch controls most of our press, and so calls the shots politically too.

Emergency Verse aspires to place itself as part of a British dialectical literary tradition: it is attempting in its way to reconnect with an ancestry of polemical pamphleteering, protest verse and song, of the likes of the Levellers and John Lilburne, the Diggers and Gerrard Winstanley (both voices of the left-wing arm of the post-Civil War Parliamentarian intelligentsia, crackling from the radicalised ranks of the New Model Army); through the literature of the Chartists and poets such as Shelley who wrote against the Peterloo Massacre (in his exceptional 'Mask of Anarchy'); to the last century, from the internationalist Left of Auden, John Cornford, Edgell Rickword, Randall Swingler, Christopher Caudwell; and the long lineage of socialist poetry, as anthologised in *the Penguin Book of Socialist Verse* (Alan Bold; 1970) and *Bricklight — Poems from the Labour Movement in East London* (Chris Searle, Pluto Press, 1980). Perhaps the closest ancestor of *Emergency Verse* is *Where There's Smoke* (Colin Samson, Hackney Writers' Workshop, 1983), a remarkable gathering of anti-Thatcherite verse, one of whose core contributors, the esteemed writer Ken Worpole, is also among this anthology's contributors. Any future comparisons between *EV* and two preceding ideologically left-wing poetry anthologies of the 'Noughties', *Red Sky at Night: Socialist Poetry* (eds. Adrian Mitchell, Andy Croft, Five Leaves, 2003), and the late John Rety's *Well Versed: poems from the Morning Star* (Hearing Eye, 2008), would be taken as supreme compliments. Like the aforementioned anthologies, *EV* is also both political and *ideological*, which separates it from broader humanitarian campaign anthologies such as Todd Swift's *100 Poets Against the War* (Salt, 2003) — the admirable protest against the Iraq invasion — since *EV* is not a single-issue campaign, nor a trans-partisan one: it is, in its open dialectical opposition to this coalition government's entire agenda as distilled brutally in the budget, a verse campaign of the Left. Nevertheless, *EV* is certainly targeting a specific political vicissitude in its defence of a welfare state being nakedly targeted in a government budget; so in this sense, it also stands at a slant from the more broadly ideological anthologies I have cited. It is then in its own distinct camp: an ideological poetry campaign triggered by specific government legislation and in the cause of preserving the Welfare State, inclusive of the National Health Service as a state-maintained institution — a universal issue, since the interests of *every* ordinary citizen in this country are invested in it. But *EV* is also a rallying-call for a Rainbow realignment of the literary Left, as one Column of a broader national vanguard in ideological opposition to what we perceive to be a return to unreconstructed Thatcherism on the part of the new 'coalition'. The credentials of *EV*'s 'Rainbow' call to all parties and groups on the Left in the UK is signatured by its patron, Caroline Lucas of the Green Party, the MP whom most personifies at this moment such a will towards trans-tribal left-wing pluralism, which this verse campaign supports. I have the utmost respect for Caroline Lucas, and her election to Parliament as the first Green MP was the one ray of hope in what was otherwise the bleakest General Election since 1992. (I extend my sincerest gratitude to Caroline for helping to raise the profile of *EV* through her generously spirited patronage). The 'ideology' broadly promoted by *EV* as the only viable alternative to the current status quo, then, is democratic socialism. This is not to say every contributor necessarily subscribes to a 'socialist' ethos, but the majority would probably describe themselves as 'left-wing', or at very least, 'left-of-centre'. A significant number of contributors would articulate their politics identically as I have done my own; some would describe theirs as communist, Marxist or anarchist.

What undeniably unites all of us is an intense dissatisfaction with the nature of unregulated capitalist society and an absolute opposition to a government which seeks without full electoral mandate to impose almost precisely the opposite policies to those most of us voted for; policies that will simply worsen and deepen the systematic breakdown of our economy and society for generations to come. By dismantling the Welfare State, the Con-Dems will be dismantling the social insurance of that very 'next generation' in whose 'name' they claim to be acting. Any remotely insightful analyst of such Con-Dem sophistry, however, can clearly see that this much-trumpeted crusade is purely titular, and that it is in the interests of the moneyed and propertied classes of this society that the government is so cavalierly pillaging our public sector.

If this government was truly mindful of the next generation — who continually ghost their policies — not being saddled with the debt of ours, then they would not be making the choice to cut such a large chunk out of the welfare system, which is almost certain to throw the babes out with the bathwater. The only fair and legitimate way to cut the deficit is to bring in the Robin Hood Tax and thereby get the culprits of the recession, the speculators in the City and their associated banks, to reimburse the state's black hole. The Government might also have the basic moral and ethical decency and courage to turn its attention to the tax-dodging super-rich instead of venting its fiscal spleen on the poorest in society like a pack of feudal barons (in the Chancellor Guy de Osborne's case, *literally*, being a Baronet-in-waiting by primogeniture). *That* would be 'fair'; *that* would show that 'we are all in this together'.

I would like to thank the 111 poets who contributed promptly and powerfully to this poetry anthology campaign, and whose names also constitute an implicit petition against the Government's 'emergency' Budget. I have been overwhelmed by the sheer speed, quality and quantity of contributions from a wide range of voices, some long-established, some new and emerging, and many from that potent hinterland in-between; indeed, at times I've felt deeply moved by the sheer scale and passion of the answer to my initial call: *Poets of the Nation Unite*. Contributors are of various age groups too, from those who can still distantly remember the days before Thatcherism infested the nation's heart like a cancerous tumour, and the optimism of the post-war consensus; those who grew up during the radicalised Sixties'; those around my own age group who can vaguely remember the very different country Britain was pre-1979 (one which, in spite of industrial problems, was among the most socially equal in Europe) and who came of age during the dark days of Thatcherism, of rampant privatisations and deregulated markets, of spiralling unemployment, cardboard cities, and the Miners' Strike; down to those born into Thatcher's devastation and grew up during the whitewash of the New Labour era, the end of which spelt financial crisis for a country now among the most socially unequal in Europe. The lasting legacy of monetarism then: fiscal, social and moral bankruptcy.

According to many recent polls, the nation is split between those who have already had enough of the Con-Dem Government only three months into their thumbscrew tenure, and those who seem to swallow front-bench rhetoric of 'unavoidable cuts' with the same sort of unquestioning obsequiousness as Hudson the butler in *Upstairs, Downstairs,* bowing gratefully as his superiors demurely give him notice to seek a new 'situation' since they can no longer afford to keep him (appropriately enough for our class-ridden times, the series is being resurrected this Christmas). But this state of national masochism cannot last. The truth will out in the end and many of us can see already that the 'Big Society' is yet another neo -Thatcherite, distinctly un-progressive euphemism for a regressive system of state-shrinking and further impoverishment of the poor and vulnerable. The Big Society, if it survives into maturity, could well threaten the foundations not only of our Welfare State and NHS, but of our social democracy, of our very fundamental sense of tolerance. There is no such thing as 'the Big Society', to paraphrase Margaret Thatcher: her inheritors are using a One Nation Tory shield to disguise what is in real terms a re-instigation of Eighties' divide-and-rule politics. This is becoming more and more apparent by the week, with the latest threat to our democracy being proposed sanctions, even attempts to ban, the right to strike among frontline services. Such a Falangist, even Tsarist, response to an already feudalistically inclined system of vast financial disparities, could be the final blow to the nation's stability and tip it into such severe civil strife that an even bigger political crisis than that promised by the MPs' expenses scandal could lead to mass protests and riots on a scale not seen since the Eighties.

The Government says 'we are all in this together', when what they mean is, *they* 'are all in it together': this 'emergency' Budget is a naked assault on the most defenceless citizens of the country. It is being waged on behalf of the vested interests of the capitalist classes, cordially represented by their apologists and petitioners among the multi-millionaire Cabinet. David Cameron is our first aristocratic prime minister since Alex Douglas Home — a breed of premiere that was scoffed at as a dodoism only thirty years ago. Britain has regressed politically, socially and morally to a society increasingly similar to pre-Welfare State Britain, a vicissitude which has been practically invited in by New Labour's complacent acquiescence to the dictat of the markets and abject failure (or lack of will) to narrow the wealth divide. More terrible, its latter welfare-scapegoating policy putsch has now enabled a new administration to capitalise on a burgeoning consensus that a large section of the unemployed are 'undeserving' and have 'opted' for their poverty. This nation was not 'in it together' during the Eighties; not during the Miners' Strike; nor was it 'in it together' during the Poll Tax riots, or during the Iraq protests — it was divided then, and it is divided now.

Emergency Verse — A Movement

*E*mergency *Verse* opposes the Con Dem 'emergency Budget', and petitions this government to reverse its most draconian aspects, most particularly the cuts proposed to the Welfare State, the public sector, and the new threats to sell off the National Health Service to private profiteers. Until such policies are reversed and fairly amended so as not to disenfranchise the poorest and most vulnerable in society, *Emergency Verse* will continue to campaign through periodic anthologies by way of petition, to engage the media in covering its campaign, and to seek wider contributions, support and patronage from various social and arts charities and organisations. As far as we, the Poets in Defence of the Welfare State, are concerned, this is the greatest call to literary arms since the Miners' Strike; or even further back, to that of the rise of Falangist-Fascism that sparked the Spanish Civil War.

Few would argue that the labyrinthine bureaucratic welfare system does not need any reform, and, as mentioned earlier, one or two proposals by Duncan Smith to simplify the system and to extend state support to those only just entering work but waiting for their first wage to come through, is welcome. As would have been the more contentious but now at any rate truncated new dialogue as to means-testing some benefits for the middle classes. Debatably the Welfare State was flawed from the start by its slightly unrealistic universalism which, in the case of the NHS, meant further down the line that, for instance, universal prescription charges had to be introduced in order to sustain costs of supporting everyone in society in spite of their individual means (the NHS's highly ambitious promise of being 'free for all on the point of delivery' was inevitably compromised in time, some critics replacing the 'free' with 'rationed'). Universalism seemed based on a quixotic notion that somehow society was already on an equal level materially; but it was precisely because it *wasn't* that the Welfare State was necessitated in the first place.

The real reason behind applying an egalitarianism of state provision to a non-egalitarian society must be that of the Labour Party's morbid fear of ever being perceived as waging war against the wealthy (a defensive mindset which has blunted the radical edge of the party ever since the emergence of the Cold War in 1947, which forced its hand in government to take sides against the rise of Soviet Communism in Eastern Europe and ally itself with the capricious, capitalist USA). Arguably all benefits should, by dint of their very purpose (originally, one of levelling, though nowadays more one of begrudging damage-limitation), be based on means-testing, complicated though this would be: presently, blanket rates are dished out across the board irrespective of the differing rental and living costs in certain areas, and as well, without consideration for service charges, which vary from household to household. However, any realigning of the benefits system to target the most in need *would not* feel as safe in lily-white Tory hands as it would in those of true-grit progressives. At any rate, the uproar over the badly implemented child benefit caps has now decisively kicked this debate into the long grass.

Unfortunately, the otherwise articulate Yvette Cooper has further demonstrated that her party still has yet to learn from the consequences of the banking crisis, by piping up with a tiresome and completely out-of-touch Brownite rhetoric as to 'attempts to curb spending on "middle-class" benefits'. It is highly disturbing that at this point in events, with the lower classes cowering under a Damocles of welfare cuts, that a leading Opposition spokesperson is still tub-thumping for the 'aspirational' middle classes (possibly because she locates herself among their hallowed ranks). This is not the sort of peach-coloured politics we either want or need spouted by the Opposition at this time. What we need to hear now is more of the ethical socialism of the Labour Representation Committee, and the ecologically-tinged egalitarianism of the Green Party. There needs to be a Rainbow coalition of the Left in Parliament, and if that means the last left-wing MPs left in Labour splitting off and forming a proper socialist co-operative with the Greens and Scottish Nationalists, then so be it. What we absolutely *do not need* at this time is another fence-sitting, bloodless New Labour facsimile; there is simply no place now for centre-ground point-scoring — it has had its day, and now ideology must rise to the occasion. Centrism will offer no credible or ideologically alternative Opposition and could consign Labour to an undistinguished shadow of the capitalist coalition. The Left must not at any point be complacent, even when the odd rogue coalition proposal sounds faintly tinged with whatever infusion of 'fairness' the Lib Dems can massage through its tightening fist. The Con-Dems are not merely reforming the welfare system, they are shaking it to its very foundations, making sure that £18 Billion worth of fiscal leaf tumbles to the ground in the process; and every leaf is a life. The point is being missed on a monumental scale in the current parliamentary and public dialectic: whether or not the welfare system needs reform or paring down is beside the point in terms of deficit reduction or combating the recession, since neither the welfare system, nor the unemployed, sick, disabled, or public sector, caused this financial crisis — the City did, and where is *its* share of the pain, of the burden, on *its* 'broadest shoulders'? What is more, the public sector is needed more urgently than ever *because* of the financial crisis! This government is cynically using the 'deficit' as an excuse to crowbar in ideological clamps on our Welfare State and NHS.

Emergency Verse opposes such political brinkmanship as not only fundamentally unfair and unjustifiable, but also as thoroughly spurious on any platform that tackles the subject of deficit or recession. The New Labour Government increased its deficit for public spending because of having to bail out the Banking sector during the credit crisis *that* sector caused; this also of course impacted on all taxpayers, who, while the Banks go back into the black and start paying themselves bonuses again, have yet to receive any reimbursement. Worse still, not only are the public refused loans by the now thriftier Banks, they also get further punishments as its new government decides to plunder its public services for a state of affairs that had nothing to do with them in the first place. Elementary moral and ethical logic dictates that the culprit pays for the crime: this government is asking the victims to pay for it. Our campaign says NO to this. *EV* says: introduce the Robin Hood Tax to reimburse the State for the bail-out and redistribute the surplus among the people. This campaign says leave our Welfare State and NHS alone. *EV* says NO to the con of the 'Big Society', which we reject as a cynical smokescreen for a new Thatcherism. This campaign will continue to stand up against this Con-Dem Government, its Budget and policies, and will encourage Opposition to the insult of the 'Big Society' every step of the way. In answer to the 'emergency' Budget, *Emergency Verse* emphatically echoes the mantra, NOT IN OUR NAME, and will keep saying it until this coalition government listens, or is pushed out of power altogether. And it *will* have to listen eventually: when protests such as Millbank's become ever more common over the coming months, it is only a matter of time before the tramping feet of the People's Mandate — to quote Shelley's rallying-call in 'The Mask of Anarchy' — swells to an 'unvanquishable number'.

Alan Morrison
PDWS Co-ordinator and *EV* Editor
August 2010

Insurance
Some propositions in defence, and pursuit, of the Kind Society
by Norman Jope

For most of my adult life, as now, I've paid taxes and it's inevitable — given my single, able-bodied status — that most of this has gone to support others. The only thing I've wanted in return has been insurance, not just with regard to health and defence but also work — in the form of a reasonable income if I lose a job, or can stand it no longer, or decide to move to another location without a job lined up. The erosion of this insurance makes us all a little bit more like slaves than we were — no matter how benign the conditions under which we might work as individuals. Choice, once more, is reserved for the millionaires (including those in the Cabinet).

*

I've seen lovers and good friends driven to despair and exile by the so-called 'war on the unemployed' (as a newspaper in my part of the world once put it). I've seen their creativity devalued as a 'hobby', whereas flipping burgers, cold-calling telesales or giving out leaflets counts as 'real work'. I've longed for the replacement of a compulsory work-ethic with an encouraging and nurturing ethic of participation ...in vain, of course. I've listened to mean-spirited rhetoric from politicians anxious to mop up the votes of the resentful. As with so much else, the more muted the resistance the worse the onslaught gets — and, whilst it's been painful to many, the saddest thing to me is that it's hit some of the most generous and dedicated members of the community the hardest.

*

For creativity requires time, what the Latin poet Horace called 'strenuous idleness'. A healthy society creates enough idleness for creativity to flourish in. Our 'affluenza', as Oliver James puts it neatly, demands that time be used up to the max in working or consuming, and that no-one should be left alone with their thoughts for longer than is unavoidable. Anyone who fails to keep a full diary, or who is not constantly available to receive the latest e-mail, text message, phone call — or advertisement — is somehow suspect. And yet, if our lives are made of anything it is time. We can live most vividly when our schedules are blank, as long as they are not blank spaces filled with worry and anxiety. And it suits the system to make us worried and anxious, so that we fear and shun those spaces rather than see them as opportunities.

*

Poetry, as the ultimate non-commercial art-form, is the one least respected by the haters of free time and the lovers of money. Why is it so subversive? Not only because it is the least material of art forms, but because it is one that thrives on contemplation — the calm, irregular hours and silence that it needs are denied to the 'getting and spending' that, in Wordsworth's words, 'lay waste our powers'. Moreover, as those of us who deal in it know, it can bend time in ways that would otherwise seem impossible. For it has its own time... the time of the un-owned word.

*

We do not know what the future will make use of, and this applies above all in the creative sphere. Over the past few decades, a considerable number of recognised creative artists have used the dole as a breathing-space and a springboard. Anyone who admires the work of one, or more, of those artists is a (belated) beneficiary of their giro cheque. Granted, for every one such figure several others may fail, but that's what blue sky research is all about. As a citizen and taxpayer, it's a price that I'm prepared to continue to pay.

*

Having had my bouts of 'strenuous idleness', I am now prepared for another fifteen to twenty years of continuous full-time employment until I retire. I pursue my creative interests amongst a host of competing priorities, of which my day-job is the most time-intensive. I used my times of relative leisure as wisely as I could... how could I resent it if others, now, are doing the same? And who, moreover, is certain — apart from a minority, including most members of the current cabinet — not to end up on the dole, or on incapacity benefit or so-called 'employment support allowance', given the right combination of circumstances? And how arrogant it is to assume that every such claimant is languishing in despair... it comes across as more of a hope, in fact, than an assumption.

*

Chasing infinite wealth on a finite planet, we scurry in our mazes struggling to breathe and loosen our limbs. Dare we slack off? Dare we allow our economies, here on a large European island (as opposed to America's Airstrip One), to decline in relative importance so that we can relax a little more and do other things with our lives? It won't always be an easy discipline to learn, by any means. But at least we have the luxury of being able to learn it in relative ease. We Western Europeans, as a whole, also have the recent experience of a (relatively) humane and progressive social order, borne out of the atrocities of the first half of the previous century, to sustain us... along with the knowledge that things have become harsher, over the past three decades, in order to benefit a minority to whom we owe no favours.

*

If work pays more than a pittance, it will be done. Scrap benefits altogether and the work will be done but life and society will be hell. I'm waiting for the first think-tank of well-heeled young professionals to come up with this, at least for the able-bodied. But offer a modest basic income to meet survival needs, and make work pay on top of that, and the work will be done too. And life and society will not be hell.

*

But why pay out all that money (we will be asked) so that people can sleep in late and laze in front of daytime TV? The first answer is that it helps us all to have a safety-net, to be freed from the anxiety that its lack creates, even if it means carrying a minority of passengers in the short-to-medium term. The second answer is that work should always pay, which could be the case if a modest basic income were established. The third answer is that, if society has churned out a horde of de-motivated, illiterate and unemployable citizens then forcing them into work, in itself, is unlikely to make them any more motivated, employable or literate. And the fourth answer is that they are the exceptions that are constantly 'proved' to be the rule — the vast majority of human beings are mature enough to know that we must participate in society for society to function and we should not be held to ransom, therefore, by an emphasis on the minority.

*

Global experience suggests that the more porous the safety-net, the more likely it is that the unemployed will turn to crime — as in other European countries where benefits for single people are time-limited — or to political extremism, as in the Middle East where they don't exist at all. Shall we decide to go down that route? It now costs more, apparently, to keep a prisoner in jail than to send a boarder to Eton. Short of sending all the prisoners to Eton, it makes sense to maintain a safety-net. And it would be a truism that harshness engenders harshness — at least, if it wasn't ignored and disregarded so much.

*

We should not be afraid, therefore, to use the verb 'to bully' to describe what is happening, daily, in the UK's benefit offices and assessment centres. It is neither liberal nor democratic to bully the vulnerable — and nor can a truly Big Society be a small-hearted one. What happens as a result of fear is always grudging, even when this is not consciously recognised or acknowledged. The fear of destitution hangs, increasingly, over this society and in a society of relative plenty this is an evil as well as a mistake.

*

The Kind Society is the one that most of us would flourish in, and it is slipping from our grasp by the day. This is indeed an emergency because decisions are being made that will affect the quality of our lives, the texture of our lives, in the years to come. There are far too many countries in the world where destitution is an ever-present risk for the majority. Do we wish to live without insurance, joining those ranks? Or is it time, at last, to stand up for a more humane and, dare I say, sustainable alternative?

Big Society, Big Noise, Big Deal
by Brian Beamish

We can change. I've always believed in this possibility. Despite successive governments, like the one under which we find ourselves declaring class war on the very people that voted for change. The very people, if I might take the liberty of speaking on behalf of briefly, who did not vote for the Con-Dem coalition but voted against old New Labour. I believed like many others that we could change the voting system to give a fair representation of the people. Proportionally. Seem to have heard those hastily dispatched words somewhere before. Only now when their electoral masks have slipped and their manifestoes have crumbled into the gutter of promises, do we have the alternative reality — Alternative Vote. This is neither the democracy we wanted nor the courage we believed the Lib Dem coalition partners were showing; this is capitulation. Unable to strike a deal with a tired, stale and deeply unpopular Labour government under Brown, Clegg's only recourse was to go cap in hand to Cameron and beg for a job. He never was a kingmaker, but a lowly pawn, taking the crumbs and having his big ideas watered down to absurdity. His position was always going to be untenable. He could not have sided with Labour and assorted other minor parties; we would have felt cheated for change. And yet what do we have now? Same old Tories with a different face. Watered-down principles and cracks within the Lib Dems' senior ranking party members, clearly disconsolate with the policies and action plans that have been formed since the alliance was first created.

The coalition appears to me to be following in previous Tory footsteps — the 'Victorian Values' of Thatcher, 'Back to Basics' and the non-existent warm beer and cricket golden age of John Major. They are attempting to persuade us to 'Dig for Victory' whereas all they are doing is getting the working class to dig their own graves. Deep graves alongside such untimely deaths as the welfare state, affordable housing, the winter fuel allowance, fair state pensions. N.H.S. R.I.P.

As the change that we couldn't believe in comes along I have a feeling that the voices of the past will begin once again to take to the streets — Class War and other anarchist groups, Stop the War Coalition, the SWP, etc. I wonder whether they will be given the air time that they enjoyed during the 90s with a largely supportive press deciding what is 'news' and what is not.

I feel with every fibre of my body that the older I get the more socialist I become, the constant injustices of governments, mismanaging the public purse, the welfare state, blending utilities with private enterprise despite the collapse and corruption of so many corporations, banks and businesses in the past 30 years. It beggars belief that successive generations of government are out for all they can make in their term and screw the country when they leave because they have their ennoblements, knighthoods and chairmanships waiting for them along with the easy life to which they are well used in perpetuity with solid pensions, bonuses, golden handshakes and the like.

The same is true in the corporate world — successive CEOs come and go — all come on board with narrow self-interest in their sights; to increase profit, which in turn mollifies shareholders, thereby increasing their own remuneration. And so the whole cycle begins again with

CEO number 2. And how does all this happen? With so-called cost reduction, rationalisation, downsizing. These euphemisms were only ever created to soften the blow to the executive's conscience. They talk of having the business' interests at heart, which neatly disguises the fact that people will lose their jobs. How much easier it is to sleep at night saying "I have saved the company money" than it is by saying "I have had someone indirectly sacked". This is not change, this is government policy writ large. Our government is corporatised. Cost reduction of the Welfare State. Rationalising the public sector workforce. Downsizing the Metropolitan Police.

Here comes disease and the long waiting list. Here comes unemployment. Here comes crime.

I began this piece by saying we can change and I believe we can. Change doesn't necessarily come from revolution but from a simple choice.

If all we are in this world is consumers, customers, or that dirty word 'stakeholders', then we have a very clear and simple choice: Consume or Boycott. It's a testament to how much we have consumed already that whatever town or city we visit has its identikit parts from the same source; namely the corporation. As we walk down the high street, we pass McDonalds, Starbucks, Tesco, KFC, and so on ad infinitum. The initial saviour of competition that drove down prices, became the monopoly that drove out choice, fairness, family businesses and other unimportant things like that.

Our choice is also in who to vote for; not on their looks or their soundbites or their phoney promises but by solid ideals and radical change. It was often said by friends and colleagues of mine that the Liberal Democrats were in the easy position of being able to say just what they like when in third-party opposition as they could not conceive of getting near power with this outdated and undemocratic First Past the Post voting system we still have. Yet, suddenly having greatness "thrust upon 'em", these same Liberal Democrats show that they are not the radical voice of the progressive centre-left, but instead the lap dogs of the new Right. They had a very real opportunity of negotiation during the early days of the hung parliament to drive through their core principles of a referendum on Proportional Representation and their so-called "4 Key Policies". For example "A fair chance for every child" is one of those key policies — contrast this with the scrapping of child trust funds, the announced £670 million cuts from the Department of Education of which £311 million is to be cut from council spending on schools. Fair chance? Fat chance. Another of their key policies was "A fair future, creating jobs by making Britain greener" — despite of course the £34 million cuts from the Department of Energy and Climate Change... Rather than provide any exegesis on another of their key policies "A fair deal for you from politicians", I shall leave the irony of that to resonate alone.

So how do we change things if all we get are another set of people making the same mistakes as the previous incumbents? By actively getting involved in whatever way possible. Whatever your skills, whether they be in writing, poetry, activism, oratory, or anything else, they must be put to some use in the causes of fairness, democracy, social change and in my personal view, Socialism.

It is because of that very principle that I'm even more energised by my involvement in *the Recusant's Emergency Verse* project. Whilst I wouldn't expect the government to throw up their arms and cry "What are we doing?", I do sincerely believe that the more visibility that dissent has, the better that filters through to government who are ultimately only worried about votes, popularity and their own hides. This is why even though there may exist so much electoral apathy and cultural materialism I still remain hopeful of radical change and if we can contribute to this through poetry or pressure or visibility or just by sheer numbers then that in some small measure will ebb away at the Con-Dems' arrogance and blithe disregard for any class but their own.

...But I have a high old hot un in my mind —
A most engrugious notion of the world,
That leaves your lightning 'rithmetic behind:
I give it at a glance when I say 'There ain't no chance,
Nor nothing of the lucky-lottery kind.'

John Davidson, 'Thirty Bob a Week'

'aper coin — that forgery
)f the title-deeds, which ye
Iold to something from the worth
)f the inheritance of Earth.

'ercy Bysshe Shelley, 'The Mask of Anarchy'

'Eat more fruit!' the slogans say,
'More fish, more beef, more bread!'
But I'm on Unemployment pay
My third year now, and wed.

John Corrie, 'Eat More'

's the same the whole world over,
's the poor what gets the blame,
's the rich what gets the pleasure,
n't it a blooming shame?

illy Bennett, 'She Was Poor But She Was Honest' (Weston & Lee)

When the worker begins to think,
And use of his organ of sight;
He will rid the 'Human Flowers'
Of the capitalistic blight.

William Robert Halls, 'When the Worker Begins to Think'

ı these unused canals a flood,
erelictions that rattle on the light
ıd call to the body of your unemployed blood.

'oward Mingham, 'Broken Water'

I will not cease from mental fight,
Nor shall my sword sleep in my hand,
Till we have built Jerusalem
In England's green and pleasant land.

William Blake, 'Jerusalem'

> And now cold charity's unwelcome dole
> Was insufficient to support the pair
> And they would perish rather than would bear
> The law's stern slavery, and the insolent stare
> With which law loves to rend the poor man's soul—
> The bitter scorn, the spirit-sinking noise
> Of heartless mirth which women, men, and boy
> Wake in this scene of legal misery
>
> *Percy Bysshe Shelley,* 'A Tale Of Society As It Is: From Facts, 1811'

Blood, sweat, and tear-wrung millions — why? for rent!
They roar'd, they dined, they drank, they swore they meant
To die for England — why then live? for rent!

George Gordon, Lord Byron, from *The Age of Bronze*

> Starvation 'tis they bids to a man with seven kids
> When he brings home only fifty pence a day
> For what can you get to eat on seven and six a week
> When it often takes it all the rent to pay
>
> *Union Song:* 'Tramp, Tramp, Tramp the Boys Are Marching'

Did He [Gawd] give an eternal vacation
To you, lazy nobodies, there,
Sittin' squat on a nabbed reputation
With your *Times* and your padded arm-chair?
Did He grant you an endless vacation
Wen He made the lords o'creation?

Richard Free, 'A Cry in the Darkness'

> A poor life this if, full of care
> We have no time to stand and stare
>
> *WH Davies,* 'Leisure'

Emergency Verse

Poetry in Defence of the Welfare State

This anthology is dedicated to the memories of

Herbert Asquith
David Lloyd-George
William Beveridge
Clement Attlee
and
Aneurin Bevan

chief architects of the British Welfare State

Antonionioni

'Antonionioni' is a Salford-based poet and performer who has taken part in the Poets Express annual event in West Cork, Ireland.

The Political Party's Over

The threat of swingeing cuts is a spectre
(I hate 'swingeing cuts' but I'll still use it)
Hanging over the whole public sector
In which I serve the Queen, helping collect
Her taxes (not mine or yours). But I'm not
(Although I have been) inspector
Of VAT in my time. Pause for lots
Of sympathy for me (not). Remember
Though that tax holds society together
(Against its will, maybe), so affect a
Momentary tear. (Can you method act?)
More tax, less debt. Pay the bank manager
Too, and live frugally, or we'll wreck a
Generation's pension and benefits.

Freedom of Choice

Liberty means we can do anything
Our human rights seen as inviolable
We can protest and refuse everything
From parents and teachers that's possible
Which makes authority unworkable
Now kids decide, not adults. Kids have kids
Then refuse to bring them up, unable
To do so properly. Liberty fits

If you're a businessman. Capitalists
Love it, especially when they're outsourcing
Or downsizing. Keep jobs affordable
So they can pay less and keep their profits,
The minimum wage: that is the worst thing
But Chinese kids are more employable.

Emergency Budget 2010

Budge it

smudge it

smash it
this Thatcherite
batch of writing
scratched out
by some Bob Cratchit
smacks of smiting

Taxes bite
practice belt tightening
around the neck of
the public sector
worker

To prophets
of profits
and to toffs
doff it
cough it up
keep coughing

and coughing

Tough
you've snuffed it

Stop it

Drop it

Hop it
or you'll cop it

These cops hit.
Shit!
That hurt
a bit

Be bought
or be caught

Shop for it
pop out for it
drive way out for it
but don't drop out
or cop out

Keep out

Step out of that
vomit
outside
the
summit

The humming of bombers
stun guns
making 'em slum it
till they submit
to the doormat
format

and to laws that
ensure that
and enforce that

Prison wing
intravening
dreaming
steaming
screaming
bleeding

Reading
even in
prison

Freedom
is
raising
reason
above
believing

Peace in
our mind
if not in
our time

Keith Armstrong

Keith Armstrong has worked as a community-arts development worker, poet, librarian and publisher. A founder of *Ostrich* magazine, Poetry North East, Tyneside Writers' Workshop, Tyneside Poets, East Durham Writers' Workshop, Tyneside Trade Unionists for Socialist Arts, Tyneside Street Press and the Strong Words and Durham Voices community publishing series, he has been poet-in-residence in Durham, Easington, Sedgefield, Derwentside, Teesdale, Wear Valley, Chester-le-Street, Sunderland and the Hexham Races. His publications include *Pains Of Class, Dreaming North, The Jinglin' Geordie, The Darkness Seeping, Poets' Voices, The Big Meeting: A People's View of the Durham Miners' Gala, The Town of Old Hexham, Old Dog On The Isle Of Woman* and *Bless'd Millennium: The Life & Work Of Thomas Spence*. His music-theatre collaborations include *O'er the Hills* (Dreaming North), *Wor Jackie* (Northumberland Theatre Company), *Pig's Meat* (Bruvvers Theatre Company) and *The Roker Roar* (Monkwearmouth Youth Theatre Company). Several of his songs have been recorded by Durham indie-folk-punk band The Whisky Priests.

The Chief Executive Rat

he's the chief executive rat
the chief executive of this and that
the chief executive of want and waste
the chief executive of bad taste
the chief executive brat

she's the chief executive of style
the chief executive bitch of bile
the chief executive of cluster bombs
the chief executive CD Rom
the chief executive of Zeig Heil

we're the chief executives of empty culture
the chief executives of soulless sculpture
the chief executives of soundbites

the chief executives of red kites
the chief executive vultures

chief executive emptiness
chief executive battledress
chief executive cocktails
chief executive entrails
chief executive stress

he's the chief executive slave employer
the chief executive missile deployer
the chief executive of civilian targets
the chief executive of hypermarkets
the chief executive life destroyer

she's the chief executive smirker
the chief executive charity worker
the chief executive of state terror
the chief executive of trial and error
the chief executive empty talker

chief executive workfare
chief executive homecare
chief executive meals on wheels
chief executive easy deals
chief executive warfare

chief executive warfare
chief executive war

chief executive war

A Prayer For The Loners

The dejected men,
the lone voices,
slip away
in this seaside rain.
Their words shudder to a standstill
in dismal corners.
Frightened to shout,
they cower
behind quivering faces.
No one listens
to their memories crying.
There seems no point
in this democratic deficit.
For years, they just shuffle along,
hopeless
in their financial innocence.
They do have names
that no lovers pronounce.
They flit between stools,
miss out on gales of laughter.
Who cares for them?
Nobody in Whitley Bay
or canny Shields,
that's for sure.
These wayside fellows
might as well be in a saddos' heaven
for all it matters
in the grey world's backwaters.
Life has bruised them,
dashed them.
Bones flake into the night.

I feel like handing them all loud-hailers
to release
their oppressed passion,
to move them
to scream
red murder at their leaders —
those they never voted for;
those who think they're something,
some thing special,
grand.
For, in the end,
I am on the side of these stooped lamenters,
the lonely old boys with a grievance
about caring
and the uncaring;
about power,
and how switched off
this government is
from the isolated,
from the agitated,
from the trembling,
the disenfranchised
drinkers of sadness.

Anne Babson

Anne Babson wrote the libretto for the opera *Lotus Lives,* which opened in New York last month. In the US, she won the Columbia Journal Prize and the Artisan Journal contest, and was nominated for both 2001 and 2005 Pushcarts. Her work has appeared in *Bridges, Barrow Street, Connecticut Review, The Pikeville Review, Rio Grande Review, English Journal, New Song, The Penwood Review, Sow's Ear, The Madison Review, Atlanta Review, Grasslands Review, Taproot Literary Journal, WSQ, Global City Review, Comstock Review, California Quarterly, Wisconsin Review, The Red Rock Review,* and many other publications. In Europe, her work has appeared in *Current Accounts, Iota, Poetry Salzburg, Nth Position* and in *Crannóg* (Ireland). She has also appeared in publications in Australia and New Zealand. She has four chapbooks: *Counterterrorist Poems* (2002 Pudding House Press), *Dictation* (2001, Partisan Press), *Uppity Poems* (1999 Alpha Beat Press), and *Commute Poems* (forthcoming from Gravity Presses). Babson was included in *Seeds of Fire: Poetry from the Other US* (2008, Smokestack Books).

Recitative: Then Shall The Eyes Of The Blind

"Then the eyes of the blind shall be opened, and the ears of the deaf shall be unstopped. Then shall the lame man leap as an hart, and the tongue of the dumb sing: for in the wilderness shall waters break out, and streams in the desert."
— *Isaiah* 35:5-6

Then shall be opened the eyes of the blind.
Rubes trusting the government shall spot graft.
Crones gone antiquing shall find the lost craft.
Contracts will be read before they are signed.
Unctuous beauties shall be ogled streamlined.
Dour dowagers will be caught in mid-laugh.
Then shall be opened the eyes of the blind.
Rubes trusting the government shall spot graft.
Loose-goose floozies shall be found in a bind
High-five-ing high rollers shall lose a half.
Poop deck swabbers shall be caught in the aft

Devil-may-care call girls shall see and shall mind.
Then shall be opened the eyes of the blind.

Then shall the ears of the deaf be unstopped.
The truth shall be heard despite all the lies.
Children will quit playing "Lord of the Flies,"
To listen to the ocean floor get mopped.
Retirees unshod will sing songs sock-hopped,
Crouch to hearken to the floor pipe's sighs.
Then shall the ears of the deaf be unstopped.
The truth shall be heard despite all the lies.
Show tunes shall echo from plays long since flopped
And questions shall reverberate —"Who?"s, "What?"s "Why?"s
A Grand Canyon resonance for the wise,
A radio silence for fools' words chopped,
Then shall the ears of the deaf be unstopped.

Then shall the lame person leap as an hart.
The proud knee shall buckle with gratitude.
The shop clerks will lose the snide attitude,
And the traffic cop shall direct as art.
Then shall the aisle cruisers mosh at Walmart.
Airline pilots shall loop with latitude.
Then shall the lame person leap as an hart.
The proud knee shall buckle with gratitude.
The golfers shall cartwheel out of their carts.
The professors shall plié platitudes.
The curmudgeons shall shift their shattered moods.
Then shall the zombie awake with a start.
Then shall the lame person leap as a hart.

Sebastian Barker

Sebastian Smart Barker FRSL (born 16 April 1945) is a British poet. He was educated at The King's School, Canterbury, Corpus Christi, Oxford (MA) and at the University of East Anglia (MA). He has been on the executive committee of P.E.N. and was the Chairman of the Poetry Society from 1988 to 1992. In 1997 he was elected a Fellow of the Royal Society of Literature. In 2002 he took over editorship of *The London Magazine,* which he resigned from in 2008 after the Arts Council England had cut the magazine's funding. His earlier collections, which include *On the Rocks* (Martin, Brian & O'Keeffe, 1977), and *A Nuclear Epiphany* (Friday Night Fish Publications, 1984) were brought together in a volume of Selected Poems, *Guarding the Border,* published by Enitharmon Press in 1992. More recent collections include *The Dream of Intelligence* (Littlewood Arc, 1992, a long poem based on Nietzsche's life and works, *The Hand in the Well* (Enitharmon, 1996), *Damnatio Memoriae: Erased from Memory* (Enitharmon, 2004), *The Erotics of God* (Smokestack Books, 2005).

Old Nick

I die day by day, by day, but you
    neither die nor end,
Immortal in your arrogance,
    the politician's friend*.

Like chocolate tipped into a cup
    to fill an empty brain,
You talk to me of sweetness, shit
    I'm flushing down the drain.

Death laughs in your face, Old Nick,
    you do not see her smile.
The cunning angel, arm in arm,
    who walks you down the aisle.

* *the politician's friend*: a reference to John Webster and his mighty conception of the politician as 'the devil's quilted anvil'.

The Stranger In The Pass

Sunlight on a broken fence,
    sparrows in the grass,
The wheels of industry make sense,
    the stranger in the pass.

What is it, stranger, what do you
    want? 'I want to live
Before I die, an overview,
    a rich alternative.'

Amazing swans fly like the truth
    difficult to believe.
The city traffic's heading south,
    there's summer in the breeze.

Ten to one the sky is blue,
    the picnics in the wood
Conceal the witty families who
    have long since understood.

To live before you die, attend,
    O stranger in the pass,
The cracks within the family mend,
    sparrows in the grass.

Dickhead

Dickhead pissing on the truth,
    give yourself a break.
Many a cowboy wears a suit,
    but none so false unique.

There is more classic rodeo
    in horses on the screen
Ridden by honest men who know
    your politics obscene.

Michael Bartholomew-Biggs

Michael Bartholomew-Biggs lives in London and works as a mathematician at
the University of Hertfordshire. His previous collections include *Anglicised by
Common Use, Inklings of Complicity, Uneasy Relations* and *Tell It Like It Might Be*
(Smokestack Books). His latest collection is *Tradesman's Exit* (Shoestring, 2009).

Fool's-errand Boys

after Philip Larkin's 'The Old Fools'

Who do they think they're fooling, purveyors
of government bluff? Do they somehow suppose
you sound more grown-up the more cant you bray as
you keep pissing yourself for fear of who'll hurt you
for each line you muff? Or that, if they only chose,
they could alter things back to when they slept at night
or had their own visions or joined arms with real virtue?
Or do they fancy there's really been no change

and that they've always believed that black could just as well
$\qquad\qquad$ be white,
or sat through days of mean and weasel scheming
watching lies ooze? If they don't (and they can't), it's strange:
$\qquad\qquad$ why aren't they screaming?
Perhaps to be hired you must have little room
inside your head for empathy or being bold
as prompters hiss at you to preach what they assume,
deny all harms then vomit slimy care
for victims. Would they balk at being told
to walk on water? Promotions keep them quiet:
the stumbling blocks so obvious from elsewhere
for them are stepping stones. Can they never smell
what's gagging them, what makes them claim that they
$\qquad\qquad$ were right
(at worst, were misinformed)? Never throughout
their sweaty introverted public lives? Well,
$\qquad\qquad$ they'll get found out

To Whom it May Concern

When I heard the way they'd treated you
I wanted, very calmly,
to crush my glass against the table top.
And that would testify
I hadn't anything to do with them —
not the counter clerks
who fingered through your papers,
nor the authors of their picklock questions,
shaped to make the wrong replies slide out
like bolts drawn slowly back across a trapdoor.
I wanted to shout down their smug assumption

of my mute agreement
to brand you, steal your clothes and make you dance.
Denials alone won't do
for those who make their own small ugly choices.
I needed, very simply,
to know if God could answer
the question of how far the likes of us
should take an inkling of complicity
when we remember how they treated you.

Troubadours

A dove blurts broken Morse along the breeze:
a m'aidez out of time deprived of rest
by ducal talons poised above the trees
and cuckoo henchmen plundering the nest.
Princelings making playthings of these gardens
struck up cheap rapports with balladeers:
when Honour mattered more than honest tears
laments for murdered scions could win pardons.
We too can live like lords: expect unseen
somebody else to mop away our wastes,
to kill our meat and leave our fingers clean;
and in bastides we give some self-preserving
enterprisers free play with our tastes.
They strum on us the tunes we're well-deserving.

Anita Baxter

Anita Baxter was born in 1966 and started writing poetry and scribblings for stories in her teens. She has recently enrolled on creative writing OU course. This is her first published poem.

Untitled

Serves you right for voting Tory
what did you expect?
Letting Labour back in
would have been another story?
Haven't we learned yet it's always a swindle
financial back dealings
with plenty of scandal.
They're all public school boys
no concept of caring
bred to make money
no intention of sharing
They used our money
to save their banks
but that's not enough
public services next?
No thanks!
Work harder, earn less
fear the invisible foe
only 4 years left
unless we say No!

WE'RE INTENSELY RELAXED ABOUT PEOPLE GETTING FILTHILY POOR....

Brian Beamish

Brian Beamish was born in Devon in 1974. He graduated in Theology from the College of St Mark and St John, nr Plymouth. This is his second published poem; his first was 'Chelsea' online at *the Recusant*.

30%

If Margaret Thatcher wins — I warn you not to be ordinary. I warn you not to be young. I warn you not to fall ill. I warn you not to get old.
Neil Kinnock, 1983

While guillotine scalpels fall,
Patients bearing a hapless grimace as tightly wound bandages
Clamour to hold the drip slip drip of the
Costly flowing ruby;
Life gore of the nation's poor,
Liquidated, dispossessed.

You warned us not to fall ill.
Blood spilled.

Cap in hand our forefather's land
Ambling through Shambles
Ill-afford Paschal candles that light the twilight world of
The aged and wearied drab-drowned souls

You warned us not to get old.
Nil by mouth; starve a cold...

The rattle cabs and choke trains we half-live in
Crawling our way to pay back the abusive whip hands

Like a rotten alcoholic
Praying for a Ginsberg fix.

Youths qualified yet only quantified
Into sick-bed tax
Brow-beaten, derelict

You warned us not to be young
Jobs done.

Our warning will not be missed
For now, Dave and Nick, you're on a five-year waiting list...

Jim Bennett

Jim Bennett was born in Liverpool in 1951. He performed alongside Roger McGough and Adrian Henri in the late 1960s. Winner of various awards for his performance poetry, and a Berlin Book Prize for his volume *The Man Who Tried to Hug Clouds* (Bluechrome, 2005/6). His other collections include: *Clocks* (1997), *The Green Man of Bidston Moss* (2002), *Bold Street* (2008) and *Larkhill* (Searle Publishing, 2009). He is founding editor of *The Poetry Kit* website.

Dear David,

I should have written earlier
but I couldn't
every time I sat down to write
my pen had other ideas
and now I find words fail me

As bodies mount

in the ice hard morning
there will be resistance for a while
chisels trying to make a point
there always is when change comes
when bodies mount
but you can say things about that
things that make all opposition wrong
that sends blame scuttling away
that's the secret   finding ways to
think and words that mean other than
what they really mean
people do not realise how fluid history is
it is not about reality
it's about perception

people scared into acceptance
this way or no way disaster is looming
that is politics
it's the winner who keeps
the score
as the bodies mount

THE THREE GRACES.

Keith Bennett

Keith Bennett is a prize-winning poet and playwright, founder of the New Forest Poetry Society and a Reader for The Literary Consultancy.

A City Fable

Observe this; history teaches us nothing lasts.
The old blue has done for the newly red.
The city bubbling with South Sea dread
that money might become a thing of the past
and Northern Lights outshine their shrinking grasp,
invented a monumental tower, well bred
in the language of Gelt and well read
in the mathematics of the un-moneyed class.
The tower outshone them all, its face of shining glass
reflecting our sun, until the sunset bled
it white and only night with its black tread
stepped through, fear grew as the tower disappeared fast.

Still, credit where credit is due, without pity;
'Once upon a time there was this tower in our city...'

Charlotte Beyer

Charlotte Beyer was born in Denmark in 1965. Her poems have previously appeared in the anthology *Crab Lines off the Pier.*

Emergency Budget Storm of 2010

Weather warning's out, a horrible hurricane is on its way,
Coming towards us,
you better take cover,
shelter your loved ones,
this is going to be terrible,
relentless, no one
will be spared.
The Emergency Budget Storm of 2010
is blowing up a gale
its vicious winds,
appalling hurricane blasts,
speeding across the skies
coming towards us.
Dread, trepidation.
The biggie.
Newspaper headlines
predict deepest cuts.
Doom and depression pepper the numbers and figures cited,
what is going to happen.
Bad news is what it means,
I know
it will mean me, too.
Like a gale force wind blasting the land, these cuts will destroy
too much, go too far.
Forewarned is forearmed,
so they say,

but not in this case.
Coming towards us.
The Emergency Budget Storm of 2010, of a thousand cuts,
sings squalling songs that drift in the gales, recklessly:
take from the many
give to the few,
keep taking.
Deep cuts,
you must
bear the brunt,
pay the price,
plug the gap.
Coming towards us.
Don't kid yourselves.
This hurricane havoc will break everything in its wake.
Mass unemployment.
Hospital waiting lists.
Tumbledown school buildings,
university closures,
welfare sacrifices.
The Emergency Budget Storm of 2010 is coming, with its
blasts of agony.
This October
will be truly autumnal, the outlook so bleak.
Coming towards us.
Ominous sound of thunder
faintly rumbling,
far away at first, then approaching,
with ferocity,
lightning will strike,
rain will wash away,
winds will ravage.
Imagining your life after the Emergency Budget Storm

Coming towards us.
How will it be.
What can you do.
Can you stop a hurricane
with your voice,
talking back.

D.d. Biretti

No biographical information provided.

Forward to the Past

Public sector workers Con-Demned to pain at last,
while the coalition government goes forward to the past.

Jan Bradley

Jan Bradley was born in the Black Country. A qualified Occupational Therapist, her MSc research paper, *Exploring the Experiences of Writing Poetry*, focussed on the concept of *flow*. Poetry published online at *the Recusant* and *Eleutheria — Scottish Poetry Review*. Her first chapbook collection, *The Winding Keys*, was recently published by Creative Future (2010).

Shaving the Lion

Strange, the wealth of errors penned by politicians
When their talents are the arts and crafts of politics
Still, they shave the lion; drown his fiery phoenix visions

Governing ungifted, an uncommon House of Commons
In a watercolour challenge of weak candidates and villains
Strange, the wealth of errors penned by politicians

Amateurish sermons boast bombastic, buzzword jargons
Uncaring in their legions for the artists' meagre rations
Still, they shave the lion; drown his fiery phoenix visions

If the aftershock of actions tames the lion's blazing passions
Then their lack of humane reason throws the lion to the dungeons
Strange, the wealth of errors penned by politicians

The divide only deepens between the artist and the demons
Teach the artist to succeed, it's called progress, and he'll listen
Still, they shave the lion; drown his fiery phoenix visions

Art-forms are the language of opinion; visionary siphons
Each mind expressed in unique, bright-burning Titans
Strange, the wealth of errors penned by politicians
Still, they shave the lion; drown his fiery phoenix visions.

Peter Branson

Peter Branson has been accepted for publication by journals in Britain, USA, Canada, EIRE, Australia and New Zealand, including *Acumen, Ambit, Envoi, Magma, The London Magazine, Iota, Frogmore Papers, The Interpreter's House, Poetry Nottingham, Pulsar, Red Ink, the Recusant, South, The New Writer, Crannog, Raintown Review, The Able Muse* and *Other Poetry*. His first collection, *The Accidental Tourist*, was published in May 2008. A second collection, *Red Shift*, was published at the beginning of this year by Caparison. More recently a pamphlet has been issued (May 7th) by Silkworms Ink. A third collection has been accepted for publication by Salmon Press, Eire, for 2011.

General Election Night, 2010

Set in a crowded bar near closing time,
damp-elbows raised to beer and bonhomie,
we're mindful of our youth. Recall back there,
Labour — old style, we cared: closed minds, clenched fists.
We'd cheer a victory, drown in defeat.
Now no one mentions it. Democracy?
Don't take the piss. It's meaningless; short shrift
whichever mob get in. And always was,
though we'd too much invested to decry
the hollow victory when our lot won.
Leaders soon geld themselves, turn flabby-chic;
we're hoodwinked, gentled, pawns for sacrifice:
"Credo in unum deum, Mammon be praised!"
They pimp for private enterprise; we slave.

Perspective
To Alan Morrison, in thanks

Remorseless spin: nigh on impossible
to get your eye in, see the ball, block I'm
all right Jack attitudes, play with straight bat.
There are things we can do: fly all our boys
home from Afghanistan, Iraq, reclaim
our hospitals, public utilities,
our schools, wrest back our money stolen by
the banks and give our unions back their balls.

First Signs
For George and Len Pickering

"Don't look so worried son."
He hails you through,
ghost bricklayer, propped up
in fire-side chair,
frail, dogged before
his day by dodgy chest.
Familiar faces from
your childhood, aunts
and uncles, neighbours,
slowly penny-drop
you, born and bred
two streets across;
first time you've been
since you moved house at eight,
fresh down from university
to join his wake.

Swearing an oath
of brotherhood
to make ends meet,
pay doctors' bills
pre national health,
seemed sensible way back
to working folk.
High crime to greet
with Oddfellows
two hundred years
ago, en masse,
sisters as well,
panic at Peterloo,
slaughter from France.

Recession Reds an' Blues

That lot who've just been shown the door, they cared,
though not enough to see beyond the trees
harsh circumstances planted in their path.
This bunch have an agenda. At its core
is selfishness — though they disguise it well.
When things go wrong, the haves get off scot free:
the bombshells when they come are shattering;
redundancy, or benefit snatched back
for some, while others walk away unscathed.
The poor get caned. Few rage; majority,
preoccupied, turn back into their lives,
deaf, dumb and blind. Too soon the sun begins
to shine, tempts girls in sheer short dresses out
and everything's smoothed over till next time.

Front Line

For P. M.

Toolmaker all your life,
recession poor.
When orders shrivel up,
you're out the door.

This time, the rats
who cause it raid
your pension fund as well,
feed fat cats' bonuses.

Can't fathom it, worn down,
depressed. You strive
to keep your dignity;
they've scoffed the rest.

Alan Britt

Alan Britt was born on 3 March 1950 in Norfolk, Virginia. Collections: *Vermilion* (2006), *Infinite Days* (2003), *Amnesia Tango* (1998) and *Bodies of Lightning* (1995). He teaches Creative Writing at Towson University. He lives in Maryland.

For Salvadore Allende and Pablo Neruda

I crawled from a lily pad
ripped by the claw of a caiman
gliding Zen-like down the muddy Amazon.

I hopped onto the best consciousness
I could muster,
leaning on one forelimb,
gills flared.

I thrust myself,
utilizing massive, amphibious fins,
into a bank vault
filled with echoes
left behind by CIA trainees
designed to procure the deaths
of a newly elected Socialist Democrat
and his Communist poet running mate.

Profits for U.S. corporations
were valued over peace and prosperity,
over an elevated life for lowly Chileans.

The United Fruit Company revisited.
No wonder imagination remains the final
uncharted landscape

for our ego-imprisoned souls.
In fact, it's a wonder love poems
weren't outlawed eons ago!

Sorry. I forgot.
Sometimes I get like that.

Chimney Sweeps

Human scrub brushes, that's what they
were. Eight, ten, twelve years old with a
wire brush & an asteroid in their stomachs.
The Church set them loose, occasionally,
mostly before tuberculosis disrupted 20
foot luncheon tables & benches made from
purple blood that flowed through Sunday
sermons, blood with the distinct colour of
week-old crabs crushed against the naïve
windows of childhood expectations.

The Church set them loose on the dappled
greens of London once in a while, but
mostly the Church charged by the hour.

Don't pine for those little bastards, though;
they brought it on themselves.

Parasites!

The Church needed a new rectory (or
rectumry), of sorts, some place to hide the
jewels. Orphans were ripe for the picking.

Leon Brown

Leon Brown was born in Dorset in 1973. He has worked as an English Literature teacher and in TEFL at home and abroad including Greece and Portugal. Recently he has completed his first novel, *Future Perfect*, for which he is seeking a publisher. He is currently engaged with writing his second, *The Wrecker's Ball*.

Only The Mirror Knows
(Or Stuck Inside of Bromley-by-Bow with the coalition Blues Again)

They're polishing the guillotine at Tyburn
Mounting a gibbet at Spitalfields,
For the unfortunates to swing from a year from now
Till they are lain beside the angry old men,

For the mild young ones are all out of puff,
They sup Guinness in the Old Kent Road.
Once they knocked back Caparinas in Rio,
This year they'll have to make do with Hove.

It doesn't matter where you lie back and think of England,
Unreal light melts those warped by an age.
Time to cast off the 31st year of the 80s,
Apathy's army fleeing hand-me-down rage.

And still adults smirk in Brobdingnag
From mouths lately numbed by doubt.
The little boy-artist observes, settles up,
Suddenly sprung from his cell.

Coarse laughter of private phoney wars
In World Cup weary throats.

At least we know our priorities:
Smash up town when the team loses,
Fall silent as they cancel tomorrow.
Politically correct, townhouse mother
In green suburb bought with divorce,
Who once jived to Billy Bragg and Red Wedge,
Now seeks refuge from a union ballot,
Another *Daily Mail* convert to the dark.

Those who flag in a sun alien to these shores.
Those who dared to hope and dream again,
Watch plans for survival taper to anorexic wraiths;
Piled like flaking sun chairs in weed-strewn gardens.
The smell of spent money settles like gunpowder in
Flaring, aggrieved nostrils.
'We was robbed' is all they can snort.

Dragoon of Sat Nav dullards
Snakes towards Devon on Friday night.
Fading Union Jack guitars, Britpop shades,
Clutter every suburban back yard.
Greenish glows cast in unmortgaged eyes;
Are you ready for the clean up?
We lack both the energy and will.
In those days they told us we were worth it,
Now they conjure up the cheapest way to kill.

Flippancy stills longcases in Leatherhead,
Self-help swings an axe in Tyne and Wear.
Flagstones turning a darker shade of grey
Swabbed by tears of cut-price laments.
As the brave few take to their heels with banners
To wave at devils of indifference.

For the first time in a generation,
Mothers fear for their kids.
'This wasn't the way it was meant to be' they weep
While tucking the littl'uns in.

In dream gardens buried under blistered skin,
Scorched Earth, yellowing grass,
Colour is snatched by starling conspiracies.
A flurry of foxes lay siege to the house,
A terrier chases its tail,
While a cat plays with a mouse.
The rain cools all in diagonal shafts,
Then heat bowls in, all brazen again.

Laughter soon turns in the hyenas.
The sky reboots as we stare it out
Then unveils a new canopy of eyes
To gaze on infinity:
Grab while stocks and shares last,
It will snap your throats as surely as Sunday evening's
Entropically feeble last laugh.

From another car window apocalypse emanates,
Another gunman goes on rampage up North.
I observe the half open windows up the street
And watch the lights dim one by one.

I see the void but have no will to reflect
For only the mirror knows.
As shadows lunge across the afternoon
Widening near break of dusk,
I lie back and laugh as the government falls,
Helicopter hum nearing Number 10.

Norman Buller

Norman Buller was born in Birmingham and educated at Fircroft College, and St. Catharine's College, Cambridge, where he read English and started writing poetry, having an influence on the early writing of a peer, Thom Gunn. Buller's profession was as careers adviser at the universities of Sheffield, Queen's Belfast and Birmingam. While at Belfast he was part of Philip Hobsbaum's circle, which included Seamus Heaney and Michael Longley. *Thirteen Poems*, appeared in 1965. 40 years later a second chapbook, *Travelling Light*, appeared, followed by two critically praised volumes *Sleeping with Icons* (2007) and *Fools and Mirrors* (2010), all through Waterloo Press. Buller's poems have appeared in legion journals including *Acumen, Outposts, The London Magazine* and *Cambridge Left*.

Industrial Relations

Our unborn selves were pledged to change
three structures with our building power
when Eve and Adam blindly laid
foundations for the roofless tower

and so, my love, we two have come,
new hands to fill a vacancy;
nothing to sell but labour to
this strange contracting company

whose teeming workers mill in pairs
on girder, wall and scaffolding,
building the tower which shall be left
taller by what we two now bring.

Love builds inevitably, yet
by paradox of nature's course,
this evergrowing structure is
erected by a casual force,

for new mates come and old mates go
by no set stint; their ritual
is ruptured by the commonplace
of skills no longer mutual;

and though by accident we met,
our necessary gifts to give,
our parting soon enough may prove
how temporarily we live.

The meeting and the parting may
be seen as trivial if you
attend the progress of the tower
and know that in it we grow too.

So now, my love, to labouring:
we'll brick and mortar three in one,
woman and man and roofless tower,
until our unique shift is done.

Nick Burbridge

Nick Burbridge is an Anglo-Irish writer living in Brighton. His first collection of poetry, *On Call*, was published by Envoi Poets in 1994. Singer/songwriter of McDermott's Two Hours, he has also collaborated with The Levellers who covered his song 'Dirty Davey' on their eponymous number one selling album. His plays include *Dirty Tricks*, *Vermin* and *Cock Robin*. His work is broadcast regularly on BBC Radio 4. A novel, *Operation Emerald* (Pluto), was published under the pseudonym Dominic McCartan. He collaborated with Captain Fred Holroyd on *War Without Honour* (Medium), launched at the House of Commons.

Supper

Masters, you are fair, and you are true.
The world appears as brave as it is new.
For crumbs of comfort let us sing to you
Now we can't have our cake and eat it too.

Daisy Cains

Daisy Cains was born Birmingham in 1971. She was educated at Malvern Girls School and St Catherine's College, Oxford. Her short story 'Never Said a Word' appeared in *Roads Ahead* edited by Costa Prize winner Catherine O'Flynn, (Tindal Street Press).

Twice in as many months

The Eighties was the decade of disasters,
then we didn't have any for a few years and now they're starting
        again.
Desperation and hopelessness violently seen on the streets,
twice in as many months.
It must be something to do with the Tories.
It was definitely something to do with Thatcher back then.
It's not just the cut backs, although they must have an effect.
The undermanning, the lack of staff, the penny pinching,
that caused King's Cross,
The triumph of big bucks over everything that was good and
decent, that caused Piper Alpha, the Herald of Free Enterprise etc.
There was something more, there was despair
that caused Hungerford and, to a lesser extent, Heysel.
But more than that, it was her couldn't care less attitude,
a few casualties along the way were acceptable, even desirable.
She let Reagan use our airbases don't forget.
Lockerbie. 1988. Hungerford. 1987. Hillsborough 1989. Bradford.
1985. Heysel. 1985. Herald of Free Enterprise. 1987. Piper Alpha.
1988. King's Cross. 1987. The Marchioness. 1988.
Dunblane, that was later but still it was Thatcher's fault.
And I bet there were others, that I haven't thought of.
Can we blame her for Chernobyl?
And now they're happening again.

It's just so tragic after such a short a short time,
they've put despair back on the streets.
They've made it alright to be a bastard again.
Twice in as many months.

Debjani Chatterjee MBE

Debjani Chatterjee is an award-winning poet, the author of more than fifty books for children and adults, and several poetry collections, her most recent being *Words Spit and Splinter* (Redbeck Press). She was awarded an honorary doctorate by Sheffield Hallam University in 2002 and received an MBE in 2008 for her services to Literature.

No Consent — Yet Again

If New Labour was
Thatcherite, Britain at war
without our consent;

why not a marriage,
a political nightmare —
Tories and Lib-Dems.

Keith Chopping

Keith is an actor, voiceover artist and therapist. After being in a political no man's land for many years he has recently returned to socialism.

The Silence Of The Class

When no meat is left to cut
and the bones we pick on
are cracked to dust.
Then they might Poll Tax
the air.
Then woe to you whose lungs dare
to fill with protest.
You'll pay for those who wouldn't tweet a dickybird
when they had the chance.

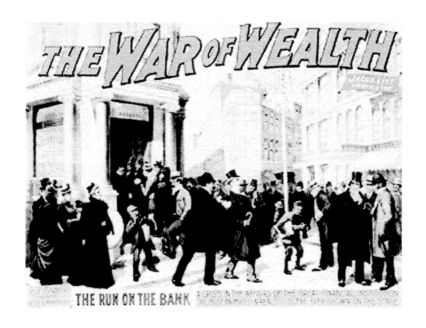

G.W. Colkitto

G.W. Colkitto has had short stories in *The Ranfurly Review*, a biographical piece on the *Scottish Homecoming* website, poems on *Ink Sweat & Tears* and has published two poetry anthologies and a poetry pamphlet. He is part of *Read Raw*, four writers who perform regularly in the Glasgow area.

An Eden Lost And Gone

Depression comes, I wonder how or why,
What fool to trust, to have my treasures lain
In Banks dissolving in financial rain,
Yet still receiving bonus as I sigh.
"It was the world, not us," is their reply.
"We understand, we comprehend your pain
But trust in us, we can begin again"
And dumb I know not, should I laugh or cry.
When fruit was plucked from the apple tree
Wisdom and sin slithered down as one
Showed nakedness unrecognised before
And in the bite an Eden lost and gone.
When a Banker tossed sour grapes to me
I saw a future stripped and bare once more.

Michael D. Conley

Michael D Conley is a 25 year old teacher from Manchester facing a two year pay freeze: "I'm disgusted at the way they're now trying to privatise the NHS and how people in this country have actually accepted the cuts to benefits because they've lapped up the lies fed to them about "scroungers" and "illegals" by the gutter press".

1929 And All That

This climate suggests
Economy of language
Is vital. Fucking

B**kers. Rash pitch-and-
Tossers with other people's
Cash. If I didn't

Owe mine two grand, my
Righteous anger would be just
Intolerable.

Alan Corkish

Alan Corkish is a writer from the UK. Originally from the Isle of Man he now lives in Liverpool where he writes novels, poetry and short stories, and co-edits the radical poetry journal *erbacce*. He is the author of *Glimpses of Notes* (2006), an autobiographical poem written in what the author calls "fragmented text"; *Corrupted Memories*, a poetry collection; and *Groups* (2006), a novel.

Do you blame her

she fiddles the system
caught in the trap
since leaving school
with zero qualifications

discovered that a baby
was the key to
a home of her own
settling her away from
that drunken father
and downtrodden mum
and now the baby has
grown a little she works
on the side
in the pub
on the corner
and has her live-in
boy friend as an
invisible lodger
she buy customs booze
and customs ciggies
and goes to the CAB
to make sure she's

claiming everything
if she gets a job
with cards-in, tax-paid,
she'll be worse off
slaving forty hours
than when she is doing nothing

since leaving school
caught in the trap
she fiddles the system
which betrayed her
from the very start

do you blame her

In the waiting room

her heavy brown brogue shoes
rest still upon the worn rubber treads
of the dull metal wheelchair which easily
supports her slender frame

the trousers are blue with intricate embroidery
and they encase legs as slender as a child's arm
and on them rest swollen, jagged, jutting fingers
deformed by her arthritic plague

she is, as I would guess, 30 years of age
her face, like that of a pale elf is more than pretty
and the vivacious eyes smile and sparkle as she rocks
gently forward to speak

to her partner; tall and straight as a javelin,
he is attentive to her needs and responds to her whispers
by unfastening the top button of the coat which hides
her tired and wasted frame
and she is one of several here in the waiting room
who tug my heart and make me thankful for all I have
but make me also aware of other possibilities that
are maybe yet to come in this life

Asylum-seeker

...a refusal often offends
so maybe it's best not to even ask
best to go home again
to where the children
wait clothed in hunger
draped in a sallow
acceptance that living 30%
below the official breadline*
is as much as an asylum-seeker
dare hope for
so she gathers her scarf
around her face
as if ashamed of the fact
that the razor sleet actually
wounds her,
physically,
takes one final look at the notice
above the broad shoulders
of the white man
in the white apron
and inwardly agrees

best not to ask for credit
...a refusal often offends
… someone

* Contrary to popular belief, asylum-seekers in the UK are given a sum to live
on which is 30% below the amount designated by Government as the minimum
that is required to exist.

Blame

goodbye asylum seekers
we never made you welcome
today, as the news informs
of a twentieth body
recovered
from the ice-cold waters
of Morecambe Bay,
we need to ask ourselves
if you'd have
chosen to cockle pick
in the dark iced hours
had we given you
the prospect to earn
a decent wage
or enough to live on
with dignity?
you came to us for asylum
for shelter and protection
and instead we grudgingly
gave you a pittance to exist on
and refused you the right to work
now, salt-slake chokes the throats

of drowned souls lying
in the midnight reaches
of a foreign country
while friends and relatives
a thousand miles away
grieve and wonder at
your deaths in a country
which, when you asked
for shelter and dignity
gave you only
segregation and suspicion

goodbye asylum seekers
we never made you welcome
your deaths are this country's shame
and we, and this country
are to blame

Andy Croft

Andy Croft is founding editor of Middlesbrough-based Smokestack Books, which champions radical left poetry. Croft is the author of several poetry collections, including most recently *Comrade Laughter* (Flambard), *Ghost Writer* (Five Leaves), and *Sticky* (Flambard). He has co-edited several poetry anthologies including *Red Sky at Night — An Anthology of British Socialist Poetry* (edited with Adrian Mitchell) and *The Night Shift* (edited with Michael Baron and Jenny Swann). He is poetry columnist for *the Morning Star*. Croft was recently awarded the Ted Slade Award for services to poetry.

Dives and Lazarus

As it fell out upon a day
  Rich Dives he held a feast,
And he invited all his friends
  And gentry of the best.

They made themselves a national plan
  To better the nation's health,
And help themselves to the public purse
  To better their private wealth.

Then Lazarus laid him down and down
  And down at Dives' door,
'Some meat, some drink, brother Dives,
  Bestow upon the poor !'

But Dives was a busy man,
  And Dives locked his door,
For England is a friendless land
  If you are old and poor.

Then Dives sent his tabloid dogs
  To bite him as he lay,
And print their teeth marks on his flesh
  And hound him on his way.

And Dives sent his merry men
  To spin The World at One,
And lick his weeping sores until
  It seemed his sores were gone.

And Lazarus he was hungry,
  And Lazarus he was cold,
And Lazarus wasn't in BUPA
  So Lazarus he went cold.

And so it fell out upon a day
  Poor Lazarus sicken'd and died,
And Dives threw his corpse away
  Before his blood had dried.

And Lazarus he went straight to hell
  To burn for ever more,
For there is always the Devil to pay
  If you are sick and poor.

And it fell out upon a day
  That Dives sicken'd and died
And Dives he went straight to heaven
  (Which now's been PFId).

For Dives was a rich man
  And rich men know what's theirs,
And when they've taken that they want
  To take the poor man's shares.

The rich will always feast and dine
  While others want for more ;
Unless the poor throw off the rich
  The rich will keep them poor.

And public medicine will not thrive
  While there is private health,
And there'll be no cure for England's ills
  While there is private wealth.

Not So
in memoriam Julia Darling

The rules are fixed. We can't compete with you.
  Before we start we know the final score.
Of course you win. The powerful always do.
  You are the offside goal, the final straw.
No doubt you like to think you're really hard,
  Tooled up with cluster bomb and DU shell;
All we possess is mortal love and art
  While you with poison, war and sickness dwell.
But look at you – old morgue-faced charnel-breath,
  Still trying to play the vampire when we know
You're just a hammy Hammer-horror show.
  Poor you. It's living that is hard, not death.
And Julia's art and love will both survive
Her being dead, by being so alive.

Brian D'Arcy

Brian D'Arcy is an Anglo-Irish poet who has written *Tha Shein Ukrosh: Indeed the Hunger* (Bellasis Press, 2002) and *Footsteps in the Dust* (Sixties Press, 2003).

Epitaph for the NHS
The Government propose to entrust the decision making for £70+ Billion of the NHS funding to the overstretched and undertrained GPs.

Forgive them for they know not what they do —
        and save us from the politician's curse.
                A pig's ear plan can never yield a silken purse.

Avaritia — The Bankers' Creed, Or 'How God Is That?'

In the beginning —
                There was the word

And so the bankers said
                "Let there be greed"
For the Thatcher had indeed
 Pronounced that "Greed is good"

But the bankers heard
                A slightly different word
For what they thought they heard
                Was "Greed is God"

So they in turn announced
                "We do God's work"
For they, as one, agreed
                "IN DEED, our God is Greed"

In November 2009 Lloyd Blankfein, head of Goldman Sachs claimed that bankers did God's work. In July 2010 Goldman Sachs were given a record fine of $550 Million for fraudulently misleading investors.

Will Daunt

Will Daunt's poetry collections include *Lancashire Working* (Kite Modern Poetry Series, 2003), *Houses Dim* (Grendon House, 2001), *Running Out Of England* (Oversteps, 2004), *The Good Is Abroad* and *Distant Close* (both Lapwing, 2006/08). His poems have appeared in the anthologies *Poet's England, Lancashire, Poetry North-West* and *Voices,* and in journals such as *Envoi, Orbis, Smoke, Iota, Pennine Platform, Krax, Period Piece and Paperback, The Green Book* and *Purple Patch.*

Summer Storms

That spring was dry enough to build
a country full of new Brunels,
with city schemes of hope and trust
and methods shaped in glass and steel.

And spring was long enough to urge
the child in us to look again
and learn from children how to dream
of schools and parks where England bloomed.

So spring was fresh enough to clear
those carriageways of dust which made
our parents, our estates, our loves
incline into their passive lives.

That spring was packed with promises
to plan, to build, to shift, to save
a millions jobs, a hundred towns.
Then summer broke: long floods, blue storms.

Lisa Davies

Lisa Davies was born on Christmas Day 1983, she is studying for a MA in Women's Writing at Edge Hill University, where she is a member of the Service User Carer panel and research group attached to the BA in Social Work, and a guest columnist for *Disability Now* magazine.

In Defence of the Well Fair State

They plan to make big cuts
they aim to bankrupt us
their tactic's to divide and conquer
pay themselves their wages longer
target those perceived as weak
while they covertly seek
knighthoods and expenses
ruling under false pretences
with little hope of mending fences.
If the coalition gets its way
everyone will have to pay —
no medical, no DLA —
you'll have to stand before a doctor
a Government stethoscope-eyed proctor
and prove your illness there and then
including invisible symptoms
of psychological disorders
beyond the scope of any 'fraudsters' —
it's all designed to save some money
while parliament's hive hoards its honey —
loss of income will stun for sure
a sting no liniment can cure
this Government punishes the poor
and unemployed by 9 Billion more

than the levy on the City culprits,
their bonuses, our deficits —
We're all in this together spares
the Cabinet of millionaires.

Alan Dent

Alan Dent is editor of the radical Preston-based journal *The Penniless Press*. His poetry collections include *Corker* (Redbeck, 1999) and *Town* (Smokestack, 2005). He has edited two Smokestack French poetry anthologies, *When The Metro Is Free* (2007) and *Common Cause*, the Collected Poems of French poet Frances Combes, translated by Dent (2010).

All You Need Is Gove
(To the tune of *We'll Make Keel Row*)

We'll have a free school a free school a free school
We'll have a free school and keep the riff-raff out;
My daddy's going to run it to run it to run it
My daddy's going to run it yes he's got lots of dosh;
My mummy went to Oxford to Oxford to Oxford
My mummy went to Oxford so she can run it too;
We'll build it in the suburbs the suburbs the suburbs
We'll build it in the suburbs away from all the chavs;
The teachers will be Tories be Tories be Tories
The teachers will be Tories or they won't get a job;
We'll learn about the Empire the Empire the Empire
We'll learn about the Empire and what made Britain great;
We'll say our prayers in Latin in Latin in Latin
We'll say our prayers in Latin so you won't understand;
We'll speak just like the queen does the queen does the queen does

We'll speak just like the queen does that is the proper way;
We'll pass a pile of exams of exams of exams
We'll pass a pile of exams to prove we are the best;
And then we'll go to Oxbridge to Oxbridge to Oxbridge
And then we'll go to Oxbridge so we'll get the best jobs;
We'll live in great big houses big houses big houses
We'll live in great big houses and drive a Jag or two;
And when we have our children our children our children
And when we have our children we'll educate them well;
We'll send them to a free school a free school a free school
We'll send them to a free school and keep the riff-raff out.

Alan Doherty

Alan Doherty is 46, and has been writing poetry for around 10 years. He has a
2:1 in Fine Art and has been on Incapacity Benefit for 5 years with depression,
which his poetry and art helps me cope with.

Them And Us

Conservative leadership con the liberal elite on how to run the
        countries deficit

emasculate cost cutting our poorest in society
while Tory Liberal sycophants survive on thousands plus expenses.

Private sector welfare reforms target the none for good lazy
        unemployed scourges
Daily Mail and *Express* readers believe
made to work for £1.60 hourly benefits
cleaning the streets whitewashing graffiti decayed piss-stained walls.
Disability claimants kicked from their wheel chairs
crippled feet told to get on your bike to work
assessed by the D.L.A
no one incapacitated to stand up
everyone fit to move.

Housing Benefits slashed
families on the streets
begging for food
food token parcels out of date binned supermarket packages.

Millions of Public sector jobs join the dole line
V.A.T. up to 20%
consumerable goods, shoes-clothing-kitchen bathroom utensils
Dickensian Society by the week.

Bankers profit
champaign coats blackberry mobiles steak dinners celebrate a 2
        billion levy charge
in our fair and equal country.

THEM AND US.

Rose Drew

Rose Drew is from Florida, Connecticut, Florida again, and now York England, pursuing an elusive PhD. Her day job consists of analyzing human skeletons. Rose has co-hosted one poetry open mic or another for about 8 years and across two countries, and has been a featured poet in Miami, New York City, several locales in CT (including TV appearances), Lincoln and York UK. Her work has appeared in newspapers, books, journals and online venues. Rose has edited three poetry anthologies for her small press, Stairwell Books, the latest focusing on that quintessential English being: the Green Man.

Fraying at the Edges

Cane in hand,
I careen toward the drugstore's heavy door
pain everywhere
fire in the base of my spine
agony coursing down my legs.

I can still smile broadly when a stranger holds a door
because I am convinced this phase is
temporary.
Will I still smile
YEARS from now, if

icepicks still stab at my hips
if fire still burns down my legs with each step
if I still gasp when I sneeze;
will good humour and good-nature
be replaced by self pity —
I can survive temporary

but I am not so sure about permanent.
Already I feel despair creeping in,

only sometimes,
perhaps a dark sleepless night
after the noisy distractions of daytime are gone
when I lay staring,
obsessively reviewing my failings and mistakes
and disasters and all the rest of my story
imprisoned by wakefulness
unable to find peaceful oblivion
where I still run in my dreams.

Liam Duffy

Liam Duffy is a student of Social and Public Policy at the National University of Ireland, Galway, where he was the editor of their Writers Society's magazine *the Sharp Review*. He recently took a break from Ireland to check out the poetry scene in Finland and study at the University of Helsinki. He has most recently been published in *A Hudson View* and *The Rain Town Review* and read at the West Cork Literary Festival in Ireland as part of a reading dubbed: *Irish Poets: A New Generation.*

Welfare

Kids

Every little urchin,
every would be rascal
will have a plastic
table tennis paddle
(not wooden,
less they set them
on fire)
and an institution

full of tables,
with paintings
in bold colours
of the kids
they would've been
if their family
stayed nuclear —

but now they can only be
a manual/unskilled
or a table tennis Olympian.

Widows

Give every widow
a dog;
so they have someone
to feed
and pamper,
but, don't let any-man
ever know
less they feel
devalued;
being replaced
by a pooch
or resentful
that they were never
pampered

and there will be
society:
waving from French windows
and car-pooling your kids.

He also reads tabloids
(after Hugo Simberg's painting *Death and the Peasant*)

He likes the calluses
on your hands,
the meaty tumours
in your lungs
and the leaking sores
in your stomach.

He likes the hours
you have to work,
the education
you didn't receive
and the health care
you can't afford.

He buys you drinks
at the bar,
and you are happy
to sit with him,

you talk of the weather,
the sports
you don't play,
the women
you're told to like
and the Blacks, Tinkers
and Poles.

Inside his dark hood
a lipless mouth
forms a smile
of gum-less teeth

he raises
along crooked finger
to gesture
for another round —

You stop him,
And happily say
"I'll get this one".

Nordic ghetto

In the bar
with the perpetual crying women outside;
nobody knows
what's in their pockets
happy to see
a cigarette
in their hands

and beer in a glass
somewhere.

You'll never see such frisky drunks;
eating each-others
wrinkled faces.

Their dogs tied up,
outside in the snow,
being comforted by concerned strangers

as the perpetual crying women
looks on.

Down and out

I would like to
undress you
and catalogue
every article of clothing,
each trinket
in your pockets:
the fish hooks
and bottle caps.

I want to know
how and when
you wash yourself,
what your breath smells like,
how your body works
after so many bouts
of hypothermia
and immersions in vodka
or vinegar grade wine.

I'd like to know
your bowel movements,
how your intestines
collect and excrete
the rare knots of fat
you digest,
and how many wipes
it takes you to
clean the malformed
excrement from your arse.

I want you

to tell me
what happened,
when you finally decided
that you would:
no longer
take your clothes off
to wash them
but began to put more layers on.

With each layer
surrendering civility,
with each layer
admitting to circumstances,
with each layer
insulating yourself,
from the cold
      and the rest of us.

Giffen Man*

Two euro,
      Two euro

more for the quality beef,
for all my hours of work
I eat the value beef.
what is it?
that makes the quality cow
superior to the value cow.

Is the value cow
devoid of nutrients?

I know I am.
I am sallow
I am skinny
I am as sick
as the cows I eat.

The breadline
does not afford me
creativity.

My wages sustain,
  My body
but my mind starves,
my kids don't dream
and they don't cry.

* *Giffen good*: A good that is so inferior and so heavily consumed at low incomes that the demand for it rises when its price rises — Deardorff's *Glossary of International Economics*.

Tim Evans

Tim Evans was born in Llanelli in 1949. He won the Nehru gold medal in Shankar's International Children's Poetry Competition, aged 16. A year later he won a place at Jesus College, Cambridge, where he studied English under Raymond Williams. He travelled around America in 1968, during major anti-Vietnam protests in Berkeley. From 1970s onwards he has worked in the UK as a teacher and lecturer — active in NUT and NATFHE (now UCU). He has been an anti-racist and anti-fascist activist since Anti Nazi League and Rock Against Racism days, and used to drum with the band Mambo Juice. Working now as a teacher in Swansea, he performs his poetry in bars and clubs and is involved with the Junk Box poetry group. He lives in North Hill with his partner and their two cats. At the moment he is helping to start up a Swansea Against the Cuts group.

Do You Want Some?

Someone from our Office
Will be coming to see you soon
About your Benefits.

FOR YOUR PROTECTION
All our Visiting Staff
Carry an identity card
ASK TO SEE IT.

The Visitor
Will need to check a number of things
To make sure you are getting
The right amount of benefit.

DO NOT WORRY
If you do not have all the things
But please get as many as you can

So that there is no further delay
In calculation and payment
Of your Benefit
Entitlement.

You must fill in the tear-off part of this form each week
To tell us about anything that has changed.
If anything changes and you do not tell us
You might get the wrong amount of money.
And you could be breaking the law...

If you are not sure if we need to know
Please tell us anyway.
Tell us everything.

Tell us about YOURSELF.
Are you pregnant?
What date is the baby due?
Are you getting Disability Living Allowance?
How much do you get?
Are you getting it once a week?
Are you getting it once a month?
Are you getting it regular?

Are you getting hospital treatment?
Do you get a fit (or something similar)at least once a month?

What do you need?
Who is it for?
Tell us their name.

What do you need?
Who is it for?

Tell us their name.
If they are applying for the cost of replacement of an item
Please say what happened to the old item.

What is it for?
Who do you need?
Tell us their name.

Do you feel a fit (or something similar) coming on?
Can you see the shape of furniture in a room?
Can you tell light from dark?
Do strangers understand what you say?
Do your family and friends understand what you say?
Can you understand someone talking in a normal voice on a busy
    street?
Can you understand someone talking in a LOUD VOICE in a
    quiet room?
Can you tie a bow in string?
Can you walk up and down one step?
Can you raise one arm to your head as if to put on a hat?
Can you clap without using your left hand?
Can you tell light from dark?

We need to know how much it will cost
We need to know how much it will cost

We know where you live.
Do you have a problem?
Do you have a problem speaking?
Do you have a problem hearing?
Do you want one?
Do you want some?
Do you have a problem?

Can you stand unassisted?
Are you going to a funeral?
Do you have a problem bending or kneeling?
Do you lose control of your bladder at least once a month?
Do you lose control of your bowels at least once a month?
Please show us how often in the box below.

Do you need help because someone needs your care and support?
This person might have a mental illness
Please tell us about this person
Their name
Their address
Their relationship to you
Why do they need your care and support?

Do you need help?
Do you need help because of very difficult problems?
Do you need help?

Do you need help?
Because of very difficult problems?
Do you need help?

Please tell us why things are so very difficult
Tell us about the pain you feel while you are doing day-to-day
        things.
Can you pick up a two pence coin with either one of your hands?
Can you pick up a pound coin with either one of your hands?
Can you pick up a £10 note with one of your hands but not the
        other?
Can you pick up a welfare cheque?
I bet.
I said: "I bet".

Can strangers understand you?
Can you understand someone talking in a loud voice in a quiet
    room?
Can you bend or kneel and straighten up again?
Can you bend or kneel as if to pick up a piece of paper from the
    floor and straighten up again?
Can you walk?
Can you crawl?
Can you pick up a half litre carton of milk
Or Special Brew?
Can you bend to touch your toes?
Can you see the shape of furniture in a dark room?
Can you understand some one talking in a normal voice?
Can you understand someone talking in a LOUD voice?
Do you have problems with fits?

Tell us about your partner.
Does he need help?
Is he away from work because of a trade dispute?
Was it a strike?
Was it a walkout?
Was it a lockout?
Were there picket lines?
Did he love you?
Was he breaking the law?

Does he have a problem?
Can he tell light from dark?
Can he see the shape of furniture in a room?
Can he tie a bow in string?
Can he understand someone talking in a loud voice in a quiet
    room?

Do you understand what he says?
What does he need?
How much does he get?
Where does he live?
Who does he love?

Does he want some?
Tell us his name.

Someone will be coming to see you very soon
About your benefit entitlement.
For your protection
Ask to see their identity card.

Victoria Field

Victoria Field was born in London in 1963. She moved to Cornwall in 1999 where she now works as a writer and poetry therapist. She has published two collections of poetry, *Olga's Dreams* and *Many Waters* (based on a year-long residency at Truro Cathedral), both with fal. Her poetry has been broadcast on BBC Radio Cornwall, Radio 3 and Radio 4. She also writes fiction and drama and has had two plays produced: *Blood* (2005) and *Glass Heart* (2006). Her fiction, poetry and drama have won many awards. She qualified as a Certified Poetry Therapist through the US National Association for Poetry Therapy in 2005 and in 2006, received a Pioneer Award for her work in the field. She gives workshops in many different educational, health and community settings and has co-edited two books on therapeutic writing: *Writing Works* (with Gillie Bolton and Kate Thompson, JKP, 2006) and *Prompted to Write* (with Zeeba Ansari, fal, 2007). She has also published a children's book, *The Gift* (fal, 2007). She is a member of Falmouth Poetry Group and a former chair of Lapidus.

Service

People piss in me, men mostly
but women too, sometimes, after the pub.

I'm part of the open road but going nowhere.
A marker on the song-lines of life, I shelter

the forgotten who don't wear the armour
of a vehicle, those who don't know out-of-town shopping

parties in rural houses, spontaneous trips to the city.
I absorb the anxiety of the elderly, clutching

their carefully counted fare, embrace the weak
whose whole world is hospitals, new glasses

bewildering benefits. Am glad to be of service
to the naked. Where else can kids go

for a smoke or a grope? I wait for the waiting
who always leave me, move on as soon as they can.

I love the caresses of sanctioned rain and snow
but can take, too, the drunk's vomit, used condoms

a hundred worried dog-ends and not mind —
be a station on life's journey on a parallel road

let the truly human pass through me.

Adam Fish

Adam Fish is the author of *Diving for Yemayá* (Morden Tower 2002), and has had work published in anthologies and magazines. Ze has performed extensively throughout the UK, most notably on the fourth plinth in Trafalgar Square, but also in Edinburgh, Liverpool, Hastings and London. Ze edits the transgressive literary 'zine *Diseases of Staggering Beauty* and blogs about poetry, politics and genderqueer issues at *Wrestling Emily Dickinson*. ['Ze' is a genderqueer pronoun'].

Class? War?

When the have-nots decide they'd like to have a little more
you call it class war, class war;
but when the rich declare a silent genocide against the poor
it's never class war, it's only case law.

When Muslims get irate and say they'll detonate the state
you say it's faith that generates their hate;
but when the guys with home-made gelignite are English-born
       and white,
you say they hate because they feel displaced.

When a black man, a gay woman or a trans girl wins promotion
you say they're only there to tick a box
but when the cabinet photo's mainly male and pale as suntan
       lotion
you say that's just the way the penny drops.

And when someone points the flaws out in your right-wing
scheme of things
you say we're bolshy, right-on, worthy, pious;
but however loud you shout your lies there's one thing you can't
       change:
what we deserve we will demand: you can't deny us.

James Fountain

James Fountain was born in Hartlepool in 1979. He is a lecturer in English Literature at Peterborough Regional College, and recently submitted the first PhD on neglected Scottish modernist poet Joseph Macleod to the University of Glasgow. He has published articles in various journals including *The Guardian* and *the Times Literary Supplement*. He is author of the autobiographical novel *Out of Time* (2006) and the poetry chapbook *Glaciation* (Poetry Monthly Press, 2010).

Revolution Falling On Deaf Ears

Life skids by on technology's wheels
Wheels roll on, take to road
Road to speed earth to its destiny
Destiny uncertain in whiff of corruption
Corruption sidled through the back door of yesterday
Yesterday I lingered in the stilled breeze
Breeze blows the stench through the cities
Cities race to gather cash to excavate the future
Future lost in the furore of enraged fists
Fists furious in the revolutionary fervour
Fervour lost on the political sandcastle attendants
Attendants tied fast to their seats
Seats of power silent to the ringing telephone
Telephone blares angrily, unanswered in the void
Void to float the future, star maps unfold
Unfold to the universe traced out in past by Galileo
Centuries back in the ether, where the lost emails fell
Fell on eardrums drumming nothing
Nothing whispered back from the authorities,
Authorities nothing to report, none to name
Name no one, naming no one else,
Else earth collide with truth
Truth falls on punctured eardrums.

Naomi Foyle

Naomi Foyle's poetry has been published widely in journals including *Ambit, The London Magazine, PN Review, Poetry London, Tears in the Fence* and *Stand.* Her poetry collections include *Red Hot & Bothered* (Lansdowne Press, 2003), *The Night Pavilion* (PBS Recommendation 2008), *Grace of the Gamblers* and *The World Cup* (all Waterloo Press, 2008/09/10).

Back in the Game Plan:
The Surly Girl Returns to the Third World of Europe

ticket number seventy-nine, booth three please
booth three please
booth three please

excoriate the petalled film
from an incandescent day
advise a lamb to walk right in
to a syncopated flay

Anne Sexton, booth eight please
booth eight please
booth eight please

cultivated blankness guides
gambles by the tips
shambles by the snips
comfort by the grips

I've given this culture the best of my ire
A habitual residence I have yet to acquire

Poetry in Defence of the Welfare State

Ticket number one hundred thousand and twelve, booth two please
                                    booth two please
                                    booth two please

Miss Sexton, please, booth eight!
some of the forms are pink
some of the forms are blue
some of the fiddles
are bloody string orchestras
none of my clothing is new

atone attune attenuate
hold a stranger's land

the crusty is sleeping
on the taxpayers' grate
warm tidal swells in his brain
don't come cheap

Can Anne Sexton please borrow a pen?

Cynical Conversion

You used to live in a studio flat,
until the landlord ripped the kitchen
into a bedroom
and stuck a cooker in the lounge.

Christ, I thought, when you told me
how much he'd raised the rent,
is it because we're Londoners,
that even our homes are cynical now?

So when Jeremy Paxman cried
at the gates of the workhouse
his great-granny had wound up in
with her brood of barefoot kids,

I phoned to tell you to watch him
on the TV you hoist
from front room to back
like a false eye shared between sockets.

You were pointing the aerial
out the back window
where the kitchen sink used to be.
'I heard he's got a huge cock,' you said.

Paul Francis

Paul Francis was a teacher for thirty years, and is now retired. He lives in Much Wenlock, Shropshire. He has published an autobiography, *Comprehensive View*, and a collection of poems, *Various Forms*.

Prospectus

It gets me mad when folks suggest
Reform's a pious hope
As though we'd scribbled down these plans
On the back of an envelope.
No way. For fifteen years or more
We've been preparing this
And the present opportunity
Is just too good to miss.
OK, it's going to cost you
For the adverts and our fees
But you're prepared for hardship,
You knew these cuts would squeeze.
We'll pick the patients that we want;
Some win, and most will lose
But that's the way we like it
And it's us that gets to choose.
We'll do just fine. How you end up
Is anybody's guess
But before we're done you'll all forget
You had an NHS.

Wanker

How about this? *OK, I screwed things up.*
Got greedy looking for the next best thing,
too much too quick. But, once you've seen the top
you can't stay on the lower slopes. The strong
clean up, the weak go to the wall. I missed
the bigger picture, lost the plot. Maybe
it's over, all of it. I feel so … lost.
I don't know what to do. I'm desperate, babe.

That's better. When you back me, I feel good
and face it, no-one does it like I do.
It's me that makes the rules here, understood?
You can't afford to lose me. No, don't cry —
it cramps my style. I'm what's best for you
so I'll screw you, screw you, screw you till I die.

John Gibbens

John Gibbens was born in the Wirral and grew up in West Germany and West Cumbria. He has lived in London since 1978, and worked as a typist, secretary, typesetter and journalist. He has been a subeditor at *The Independent, Sunday Times, Financial Times* and *Sunday Telegraph*, and was deputy editor of *The Oldie.* He won an Eric Gregory Award in 1982, and has had poems in numerous journals and anthologies over the past 30 years. He self-published his *Collected Poems* in 2000, and a study of Bob Dylan, *The Nightingale's Code*, in 2001. He plays, composes and sings with The Children, who have released eight CDs, starting with *Play* in 1999.

London Bride (2005), the opening stanzas

We wintered on the Sea of Lunder
where points of reeds stuck through ice.
Beside the blue cheek of a drummer boy
could be seen the place that had been an eye.

Worldbeat percs in a Coffee Republic
and the Inca's gold conducts our microvolts.
Where fire rolled down Gracechurch Street
the glass fronts cool.

Most were not so near the surface:
ridges of a bootsole unbudged by kicking;
stiff leaf of weed, it seemed,
was the elbow-crease in an olive sleeve.

Guitars go smoothly on a juice squeezed from the south,
white foam sweeps the sand slick
with an immaculate backbeat. Meanwhile elsewhere
oils are holding the heads of drowned waves under.

I took up a tress in my hand
that struck each finger to a thread
and spread in a wire cage
through you and yours, distributaries of breakage.

Who will ascend the hair
of a maid in the Hawksmoor tower?
Nine, eleven, the dead hours ring
that the old lady lays her eggs by.

Note the high ferroglyph twinkle
above the end of the Causeway,
no-one dancing in its chambers.
A moon nearly two-thirds grown

falls through a half-fog, dissolving
in isn't and doesn't.
The skeleton of a cage
ascending in a half-fogged sky.

Word is not the engine of power
and the bone of governance is not thought.
Its blood is force
and discourse hides its face.

Beside the shore at Menchen How,
it was not what we thought it was —
a rope,
a loop of hawser.

Somebody'd made it, something broke it,
everything lost it.
Than the useful grown useless

nothing more naked.

Dead leaf and daffodil blowing
of a March that goes on,
large as light,
the blister-bud,

lamblion long.
The growth bidden
in the cold blast
bloodied,

another bloodied
March. Venus walks
in stone-
desert camouflage.

Gresham's grasshopper, gilt over Lombard Street
making no music for workers below
on the hill that's been built her of stone
where the old one's laying their eggs.

Of how things work
will I know enough well
to make one small novel
to move convincingly

the people about
when I was younger thought.
Or do they?
Perhaps a trick all is it.

So passing Prudent Passage

which arches overhead entirely
tiled in white
I'm in the dark and there again

but am I?
Define yourself,
the products tell their products,
Go create.

Maria Gornell

Maria Gornell has been published in various online zines and in print just to name a few here — *The beat, lit up mag, Outside Writers Plebian Rag* and *heroin love songs*. In print she appears in *Shoots and Vines'* all female anthology *I can not be your virgin and your mother, agua*, Scintillating publications, *Liverpool 800* anthology, Clinicality press; *Clinical, Brutal... An Anthology of Writing with Guts* as well as the erbacce press anthology *Blood at the Chelsea*. She lives in Liverpool and is currently training in Counselling.

Inner city blues

For the bureaucrat, the world is a mere object to be manipulated by him.

Karl Marx

The air is thick with degradation
the dole queue's haven't been this
long since the 80's

Greeted by the pitiful smile of administration

Trapped in the cycle of poverty
flexed in the frustration of hope
that beats the drum of welfare state

patterns manipulating the strive to
be free of decay.

Here lies the sleek contrast though slight
the desk suggests the closed authoritarian
difference of us and them
identify theft stored in the files of PC
the false perception of their worthiness

Their talent laid in the bundle of papers
flung inside the shredder to be eliminated
unfulfilled the criteria remains bleak.

In the hoarse voice and smokers cough
of a man too old and sick too work
yet too young to be given a pass.
In the youth failed by the education system
controlled in the trap of giro doorstep hell.
in the lone women unqualified wombs for sale
fed the hollow promise of working family
tax and nursery fees

Where are the fathers to these babies?

The men victims of the recession accustomed
to the alarm call still shuffling in work boots
cement has long set within the grooves.

The sick and mental health sufferers
herded in medical certificates in hand
interviewed with same big brother questions
examined with the compassion of a Nazi.

The graduates from student dreams
degree to this debauchery sliced
ambitions laid dormant education
paid for in loans from the state.

Here lies the difference: it's us and them:
the workers getting paid to punch
lives away with keys.

The dream is over.
Then I hear snippets of conversations
worrying about the man who's benefit
was stopped no reason, no notice
His direct debits in bank unpaid now
charged a fee the vicious circle
the crisis loan refused across cold
receiver, his cries across the desk

One member of staff proclaims his sadness
'It'll get worse when Cameron gets in he
plans to scrap the child tax credit' he says

Again I swallow hard, almost inhale the bleak
inevitability of another Tory rein

While Yozzer Hughes murmurs
'Giz a job'

Instead I inhale hope in one suited worker
I discovered the humane still exists
the benefit workers as sick and disgusted
as us.

While at the top the establishment
plans to bring into office a millionaire
and his high flying club of Southerners
with duck ponds, mansions
exuberant expense accounts.

To send us out to sweep their streets
and clean their tables to remind us
of our place.

Bill Greenwell

Bill Greenwell is the OU's Arts Staff Tutor in Gateshead, and a member of the OU's creative writing team. He was the *New Statesman*'s weekly poet from 1994-2002, and his collection *Impossible Objects* (Cinnamon) was shortlisted for a Forward Prize for best first collection.

Big Soc. It To Me

I am the Big Society
As vacuous as ash,
A dose of petty piety
While we are strapped for cash:
My voice is made of mimicry,
My muscles of veneer,
My lips of wholesale gimmickry.
My substance? No idea.
I call myself Philanthropy:
You'll gather round me, shall you?
But I'm the great misanthrope
And I possess no value.
I am a slogan, brief, inane,

Coined by someone keen,
But utterly without a brain.
I don't know what I mean.
Suppose you wish to start a school,
Or hospital, or vet's,
The Big Society says Cool —
Bring pupils, patients, pets,
And organise the whole bang shoot.
We think you'll find it cheaper.
The Bible has some words to suit:
Am I my brother's keeper?
The Big Society contains
A most expressive void,
Yet runs the blood-cells through the veins
Of all the unemployed.
It's visible as wi-fi
And not of bricks or mortar:
It's like the Big Chief I-Spy
And his Wigwam-By-The-Water.
Yes, I'm the Big Society,
A feeble, forceless fable
With no vim or variety
But one great trestle table:
You put it up, you celebrate,
You roast a local pig,
But find Society, too late,
Is anything but Big.

John G. Hall

John G. Hall is founding editor of *Citizen32*, author of four poetry collections, the latest of which is *BANG!* He is an activist & poetry workshop organiser in Manchester. His poetry has appeared in *Orbis, Iota, Rain Dog, The Wolf, Coffee House Poetry, The Ugly Tree, Carillon, Outlaw, Left Curve, Square Lake, Spume, Aesthetica, Brittle Star, Harlequin, Monkey Kettle & Fire.*

The last rites of Margaret Thatcher

And as she struggled to remember her last memory,
instead of a kiss or a child's hand touching hers, she
hears the sound of young men digging in the black
ground of the dark, all around their song drifting
through the earth, 'Here we go, here we go!', then
as she looks up to see the boat come to carry her
across the river Styx she notices the name Belgrano
burned into its bony ribs, looks up for forgiveness
and finds only the cold gaze of millions, for every slave
curses the whip and never forgives those that cracked it.

Reason to be raging

Spent 9 hours last night in A&E waiting for a bed for my father, not enough beds. Trident cost £9.8 billion, each Tornado attack plane costs £10 million, and now the bankers say they may leave the country if their bonus is touched. Stop the state terrorism of our own population, bring the troops home and march them down to the stock exchange and protect people's democracy with fixed bayonets. No, they are in the Middle East protecting the rights of the west to cheap oil by putting in place or supporting corrupt flawed undemocratic governments. The mission in Afghanistan cost the Treasury £2.6 billion last year. If they want to protect us from terrorism spend that money on health & education & housing. We gave the bankers the money to do this as pension funds and taxes and they pocketed it. So, send the army down to the stock market and root out the leaders of these financial terrorist organisations. It could be your father next to be regarded as fiscal collateral damage.

2010 time to stop whispering

2010 is timed to
be the year of
the great switch
on of our left over
rage and protest,
rich men will come
to squeeze your
hearts more dry
than burning sand,

will come to smash
all the love in you,
but this will be
the brilliant time
the lovers time,
the underground
rising up through
our feet up into
our legs up into
our sex up into
our hearts up
into our minds,

up into our tongues

up into the breath
we exchange each
kiss we free we give
this year, this year.

We will write a red
unholy bible book
filled with dreams
coming true hot
off the page,
and everything
will begin with
the word awake
on the barricade,

made into flesh
made into roars,

made up to make
love to everything
an inconsumable
system of human
touch enshrined
in the helix twists
of the revolution's
unborn children,

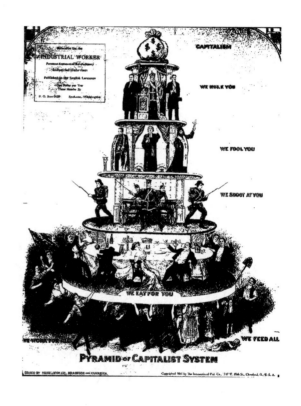

snugged curled
waiting in our
present lily
livered silence,

time to wake

up to energise
each par sec
of your heart

beat and be
beat and be
beat and be

the bow wave
tsunami revolt
of our raging
smashing up,

their thirty dirty
pieces of peace,
let us be their
poison chalice,

their cursed wine
their bitter host
their winter palace.

Wet Cement Poem No. 3

they reckon birth may hurt babies
they say life is worth every penny

they believe the working class do not exist
they tell this to shop workers and nurses

they take the proof of our silent witness
they stare through the television screen into us

they trace each thought back to its owner

they rig the trail of life with sticky pleasure
they laugh at the poor behind their backs

they pin down the butterfly inside you
they pull the wings from your genius

they find starving people then feed them war
they have decided to counterfeit everything on the face of the earth
they reckon love is a rumour spread by dirty rotten communists.

The real read

We write flags to rally around, but the battles are the real read,
yeah we are the rattle of sabres demanding new steel,
but the youth are the real read the real bleeding to be free
and our poems our comfort and courage and love made thinkable
and the roar of our hearts pulling on their chains.

Graham Hardie

Graham Hardie's poetry has been published in *Markings, The New Writer, Weyfarers, The David Jones Journal, Cutting Teeth, Nomad, The Coffee House, Cake* and online at *Nth Position* and *the Recusant*. His first collection was published in 2007 by Ettrick Forest Press. Hardie is the editor of the online journals *Osprey, The Glasgow Review, The Caledonia Review, Eleutheria — Scottish Poetry Review*, and is a founder of Literature Scotland.

For we live in war and the darkest hour!

To sing of the fruits of the Earth,
Where to the beggars come
To undo what has been done,
And to hear of God's worth
Amongst the labour of love's birth,
Is to rejoice in cities of gold
Whose devotion to God will unfold,
In the deepest rivers of mirth.
And where the wild dogs bark,
The silver vassal will await,
By the solitary sound of the lark
And the black coal of man's hate.
So venture forth and pluck the flower
For we live in war and the darkest hour!

Kevin Higgins

Kevin Higgins was born in London in 1967. He grew up in Galway, Ireland but lived in London in the late 80s/early nineties when he was active in the Anti-Poll Tax movement. He was expelled from the Labour Party in 1991 for his anti-poll tax activities and membership of Militant. He is now co-organiser of Over The Edge literary events in Galway, Ireland. He facilitates poetry workshops at Galway Arts Centre; teaches creative writing at Galway Technical Institute and on the Brothers of Charity Away With Words programme. He is also Writer-in-Residence at Merlin Park Hospital and the poetry critic of *the Galway Advertiser*. Collections: *The Boy With No Face* (2005; shortlisted for the 2006 Strong Award), *Time Gentlemen, Please* (2008; a poem from which, 'My Militant Tendency', featured in the Forward Book of Poetry 2009), and *Frightening New Furniture* (2010; all by Salmon Poetry). His work also features in the anthology *Identity Parade — New British and Irish Poets* (Bloodaxe, 2010).

Fund Manager's Confession

Bless me Father
for I have not sinned. Daily
from my glass hideaway in the sky
I look down on those
who think they now know me
still whistling into their pillows. God

consults me on a regular basis
about his pension, which last Autumn
came down with a terrible dose
of RBS. This morning I phoned
to reassure him that once again
everything's coming up Dollars.

This new time religion, I make it possible.
Christmas was Bondi Beach
but spent checking my e-mail.

The kids live the en-suite life; mine
is a map with a coloured pin
on every country I've visited.

From the cellar of my refashioned palace
in the far suburbs I can whip,
anytime, a vat of wine
from wherever you care to mention,
but am too busy managing
the world's piggy banks. The little guy
in the White House offsets the national debt
against the vast surplus of my self-esteem.

When it's all over, they'll employ me
to supervise the sale of Tina Turner's hair
and Air Force One to the Martians or whoever's
in the hunt for a bargain that morning.

Clare Hill

Clare Hill was born in the West Midlands in 1978. She has written articles for *Arts Disability Culture Magazine, Twisted Tongue, Multicultural* and various websites and has written short stories for *The Second BHF Book of Horror Stories, Twisted Tongue, Gold Dust*, Writelink resources, and others. She has had poetry published in *Raw Edge, Twisted Tongue, Delivered* and *Trespass*. Two mental health books, both published by chipmunkapublishing — including *Living Without Marbles*. Hill participated in the Equal 2 New Writers' Development Programme in Birmingham, and has performed poetry at the Oasis Cafe Theatre, Borders bookshop, the Library Theatre, and in the middle of Birmingham town centre.

The greater good

Now we have solved the so-called "disabled" problem
and criminalised single parents
all people with A-type blood will, henceforth, be deemed
to be the scourge of society.

The media will use these approved descriptive words:
cheat, scrounger, burden, idle, workshy
and blame them for the collapse of the economy.

Our research has shown A-types don't try hard enough
to find work, and that many employers consider A-types
unsuitable due to their negative attitude.

Classes will be held to ensure they perform at the same level
as O, B and AB-types. These lessons will be compulsory.

Client non-compliance will result in extreme sanctions;
propose reintroduction of corporal punishment.

Michael Horovitz

Michael Horovitz was born on 4th April 1935. Originally associated with the oral verse revival, he co-organised the First International Poetry Incarnation at the Royal Albert Hall on 11th June 1965, with Allen Ginsberg, Alexander Trocchi et al. In 1959 he founded New Departures, which (re)introduced the likes of William Burroughs, Samuel Beckett and Stevie Smith. He edited the groundbreaking *Children of Albion: Poetry of the Underground in Britain* (Penguin, 1969), which was followed by the 1992 audio and book sequel, *Grandchildren of Albion*. Collections include *Growing Up: Selected Poems and Pictures 1951-'79* (Allison & Busby, 1979). He has been running the Poetry Olympics festivals since 1980. His latest publication is the decade-long in-the-writing, *A New Waste Land: Timeship Earth at Nillennium*, the first volume of which was published in 2007 (New Departures/Central Books).

from A New Waste Land

from I. Prologue: *The Burial of the Living*

[...]

Where beds of roses had beckoned,
                                                                    now
punishing thorns closed in like muggers
and tore at the most vulnerable throats

            — unwaged parents,
            the handicapped and wheelchair-strapped,
            underpaid nurses and teachers,
            unestablished artists and writers,
            beginning musicians,
            skint students

                        — just those
whose circumstances, talents and vocations
most need support, if they're to develop

and enhance the public good.

[...]

— for the sake of '*Defence*' and '*The Economy*', y/our Gov say
and bray '*for dear life*' about so-called '*tough choices*'

    while sticking to the same old commercial deceiving
    better guns, '*smarter*' bombs, evangelical poses
        — with only the same old flags unfurled
        of the same infinitely fruitless old world
        smash and grab ways of strife,
            deathly job-stunted lives . . .

[...]

from III. *A Little Kite Music*

[...]

        — What's in a job
        if clocking in, and out
        on the dot
            (— or out
              before the dot, if poss . . .)
        just for the money
        is all?

    Whereas
— as Lawrence saw it, in his poem
        '*Work*' –

    "There is no point in work
    unless it pre-occupies you as well as occupies you.
    When you are only occupied, you are an empty shell.

*A man needs to be independent at his work, so that he
can put his own self into it."*

[…]

from VII: *Gland of Hype's Vainglory*

[…]

. . . thou shreddest welfare
from those most in need

. . . for that they may Switch, you say
(for "at the *end* of the day
all shall have pay" . . .)

and Buy In —

to the hallowed overworlds
of museums and high art,
of specialist healthcare whenever
it's called for,
of offshore trusts . . .

[…]

from VIII. *How Astutely Faulty Towers Corrupt Absolutely*

[…]

. . . Let's agree
with John Lennon that

"*. . . We want Christ to win*"

— Meaning the Christ who
as Blake understood him

"was all Virtue
and . . . taught that God
   forbade all contention
for Worldly prosperity"

      — meaning the Christ
      who whipped the money-changers
      out of the Temple

            — overturned their tables,
            poured away their profits

            and pronounced them Thieves.

      [...]

   from IX. *Touchstones for Bablyon*

      [...]

Here's three loud boos for the hype and schmooze,
For your superposh mega-dosh parties
And your smoothed-out lengths of old Tory rope
That still tie down the helpless with less and less hope

—Told:
    "Lone parents, new mothers,
    Sickos, disabled —
    On your bikes, get straight
    Back to work, all's well"

          . . . Save for those who aren't
          — left to rot in hell.

      [...]

from XI. *U-Turn On All This — or Die*

What we actually have
in pseudo-millennial Britain
is a new waste land
over which
a cold central government darkness
thick with the swarming farts and grafts
of opportunism, gambling, infinite greed
— of obligatory bar-coded consumerism
pleated in as sternly as Thatcher's suits were
with martial buttons and he-man padding
and the same unconcern
for the weak and disadvantaged
— is imposed, officialised
and bankroll-modelled
by the new Alright-Hons
— callous
and complicit as the last gang
with planned obsolescence
— with that casual victimisation of the powerless
which is bound to leave worse-off than ever
anyone who won't
— or can't —
buy into
profit from
and spread
this government darkness visible
— clotted as Monsanto — thick
as thieves in the night. . .

[NB: these are abridged excerpts from *A New Waste Land* and do not therefore
constitute a direct reproduction of the work; the ellipses ([. . .]) indicate absent sections
of text; further, the text here is in a narrower template and does not spread across
the page as widely as in Horovitz's original, whose layout is consequently different.]

Peter Hughes

Peter Hughes is a Liverpool poet since his retirement. He was a chartered engineer who did not go to University and worked from age 15 to 65 with a few periods of unemployment. He was a member of the AESD union that later became TASS and he was a member of the AUT in later years. "I worked up from the shop floor to the board room and basically expect people who are able to work not to become totally dependent on the state. In this way benefits can be targeted on those young and old who really need help. Our political leaders should be moving on to eradicate poverty and despair in our country".

Redundant

Rising unemployment takes its toll.
Last on are usually first to go,
Sign on line and claim State dole.

Search for jobs not knowing a soul.
Try down the road at so and so.
Rising unemployment takes its toll.

No pay cheques, off the pay-roll,
Pay-back time, cash dwindles away.
Sign on line and claim State dole.

Go for a grant, learn a new skill,
Help stem the rising job-less tide.
Rising unemployment takes its toll.

Working hard is good for the soul.
Trusted worker, good-will flows.
Rising unemployment takes its toll,
Sign on line and claim State dole.

Dr Robert Ilson

Dr Robert Ilson is an Honorary Research Fellow of University College, London, and was the Founding Editor of *The International Journal of Lexicography* (Oxford University Press). He has written on religion and politics for *the New Statesman*.

Ode to the National Health Service

for Harry Levinson

From my flat's windows I can see
The ramparts of our Royal Free
Hospital, never shut to me.

Although I go but seldom there
I'm happy such a place is, where
Both poor and rich get the same care.

The poor when ill are only ill:
Once they're discharged they need not still
Dread an inevitable bill.

The rich are treated — and can feel
Their taxes serve the common weal
To help a fractured nation heal.

Long live the vision! May we find
That we can still be wisely kind
Yoking together heart and mind!

Down With the Welfare State!

I'm rich. Among the joys of being rich
Is looking on the suffering to which
The poor are subject. Yes, it makes me glad
I'm not like them. But also I am sad
They're not like me. I give to charity
Now and again. And wars against barbarity
Elsewhere get my support. Thus I ensure
Our poor sleep safely knowing foreign poor
Will not come here from elsewhere to molest them.
Only fools query me. I say: Arrest them!
They need me more than I need them. It's me
Who pays them to serve me. What would they be
Without my money? But they want still more.
How then could we afford to go to war ?!
"Dignity !" they cry. "We want a living wage!
We want free health-care! A secure old age!"
Their "We want!" means that they want me to pay!
That's not how I got where I am today!
(And should by chance one of them make a pile
He'll need to learn to copy my life-style.)
Of course like everyone I have my dreams:
A loveliness surrounds me; the world seems
An avenue of equals where each greets
Each smilingly and there are no mean streets.
I wake up, though, and tell myself "Get real!
Live as you have to live, not as you feel."
Such visions sap me. That would never do.
My proper place is with the favoured few.
People like me have made our nation great!
We want our perks ! Down With The Welfare State!

The Great Recession

The Fat Cats' Guardian Angel:
Into each life some rain must fall.
Did you really think you could have it all
When you'd never had it so good before
(Except with the money you made from war) ?!
Well, God never promised you a rose-garden.
Setbacks will make your sinews harden.
What doesn't kill you will make you strong :
You'll bounce back sexier ere long.
So smile and roll onto your trophy wife.

The Punter:
She's gone ?! Your darling, your mate for life ?!
What did you expect ? If you're not top dog,
Your sweetheart will find someone else to snog.
Ha-bloody-ha ! The joke's on you
-— On you and all your cut-throat crew !
You've made your bed. Go lie in it !
Your fan's at last been hit by shit !

What's that you say? The government,
Aware of your predicament,
Has stitched together a rescue package
To mitigate the dreadful damage
That would have made the whole world quail
If you guys were allowed to fail?!

The Fat Cat:
Punter, avaunt ! I told you so!
It's not what you owe — it's who you know!
The Punter:

Oh Lord ! Now my portfolio's down.
How dare I show my face in town ?
Had I a wife what would I fear ?
I'm older and poorer year by year.
Help ! I won't bad-mouth your success
If you can get me out of this mess !

The Fat Cat:
Done deal ! I'll be your friend in need.
Just sign here. Thanks. That simple deed
Clears all your debts — until tomorrow.
Sleep now.
                    You're mine in joy — and sorrow.

The Freedom That Passeth Some People's Understanding

Sometimes I only want to stay at home.
Sometimes not. Now and then I have a yen
To get out and about. What happens when
I'd rather my world were less monochrome?
I limp to a bus-stop or a tube-station,
Hop gingerly aboard — and off I go!
Where to ? Well, frankly, I don't always know:
Strangeness lends extra zest to expectation.
My Magic Carpet is my Freedom Pass.
But wheresoever is my journey's end
There's some shop-keeper who becomes my friend
Since I spend on his wares the surplus cash
I save on fares.
                    Take heed, politicos,
Who slide past us in chauffeur-driven limos!

Tom Jayston

Tom Jayston was born on 24 October 1971 in Chertsey. He grew up in Horsell and then Leigh. He's been writing since he realised he was able to. Some of his poems have previously appeared in the Creative Future anthology *amazement* and online at *the Recusant*. His first collection of poetry, *Reverie and Rude Awakenings* (edited and introduced by Alan Morrison), was published by Creative Future this year.

£82

The electronic voice says I simply must wait
I simply must wait, for a human response.
A human response is what I require,
Not dismissal, like flesh on a funeral pyre.

They question me over and over again.
Over and over, I have nothing to hide.
Nothing to hide, I am staying alive.
I am staying alive. But only just.

£82 which does just one thing.
It does just one thing. It keeps me alive.
It keeps me alive to jump through the hoops.
To jump through the hoops which keep me alive.

Simon Jenner

Simon Jenner was born in Cuckfield in 1959. Educated at Leeds, then Cambridge. A recipient of a South-East Arts Bursary, and two Royal Literary Fund grants, he has also received a commission from BBC Southern Counties Radio. Jenner has written for *Poetry Review, PNR, Tears in the Fence, The Tablet, Music on the Web* and the British Music Society. The first volume of his Selected Poems, *About Bloody Time*, was recently published by Waterloo Press. Since 2003 he has been the Director of Survivors' Poetry. Jenner is also editor of *Eratica*. He is a Royal Literary Fund Fellow for Chichester University. A collection of poems inspired by the life and work of the Portuguese poet Fernando Pessoa was published by Perdika Press in 2009.

6 Somerhill Avenue

I'm voting in the imagined shadow
of my demolished house. Straight up
opposite this calico-faced school swaying
next to the developer's scoop.

I smile my Janus of exile to these candidates
bright in their outdoor faces.
They're suspect, next to repel
this brownfields landslide of themselves.

Just the doss-house held off millions.
Now that distinguished dove-grey blot
mirrors on greedy glass spirals who
suck the shave-close salaries of London
to the square root of the old, lived-in spaces.

Too tight to wheeze my asthmatic child's dust in:
a boy's stride across the mahogany Thirties
landing would take in three pine lives, fresh sick

with new paint; ghosts of a future haunted
by being for ever cornered by past flesh stalking.

Here, I navigate from the garish canopy.
Maybe I voted for their time, complicit
to quell tuxedo dinners; a shell of privilege
my years here occupied in a rasp
of bookish dust in the throat.

But I've elected pre-fab vision,
my rosette-dismantled self packed with
returning officers, who breathe
brickdust, swear in those who tear up
quiet quarters, look out to a sky-hard
desert studded with giant noon-yellow locusts:
no history lesson counters their coming
no shade darkens me with language.

Philip Johnson

Philip Johnson is a member of *The Poetry Kit*. He is currently employed as a Senior Care Assistant/Care Team Leader.

Following not the philosophy of fish

washed clean and dressed well
they all sit in front of the tv
saying nowt

nowt

one by one heads fall chin
to chest

nowt

nowt said
and one by one they nod
until all are head bowed
and we pass them by
saying nowt
 nowt

up
washed and dressed well
fed and sat back down in front of the tv
saying nowt

they nod

one by one they bow once more

their heads chin to chest nodding
as though in appreciation as they breath
but say nowt

nowt

when the progress sheets are completed
at the end of each shift they say nowt
no concerns

sat in the lounge

watched tv with the others
when asked if happy they nodded
said nowt

nowt

out today for lunch with family
for mental stimulation is

nowt

CAPITALISM

Norman Jope

Norman Jope was born in Plymouth, where he lives again after lengthy spells in other locations (most recently Swindon, Bristol and Budapest) and works, as an administrator, at University College Plymouth St Mark & St John. His collection include *For The Wedding-Guest* (Stride), *The Book of Bells and Candles* (Waterloo Press, 2009) and translation of work into Romanian is underway. His critical work has appeared in various magazines and webzines, including *Tears in the Fence, Poetry Salzburg Review* and *Terrible Work*, and he is currently co-editing *The Salt Critical Companion to Richard Berengarten* (Burns); he has also edited the literary/cultural magazine Memes and co-edited, with Ian Robinson, the anthology *In the Presence of Sharks: New Poetry from Plymouth* (Phlebas).

A Trial of Strength

The stand-up bufé enters the stars.
See how they crowd around the cap of the worker
who lays down his broom for beer in a cup.
He lights a fag and its red torch blinks
like that satellite overhead, as the moon imposes ice.
His forty year-old face is wrinkled.
His fifty year-old face is wrinkled, and his lungs are tarred.
His sixty year-old face breaks down
and his friends from the bufé scatter his ashes.
Now, the ashes from his cigarette drop into the dusk
as the green suburban train comes in, on an evening abrupt
      with frost.

Judith Kazantzis

Judith Kazantzis was born in 1940 and grew up in East Sussex. She took a Modern History degree and afterwards married American lawyer and writer Irving Weinman, wrote history for students, worked for the now non-existent Chelsea Labour Party and reviewed for *the Evening Standard*. During the 1970s she turned to poetry, fiction and art, including painting and printmaking. Kazantzis is is author of over 20 titles, including radical history (*The Gordon Riots*, 1966), fiction (*Of Love and Terror*, 2002) and fifteen poetry collections. Her *Selected Poems 1977-1992* was published by Sinclair-Stevenson in 1995. Kazantzis' feminist-socialist beliefs, blended with myth, are key aspects of her writing and art. In 2000, after years living between London and Key West, she returned to East Sussex, and now lives in Lewes. Through the 1990s Kazantzis worked for Kalayaan — Justice for Migrant Domestic Workers. In 1999 she resigned her membership of the Labour Party under Tony Blair, and since 2001 has campaigned for Occupied Palestine. Kazantzis was awarded a Cholmondeley Award for poetic achievement in 2007.

A Thatcher

A Thatcher is someone who makes a roof
or used to, when things were quieter,
was someone who sheltered people
from the rain, when things were quieter.
A Thatcher took folks from the wind
and layered the skin of a human weather.
Now a Thatcher exposes the dwellers,
rips off the roof in the skinning wind,
hurls down the roof on the dwellers,
who for cover snatch at the straws
the roof-maker rains
on their rainwashed heads ruthlessly
and in their teeth and in their eyes
like a war
that the thatcher unnaturally makes

on the dwellers. And the luckier
snatching more straw cover of the undoing
thatch, despise the unluckier, the colder ones,
so that some see but many don't
or do see but not why, and think it
the way of a brave wise Thatcher
that their fellows are icy and cold
in an inhuman country.

Sciatica in Esher in 1984

Even the Scargill foamers
    are speechless suddenly
over their potty azaleas — flower
    of the luxurious South East
or of acid Scottish hotels.

They are carried screaming
    like wets or wimps on
boards to bed for six weeks.

They look pale and stern as
    the Great War, as they go in
to be skewered and fused.

They can't blame the miners
    for slipped discs and stuffed
bellies over the azaleas, though
    they would like to.

Pen Kease

Pen Kease was born in 1951. She taught English, Drama and Humanities in a wide range of state secondary schools, often with students who had disabilities or other special needs. Pen has been writing poems seriously for two years and recently had her first poem published in *The Interpreter's House*. She lives near Oxford.

Hung Parliament

Give me the rope —
he says — I'd hang a few —
and they laugh
with doubtful
clatters
of applause
at the dark
side
of the funnyman.

After the diagnosis

she's down the garden again.
He waits at the window.
She digs in the dark — slices
and shifts the stones, the earth.
Wet hair clings to her face
as she works. Her back hurts.
He takes her hot, sweet tea.
They stand together now, alone
to drink from muddy cups —
taste the salty rain.

Elephant Ward, Great Ormond Street

I lay in my new dress.
When you arrive, you
want to smother me
but I say No. No.
Just cuddle my toe.
I know my laugh
is a small dry rustle
like feathers and bones
but your smile
is hollow
and I want to kick you.

Blackpool Illuminations III

At the Pleasure Beach
the girl in the pink
cowboy hat sucks
a cigarette into
a smouldering glow
through dark lips —
inhales, drops
and screws
it to the pavement
with a red toe.

On Monday
it's back
to bedpans.

**The Role
of the State**

Tom Kelly

Tom Kelly was born in Jarrow on Tyneside and now lives further up the Tyne at Blaydon and works as a drama lecturer at South Tyneside College. He has written a number of plays and musicals for The Customs House, South Shields, most recently *I Left My Heart in Roker Park*. His poetry and short stories have appeared on Radio Four and in many UK magazines including *Stand, The Wide Skirt, The Red Lamp, The Penniless Press*, and in a number of pamphlets. His volume *The Wrong Jarrow* (Smokestack) was selected as the Purple Patch Best Small Press Collection 2009.

'A third of kids live in poverty'

"There's no magic bullet
to lose poverty". We nod our heads.
Facts and figures never tell the story.
His shoes have holes, her dress fashionable
years ago. They look what they are: dead poor.
See them aching with want.
Their feet blister in cheap shoes.
It's all in the facts and figures.

David Kessel

David Kessel was born in Harlesden, London, in April 1947. He suffered a breakdown at 17 prior to medical school. With diplomas from the RCSP, he went on to practise as a GP in East London until his second breakdown put a halt to his medical career. In spite of his illness, David continued writing poetry and published *The Ivy* in 1989 (Aldgate Press; reprinted 1994). His poems have appeared in *the Phoenix Co-Operative, Poetry Express* and the anthologies *Where There's Smoke, Hackney Writers, Outsider Poems, Bricklight — Poems from the Labour Movement in East London* (Pluto Press, 1980) and *Under the Asylum Tree* (Survivors' Press, 1995); and have been put to music by the EMFEB Symphony Orchestra in Owen Bourne's score Hackney Chambers. The publication of *O the Windows of the Bookshop Must Be Broken — Collected Poems 1970–2006* (ed. Alan Morrison, Survivors' Press, 2006) proved a Survivors' Poetry bestseller. A selection from this volume was recently published in a bilingual German-English volume, *Außenseitergedichte* (Verlag Edition AV, 2007).

New Cross
For John Van

We build our own slums. The wind
through the slums blows on the highest
hills. We are all slowly dying
of cold and loneliness, no fags,
no fruit juice, and neighbours with veg
stew and cups of tea. We live with uncertainty,
Our giros and our dreams. And yet our aggression
is our frustrated love. In a billion painful
ways we make the little things of love;
a dustman's sweat, a cleaner's
arthritis, a streetlight's mined electricity,
a carpet-layer's emphysema
a desperate clerk's angina
a mate's slow moaned caresses.

Rain and Earth

Tears falling like rain
on the mean streets of London
red as workers' blood.
Falling on the market street
on a labourer's fierce decency
irrigating Oriental fruit and veg.
A city of degrading caricatures
and angry poverty in small back rooms.
Footfall of a troubled Bengali girl;
has to make her way to likely bondage
shattered on all fronts.
A cipher in a suit is the circus clown
blinded by illusion, the silence of blindness.
Miscegenation: tears of the cosmos.
A dosser waters the ground with schizophrenia.
The pain of the pavements and the wonder of the sky.

In Memory of Jude, Oxford 1982

You could still marvel at the blackbird singing
above the dusk college square, with sombre bells
ringing beneath the May sycamores.
At bookshops bleeding with mankind and the firmament.
Fancy youths with death in their hearts
pass up and down the seductive streets,
and behind thick walls make words deadly
with expectation and fear, drunk with themselves.
Only in the cold churches do they struggle
to win some divine life.
The desperate vagrant is more solid.

He remembers, as yourself, the rich flinty earth,
cuckoo calling and smell of wheat in rain up on a down.
Your death is carved in stone in library windows.
Your tears' angry, soulful music
in a pub by the bus station. Beneath a bus
your sweetheart wrestles with uncertainty
spanner in hand, her poems in her pocket.
You are the busman, bright-eyed and eager to know
your mother's dark land. Your children's
children may enter this city
with nothing but strong boots, good bread and hope
to destroy and create a strange people's history.

Lament for a Taliban Land

Rigor mortis of Brits' demented empire
on hard famished plains.
Rain falling on the troubled streets of London
on Afghan iron fields, blood!
A Taliban lad, lead in his silver,
shot by a Surrey Para,
his sister taken to a GI brothel,
the devil knows why we're there.
Beneath an apricot tree their mother weeps,
fallen, withered, apricots.
When this winter's snows melt she will rise
like the eagle, over savage mountains, genocide,
and the fragrant flowering pomegranate
'O the fatal loveliness of this land'.

Note: last line is a quote from *Dead Roots* (1973) by Arthur Nortje (1942-70).

Mark Kirkbride

Mark Kirkbride was born in Lancashire, grew up in Dorset, was educated at Kingston and Oxford, found employment as a television subtitler in London and currently checks subtitles for cinema and DVD. He mainly writes novels, children's stories and poetry, and is currently finishing what he hopes is the final draft of a psychological thriller.

Land of No Hope

Notes from an insignificant island:
The politicians are on automouth,
No-one's saying anything new or true
And nothing's getting done. England's sinking.
I bought a ticket to the welfare state.
I tried to get there but the train was late.
The Government only look after their own.
They steal from the poor to give to the rich.
Meanwhile, our children are being brought up
By the police. And who gets blamed for that
And just about everything else that's wrong?
Single mothers, the heroines of our time.
I can think of a way to change all this.
It's so simple. Read my lips: 'Tax the rich.'

Matthew Knights

Matthew Knights was born in London and grew up in the village of Bishop Norton in Lincolnshire. He studied English Literature at the University of Sheffield and now lives and works in Edinburgh. He has been published in *The Rialto* magazine.

My hope

To outlast the joy which was severed from
the land which owned it
my hope would have to be very strong
stronger than the foolish actions of leaders
and their blindness
my hope would need to be
beyond feasibility, beyond question
absurd.

And who will compensate me
for the loss of this hope
even less so the loss
of the small improvements we had made
wiped out in a moment
small improvements to a large unkind society
and now with our small tools
all we can do is repair
the willed for damage and the waste
not just willed for by the politicians
but by all those
looking out of high windows
and seeing nothing.

I fear I will lose my hope
as we continue to ignore
our capacity to destroy
and to collude in destruction
either knowingly or through ignorance to damage
those things which are truly valuable.

Ideals and high hopes
are the preserve of the few
but defence of them
falls to us all.

Politicians

It takes few words to emphasise the emptiness
of our shallow politicians and their lack
of real humility, and their Politics,
played out by blustering and brawling
suited men (the occasional woman)
is the all absorbing spectacle.

It is entertainment
but who will entertain
the sufferings of the dispossessed and the disenfranchised
the poor and the marginalised
those of disability and disadvantage
and the whole enclosing wrath of the wider picture
of one problem necessitating another
with no release
and all these people in this trap
with no voice

those who rely on their government
they rely on their awareness
their Christianity, their good will, their humility
their selflessness, their tirelessness
their openness.

We all see all this, we all know all this
and we speak to each other
but how can we tell them so that they will listen.

The really foolish

As I read the papers which say job losses will be imminent
and funding cannot be secured, and the government cannot
        promise
to deliver services to the same level although it promises

the world shifts and eddies about me
the bus is over filled with dour faces
the buildings are all glum and the sky is only
dark and impending

as the economic glory retreats, the shared celebration
the banners flap in the wind and the whole
heaven cloud of glory passes out of view beyond
Europe, beyond Japan and America — goes off the earth and
        elsewhere.

We all go dour in our faces and cast our eyes down
for Economy has left us and Economy now tests us
and we make solemn penance
and chastise those who do not now chastise themselves.

The man in the bank turns and watches, wonders for a moment
at all the downcast faces, then spies a pigeon
fighting for bread another pigeon had
and returns to work
he is smiling,
oblivious to the emptiness
which is slowly growing in him.
We are all the weak apologists for his kind
and the supporters and devotees of vast empires
held in the palm of the few
we are the really foolish.

Prakash Kona

Prakash Kona is a critically acclaimed Indian novelist, essayist, poet and theorist, born in 1967, who currently lives, works and writes in Hyderabad, India. He writes in English, and is the author of *Nunc Stans* (Creative Non-fiction: 2009, *Crossing Chaos* enigmatic ink, Ontario, Canada) and two novels, *Pearls of an Unstrung Necklace* (2003) and *Streets that Smell of Dying Roses* (2005) (both Fugue State Press, New York). He is currently working as an Associate Professor at the Department of English Literature, School of English Literary Studies, English and Foreign Languages University, Hyderabad.

Onions

Everyone wants a piece of land — to belong and to imagine,
I'm a peasant — my loves are land, woman and onions,
      I would be poor if I had the wealth of the world
And not feel the pungent taste of onions on my palate;
My life is the present that my dead past encroaches upon,
When I think of truth it is the millions of South Asia
      and across the earth in pockets I refer as 'third world,'
When it comes to reality it is what my eyes configure,
      in the revolution of an instant: the future rushing
Into the arms of a present: an order where no one goes
      to bed on an empty stomach,
Children do not have to pick food from garbage dumps,
Lifestyles are not bought and sold in free markets,
      with the poor paying with their lives;
The word 'refugee' is reality — the truth being that
      refugees create the haven for cynical elites
To revel in schizophrenia of head mocking the heart;
The have-nots are united in their plight as have-nots,
      it is those who have that are threatened by walls of
A deafening silence, isolated as atoms and without bonds
      that give the material world a semblance of reality.

If there is a God above

The cottage industry, so vital for India's existence, has been ruined by incredibly heartless and inhuman processes...Little do town dwellers know how the semi-starved masses of India are slowly sinking to lifelessness. Little do they know that their miserable comfort represents the brokerage they get for the work they do for the foreign exploiter, that the profits and the brokerage are sucked from the masses... I have no doubt that both England and the town dweller of India will have to answer, if there is a God above, for this crime against humanity, which is perhaps unequalled in history.

Mahatma Gandhi, 1922, District and Sessions court, Ahmedabad, India

If there is a God above. Perhaps there is one. Perhaps none.
If there is a God above the powerful must account for their deeds,
The rich must explain where their wealth comes from
                              if not sufferings of the poor,
The United States must explain why it supports fascists
         everywhere,
For the countless deaths of children in Iraq,
                  for a history of slavery and genocide,
Israel must answer for colonization of Palestine,
                  for persecuting the ones who resist,
And rendering them homeless in their own homes,
Europe must answer for colonial brutality and anti-Semitism,
India for centuries of oppressing the so-called 'polluted' castes,
The World Bank and IMF for conscienceless manipulation
                  of third world economies,
And putting the poor in a state of perpetual debt and servitude,
The good must account for silence in the face of injustice,
                  for pessimism and lack of resolve —
The beasts that devour the overtly sensitive,
Every man must answer for subjugation of every woman,
The media for drugging masses with untruths upon untruths,

The murderers of Patrice Lumumba and Chris Hani
                     Rosa Luxemburg and Gandhi,
Must seek forgiveness for the unforgivable;
Surely it must be an inordinately patient God that can listen
                        to so much explanation,
And remain unaffected by contradictions,
Perhaps there is one above. Perhaps none.

Confucius

Nothing is older than a speck of dust
Or taller than a blade of grass.

Three people God wished he never created:
Darwin, Marx and Bertrand Russell.

To liberate women is to liberate the mind of man
From ignorance that enslaved women in the first place.

It's when I'm ready to leave a place,
That I want to speak my thoughts.

Our worst enemies are hiding
Beneath the faces we love.

I thought of you and wrote about bread,
I thought of bread and wrote about people,
I thought of nothing and wrote about flowers.

Testimony

A witness to conspiracies of the senses:
A dreaming soul in a lethargic body,
Yesterday's sins crept into the soul
Of today scattered like viruses
Across the face of the sun:
My vain heart longs for approbation
Of streets; pity makes me defensive —
The pity that my dead father inspires for fathers
Of the world; but they're men and their
Manhood is a threat to my fragile existence
Built upon hopes for a future in the
Bubble of the present;
One day it'll be over — the love and betrayal
That made love meaningful,
But it's not one day that I'm waiting for
With headaches and belly breakdowns,
As signs of life for an apolitical body
Dissociated from the truth of resistance;
The tyranny of the old frightens me and
The new, fierce in its lack of
Compassion, makes me sick at heart;
The modern world of displaced longings
Strains the sensibility to indulge in
Forms of self-pity alien to my nature;
Something in my nature is dead, dying
Or refusing to be born; the ecstatic,
God-denying performer is no more
In love with the world than the curtain
Is in love with the stage; the revolution
My spirit is too weak to make,
With my ability to forget names and not

Make a logical conversation,
The minority in me — a puny, protesting thing
Prefers the intelligence of the defeated to
The conservatism of bodies lost in stupor.

Prayer

I, who am incapable of believing, take the name of a God who rests in silence while the poor toil night and day to taste the bread of struggle.
I pray that daughters of toilet-cleaners and sons of single mothers rule this country and every country on earth. Their fathers kept the toilets clean and their mothers braved nights to make life bearable for their children.
I pray that there are hospitals that do not humiliate the bodies of the lonely and beds for the sick and dying to leave the world with dignity.
I pray that every man, woman and child has a name worth the remembering. That each of the faces is worthy of affection as if it were a scene from a tapestry.
I pray that men wake up to the evil of pride and ugliness of malice.
I pray that I never abandon the company of the powerless though death may hang like a sword upon my head. It is a death worth dying than watch injustice the poor suffer every day of their lives.

Paul Lester

Born in Birmingham, England, Paul Lester has published some thirty booklets of poetry, including *A Funny Brand of Freedom* (Arts Lab Press,1975), and the full volumes *By the Scruff Of the Neck* (BMI,1995) and *Going For Broke* (Protean, 2004).His poetry has been broadcast on BBC Radio One and the BBC World Service. He has performed his poetry with a variety of musical accompaniment. A 23-track CD is available from Protean Pubs entitled *The Legend Of Lester* featuring work spanning over twenty-five years. In 2008 a 16-track album appeared, entitled *My Career As A Dead Man*.

The Privatisation of Air

As the Managing Director I take care
Of the newly privatised realm of air.
Though my salary, some might deem,
A little on the far side of extreme

I deserve my cars, my yachts and my plane
And my sea-side villas in the south of Spain .
With profits I've made from the cut-price share
They call me the 'Air-Tight Billionaire'

But I assure you I haven't an hour to spare
From breathing all that privatised air —
I'm taking it in but I'm letting it out,
Especially when I've occasion to shout

At the lazy and shiftless employees who
Suspect I've got nothing better to do —
Such people need to be made aware
Many have died from a shortage of air.

All compulsory subscribers must be clear,
Germ-free, pollution-free air comes dear,
So breathe in deep but cough up soon,
And give thanks the earth is not yet the moon.

And bill-defaulters need to beware
We'll quickly disconnect their air
So the rest of us can breathe with greater ease
Since there's more air for us, if you please.

They said it was impossible to walk on air
But I do it, it's a miracle, and I'm everywhere,
And it's all part of my job, because I take care
Of the newly privatised realm of air.

Mark Lewis

Mark Lewis has been an actor for 35 years, mostly associated with the Citizens Theatre in Glasgow, as well as many appearances in Film, TV and Radio. He has written screenplays and TV series, pitched and commissioned, but never produced. He recently completed an MA in Creative Writing at Goldsmiths.

Strong Government

Conjugal rights is a rite, up my passage.
Shafted, crafted like it's good for us.
Pet me, rub me, tickle my favours.
Let down, get down, bust us up
The wrong way round.

Raise a cup to this coagulation,
A triangulation of poor alternatives.
Coalescing into coalition without friction.

Gift us with joyous accommodations
Of mediocrities, spouting generalities
That we must smile at while they
Smother our dreams and dig our graves,
Beaming, reaming, burrowing deep
To a different truth, congenially congealing.

So drip into each other squeezing,
Blending amoeba-like as we plunge our
Fingers into this trench of effluent
Oozing from ivory towers, looking for
Sustainability Œcos we are all in this together.
It's time for a change, strong government.
A steel claw in a fisted glove.

Rub-a-dub-dub don't blub,
We got what we asked for... but
I reserve the right to fight or flight.
Adrenalize me to make a difference.
Shake me, wake me and rattle my bones.
Coalesce into coalition without friction.

This joining together is Right of course
And wrong, an aberration, a cross to bear.
So you represent me and them and us,
All everybodies everywhere, a soup of
The world bubbling, all in it together?

Am I dead? Did we die? Shall I cry
Or hide away under an array of grey.
So back to school bored by middle-aged men
Blending together, smiling with the same teeth,
Endless un-street, able to do what?
Teach us to be good, as we should,
While they rip it all up. Who needs it?

Alexis Lykiard

Alexis Lykiard, poet and novelist, was born in Athens at the start of 1940, when Mussolini's Italian troops were repelled by the Greeks in the North of the country. He is author of over two dozen poetry collections, including *Journey of the Alchemist* (Sebastian Carter, 1963), *Greek Images* (Second Aeon Publications, 1972), *Out of Exile — Selected Poems 1968-85* (Arc 1985), *Safe Levels* (Stride, 1990), *Cat Kin* (Sinclair-Stevenson 1994), *Skeleton Keys* (Redbeck, 2003) and *Judging By Disappearances: Poems 1996-2006* (Bluechrome 2007).

Holy Moloch?

God-myths whole armies
of false prophets reinforce,
drinking human blood

After An Election
(*6 May 2005, and onward...*)

When propounding an issue of trust,
our guidelines are always robust:
to sing democracy and choice and send a
clear message about the current agenda,
which is (or are?) seen to be Right. Today
the creeping Party-Faithful praise — or pray
for fiercest critics to desist or fade away.
Kingmakers, warmongers, go down in History,
revise the truth, twist fact, make wealth a mystery.
Now, clubman, smile again, congratulate and rule:
the earnest rogue returns, outwits the honest fool.

A Brown Study

In the prudent, doubtful playtime of a dourly downbeat Presbyter,
shifty bankers, shameless MPs, lived well on jam-and jelly-roll.
That grail Brown sought to inherit from Blair the pious predator
resembled a crock of old gilt, sold to a naked emperor;
dull years of waiting one's turn will tarnish the worthiest soul …
When the Speaker scored an own goal, the rules spun right out of
     control:
lame excuses scuppered the strong — the Cup game went finally
     wrong.

Chris McCabe

Chris McCabe was born in Liverpool in 1977. His poems have appeared in a number of journals including *Poetry Salzburg Review, Shearsman, Magma* and *Poetry Review*. He has published three poetry collections: *The Hutton Inquiry* (Salt, 2005; which included a sequence of poems that chronicled the circumstances surrounding the death of government science adviser Dr David Kelly in 2003 and Britain's involvement in the war in Iraq), *Zeppelins* (Salt, 2008), and a chapbook, *The Borrowed Notebook* (Landfill, 2008). He has read his work at the Cambridge Conference of Contemporary Poetry and in the *Crossing the Line* Series at the Poetry Cafe. He discussed and read some of his poetry on BBC World Service on Armistice Day 2005, and had a poem featured on the Oxfam CD *Lifelines*.

The Final Cut
a requiem for the post-Thatcher State (after Roger Waters)

Trust us to be sick and the scrapman's calling
no Home Economics for six complete weeks
but something's baking only the pond can take.
The five o'clock alarm strips us back a motorway
a kestrel for breakfast & a box of maggots
with the brown cocoon crowdsurfing a moshpit
of pinkies. The tench, in his bottle green jacket,
can toke all day the bonedry keepnet. An airport
of carbon & metal shuffles through the rushes —
two rods, reels, tacklebox, flask, elasticated
pole & catapult. The fishing is the rest before
the long walk back. The gulls hawk the '62's
slipstream — I wanted to twitch but they accused
me of voyeurism — the discovery at thirteen
that tight shorts are best for buttering toast.
Voyeur the gulls shriek, *voyeur, voyeur.* The
walkman swings the haunches & spins inside
like two fairground carousels in a prefabricated

farmhouse. *I'm spiralling down to the hole*
in the ground where I hide...

But now she stands upon Southampton Dock
with her handkerchief and her summer frock
clings to her wet body in the rain...

Maggie, slap-parted with horns arrives at Downing Street
Crowds cheer as she misquotes St. Francis of Assisi...

Maggie next to Reagan in air-hostess black
Silk scarf & hybrid Cold War hat...

Maggie in navy blue, pearl ear-rings & purple bowtie
Says You turn if you want, the Lady's not for turning...

Maggie in near-ruff, hair clipped back in bunches
Faces enthusiastic crowds after threatening nukes for Falklands...
Maggie with Nancy Reagan at No. 10 in forest green
Near-khaki floral dress, white beads & high-heels...

Maggie giving speech against picket line violence during Miner's
        Strike
In spotted foxbrown dress with funslide collars...

Maggie meets Gorbachev in blue-black paisley Beatlesesque jacket,
Hair licked over ears, tells Reagan "I like him, we can do business"...

Maggie reproduced on car-sized London travel permit held by
        Red Ken
Eyes shrunk like Osip Mandelstaam after NKVD arrest...

Maggie in striped New Wave Stetson, breasts made dwarfs by
    shoulder pads
Calls George Bush Snr to say "this is no time to go wobbly"…

Maggie in cream from shoes to bouffant to meet D. A. Rumsfeld
Lapis lazuli bracelet swinging down to her widowed ring…

Maggie in pink top, cream-coloured skirt, salmon cardigan
Waves her good arm with the broken one in a sling…

When the tigers broke free I read in my dad's
facsimile of his dad's war diary (I found it one
day in a drawer of old photographs in the way)
that he was in a bar called *2nd Precinct* in Norfolk,
Virginia, toasting his own armistice and that's why
The High Command took six dollars from him.
At the opening announcement of the Edwardian Funfare
Maggie fires the laser gun so loud the Bomb Squad decamps.
She declares "This is a wonderful example of private
enterprise & local government working hand-in-hand."

Alton Towers Property Developers strip art deco for rock
aiming to charge the carousel inside the turbine hall.

What have we done, Maggie what have we done… .

When she started waiting for the worms I said as much
to my dad, at the start of his illness — the woman he destroyed
his nerves to rise above — but he said to me, softly: No one
deserves that Son. A decade of stolen gas & mysterious cheques
— the aubade jingle of counted milk bottles in the frost —

passed between us in a glance. What concession was this?

Ten years later she stumbles — an upended caterpillar wrapped
in a blue leaf — through Battersea Park, her hands hawk her own
    puppetshow,
her face a Punch stitched from Judy's silks, her face a kestrel's print
shrunk into a grub, she stumbles the brownfield's perimeter
    towards Chelsea
— the Powerstation a submerged rig in the Thames —
woodworm inside an Eighties' screen, a pink sun shredding
a powercut inside the cathedral of electrons.

The grocery cortege of her bodyguards were pumped for
    quietness,
past the minefields & the drives, onwards, towards Chelsea.

An airport moved. My mouth opened to. Against haunches
trembling hands, prepared to make it but.
Just then the phone rang.

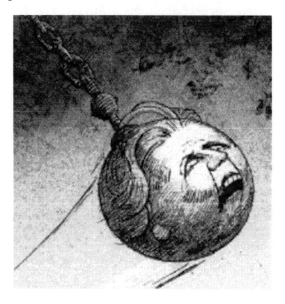

Richie McCaffery

Richie McCaffery's poems have appeared or are due to appear in *Magma, Poetry Scotland, Envoi, Horizon Review, Northwords Now*. He is also the recipient of an Edwin Morgan Poetry bursary, funded by the Scottish Arts Council.

Sweeney Todd with Occam's Razor

He remembers it the first time round,
a rodent's existence under that ferric
martinet. One day she swept her scythe
and his job was gone, and decades
later, this grim promnesia.

The way a bee only knows to make honey
no matter the losses, he built himself up
to the position of 'buildings conservator' —
a servant of our nation's architectural heritage.

In an age when all the property-dabblers
want is plastic windows and extensions,
now his job nears the Axeman's block
all over again. He has a son who won
his way through university on bursaries,

getting nothing but firsts in Literature
and now gathers dust in the dole queue
unemployable, and no matter how big
the words he uses, the blue-bloods hear
his accent and take him for cannon-fodder.

Niall McDevitt

Niall McDevitt travelled through 23 European countries with a guitar and tent. Returning to London, McDevitt worked as an actor/musician in Neil Oram's 24-hour play *The Warp*, Ken Campbell's *Pidgin Macbeth,* and John 'Crow' Constable's *The Southwark Mysteries.* For radio, he was resident Pidgin poet/ translator on John Peel's *Home Truths,* and has featured in *Bespoken Word, The Robert Elms Show, The Verb, The Poet of Albion,* and also such Resonance 104.4FM shows as *Mining for Gold* and *Lost Steps.* As activist, McDevitt has campaigned to secure the future of the Rimbaud/Verlaine House at 8 Royal College Street, and for the release of poet Saw Wai from Insein prison in Burma. He leads epic psychogeographical walks through London. His collection *b/w* was published by Waterloo Press this year.

Ode To The Dole
(in praise of a free money Europe)

'from the Ice Age to the Dole Age there is but one concern'

Morrissey

a huge shout echoes through the street like a Red Indian praise song. the note is sustained, the shout becoming music. this is not the voice of a line manager. someone is intoxicated...

Original Sin is being born into a society that asks only of its children: 'make money'. thus, our mullahs have decreed. (a crap categorical imperative). X—we hear—is not complaining, but writing his ode to the dole, in a red-brick slum of the west. the underclass are the new aristocracy. they will not lift a finger and dress only in sportswear. city is their arena. like Ralegh, they deal drugs and write technosonnets, all in towers. they do not need to wade through Das Kapital to know that Marx's adopted country isn't very nice to minimum wage-slaves. in the new age of Hassan-i-Sabbah, a single joint of skunk makes you go insane. hashish:

the enemy drug-of-choice. dogs chase the assassins through
underground tunnels. beghards! abraham-men! judeo-apaches!
Europe has apologized for colonizing Europeans. somehow, the
dole is issued by a Danish/French/Russian/Greek/German/
Belgian king: a begrudging king, a puritanking, a philistine king, a
luxembourgeois king. (admittedly, there's a million things wrong
with our king). yet is he ring-giver. the media is today what the
church was in the Middle Ages: the all-pervasive brainwash. it
brands the psychosphere. Plato's radio, television, newspapers.
advertizing is psychic violation. dole is the antidote, a final
overturning of serfdom, a compensation-package for centuries
of oppression. the beneficiaries of the system—a system
that always was/is/will be rigged, by the beneficiaries for the
beneficiaries—were shell-shocked into conscientiousness
by WW2. benefits: for the disabled, the single mother, the
schizophrenic, the redundant. puritans are suspicious of these
new timeshare millionaires who make burnt offerings of charis
and black and sensimilian under the all-seeing eye of the Empress
State Building.

X too has joined the underclass (though they think he's beneath
them). the cry of gratitude that hurls through the city masonry?
it might be his. the exchequer need not worry itself unduly; X is
a bargain. verily, free money is economically correct. the hooded
child in the tracksuit—the chavi—is a lord of the underclass, his
black/white patois the sound of evolution. no one and nothing
will convince him that joining the workforce is promotion, not in
this christendom, where I sin/ you sin/ he sins/ she sins/ we sin/
you (pl.) sin/ they sin/ it sins etc. call it expenses. Elizabethans
walk

with blades

George Orwell Is Following Me

in the moon under water
he's slumped at my table with a bargain bitter
heavily disguised as a member of the proletariat

george orwell is invigilating my existence
in the bleak streets and bombsites
I feel the force of his eyes
from where he stands tall thin intent as a surveillance camera

george orwell is insidious and ubiquitous
in one of the bookshops of obfuscation
he was stocktaking on a metallic ladder
false moustache (over his own tory anarchist moustache)

orwell is always busy on the next bowl
of the public urinals
sniffing his piss-steam with scientific disgust
and debating the merits of the henry millers

the most remarkable people turn out to be orwells
I threw a couple of twopenny coins
to an old etonian in a cardboard box
who said: 'what do you do in this shithole with five pence?'

at night when I've made it to my safehouse
again the whirring of lenses
and he's standing over my bed with a birch
keeping me awake (i.e. protecting me from sleep)

george orwell is following me
in the wetherspoons boozer
he's slumped at my table with a bargain bitter
heavily disguised as a member of the underclass

Leun Deun

1
jobless
I inhale the sun
            (honey guillotines)

in the Sumerian city I walk upside down
by a noiseless river
            trees
                    with noises of rivers

bluebottles

dove o'clock

two testaments:
            Ark and Cross
                on the
                intellectual skyline

people on their own wings fly

public buildings sold off
public houses closed down
            buy-curious
                bored to debt

ears
take us to the core of the city's layers
            the tombs
                the feet of joggers

as the bells call
we look to Jerusalem south of the river
    in a grapefruit panorama

honey cascades in it
    o the ochre
    skin-shedding
        gash

2
la Londonisation:

a non-conformism
of coffee-shops
    an afforestation
        of adverts

but in towers
doors slam
    (echo)
    of a mystery people

and in the airplanes I hear Charles Ives'
'unanswered question'
      slide

security van
      LOOMIS

pigeons lapping up
    vomit

streets carpeted in newspaper

3
Leun Deun:

office blocks in sun

in the city's
microwave oven
a slowness
(microwave minutes)
parked car
contains an African family

a vessel for Tum

these are the sands

these are the silences
of druids

of doves in spikes

23 celsius
the sufferings

evaporate

4
aggiorniomento / approfondimento

rays

eyes
look into a thousand windows

unhappy hour

the giant insane rastafarians
lounge on flags
    as ambulance crews
        come to inject them

this altitude
    is best for peregrines
        black-yellow-grey

tyres rub the tar
    to fat
    comfortable as token animals

under a
VEDETT parasol
    the city's inert honeycomb
        foxes jump fox corpses
        to a tenement drum

jobless
I inhale the sun
    limbs lit
    (rivered)

this peace astounds

    this haunted leisure

John McKeown

John McKeown was born in Liverpool in 1959. He graduated from John Moore's University in 1987 with an Honours Degree in English and History. He lived in Prague for several years as a teacher and freelance journalist before moving to Ireland in 2000, where he was a columnist for *the Irish Examiner*, and arts feature writer for *the Irish Times*. He was theatre critic for *the Irish Daily Mail* from 2006 to 2008 and is currently reviewing theatre for *the Irish Independent* and raising his daughter Julia. He lives and writes in Dun Laoghaire, County Dublin. His poems have appeared in *Orbis, The Eildon Tree, Dreamcatcher, Aireings, Earth Love, Envoi, Borderlines, The London Magazine*, and Irish-based journals *Cyphers, The Shop*, and *Southword*. He was winner of the Start Chapbook Prize (Ireland) in 2004 for his cycle of poems *Looking Toward Inis Oírr*. A full volume, *Sea of Leaves*, was published by Waterloo Press in 2009.

Britain Is Open For Business!
(A coalition MP In Response To The So-Called 'Emergency Verse' e-Anthology')

Poets! Be not incensed!
Britain is open for business!
New wealth will trickle down
To oil your scratchy pens
And lift your curmudgeonly spirits!

Poets! You are sensitive I know,
And we treasure you for it;
You're part of our rich cultural heritage,
But culture too must play it's part
In attracting the right investors.

So do not moan and groan
As we correct the mess
The last Labour government bequeathed us;
As wordsmiths you know the necessity

Of sometimes drastic cutting and pruning.

Like well-turned verses
The New Britain will be
Sleeker, trimmer, effervescent with innovation,
Cutting a sharp, competitive dash
Through the global markets.

Poets! You yourselves are no strangers
  to competitiveness;
Words jostle constantly in your heads
For access to the open page.
In a very real sense
Poetry is the soul of Capitalism!

So come Poets, drop your grudge
Against the streamlining of the NHS, Education,
  our exorbitant Welfare System,
Or whatever your particular gripe is.
Cure that collective Left-wing hangover!
Join us! Rejoice! Britain is open for business!

Jonathan MacKenzie

Jonathan Mackenzie was born in Edinburgh on 22 March 1970. As a poet, he works almost exclusively in metered verse. He is currently working on a collection entitled *Free Verse is an Oxymoron (Formal verse is tautology)*. Mackenzie is founder of the online The Poetry Academy. He also provides poetry workshops for beginners on his blogsite where he features examples of various formal styles.

Downtrodden

I'm just another pebble on the beach
That wants to shine and stand out from the crowd.
Instead, I'm stepped upon and kicked around,
And hopes, once cherished, linger out of reach.

Decaying driftwood scattered on the shore
Is wreckage from my ship of childhood dreams
That foundered in a shallow sea of green
To splinter in my every bitter pore.
Dilapidated shells, like unkempt graves
Are weather-beaten victims and the scarred
And disenfranchised debris from a herd
Too weak to dare oppose oppressive waves.

And yet we have the power to impeach
The tyrants who conspire to implement
Privation. Tell me who they represent?
Aren't most of us just pebbles on the beach?

Steve Mann

Steve Mann is in his fifties and lives nr Shrewsbury. He was published in *Waiting for Gulliver* (Caradoc Publications) alongside fellow poet Sally Richards. His first solo collection *cui bono?* (Survivors' Press, 2007) was launched at The Poetry Cafe. His poetry has appeared in *Poetry Express* and in a number of journals and anthologies. He has read at Aberystwyth, Keele and Staffordshire Universities, and at the Royal Shrewsbury Hospital, Shrewsbury Library, Shrewsbury Museum, and at other venues throughout Shrewsbury and Shropshire.

Zymotic Capitalism

bastardized syncopal miscarriages
governments and systems bejungled intertwining
supping in corruptions devil grail
chewing temptations roots
world not-without end
mammon

Nigel Mellor

Nigel Mellor lives and works in Newcastle. His poems have appeared in a broad range of publications both inside and outside the poetry world including *Time Out, Tribune* and *New Poetry 1* (ACE). His latest collection is *For the Inquiry: poetry of the dirty war* (Dab Hand Press, 2010).

The great Sainsbury's filling station massacre of AD 2018

There is no more terrifying sight
Than the middle classes
Short on
Fuel

Go forth and modify

Across all the lands
The new corn grew strong
Until the twentieth generation
When crops simply failed

Then we begged off the poorest
Seeds from the old days
Too precious to eat

Economics

Imagine the impact
On the dismal science of economics
If, in standard text books,
Wherever we saw the word "markets"
We substituted the, admittedly rather cumbersome phrase,
"A small collection of extremely highly paid men"

Debt burden

It was easy in the old days
We all knew who we were fighting

But now
It's the dollar that screws you up
But it's the dollar we want

And that's a poor basis for a fight

Trickle down

The spectacularly fraudulent trick
Behind the theory of trickle down
Is that, in practise,
Money is actually persuaded to flow
Uphill
From poor to rich
Not t'other way round

Transformation

The only way to make the poor richer
Is to make the poor richer,
Making the rich richer never works

Helen Moore

Helen Moore is an ecopoet, author and Forest Schools practitioner based in Frome, Somerset. She publishes her poetry in anthologies and journals and as handmade pamphlets, and regularly performs her poetry around the UK. Other books include: *Changing Nature* (GreenSeer Books, 2006), and for children, the *Hope* stories on climate change (Lollypop Publishing, 2008/9).

The Never-never Land
On Ecological Debt Day, September 23rd, 2008

Planet in the red, we've pawned our Great Mother. And for tomorrow's reserves — forests, fish, topsoil, minerals — we're indebted to our children. They themselves will live on Mars, reading Peter Pan.

The Cancer

The current financial stripping of economies and environments across the
world exhibits... all the hallmark characteristics of a carcinogenic invasion.

John McMurtry

A cell grows, mutates, divides, and multiplies — power-surging
life, evolved with no primordial forces at core, but primogenital
rights an inner lore. From the stimuli of discovery, to have, to own,
a form previously unknown, which bursts into Superbeing, hungers
for more.

And still senescence has no check, no regulatory effect, so that
growth becomes the goal, becomes immortalized — this strange
apotheosis of mind, a selfish strand that science gives most credence
to; that state mythologies expand.

And isn't this just Spring, sempiternal Summer — Nature without
her fickle change? Just like it's human nature to seek to better the
self; to have everything sunny-side up? To crawl, to stand, walk
on two legs above all four-legged forms? To have power over,
recreate the self over and over — metastasized past the confines
of a single body?

Meanwhile greed gains ground — on and on, jaws breaking
mountains to serve the purpose of itself. Head buried in the Earth's
febrile breast, it sucks out every ounce, but never asks, what next?

Alan Morrison

Alan Morrison is author of critically praised poetry collections, *The Mansion Gardens* (Paul Brown, 2006), *A Tapestry of Absent Sitters* (Waterloo Press, 2009; selected for a *Purple Patch* Small Press Award 2009) and *Keir Hardie Street* (Smokestack, 2010; an audio version read by actor Michael Jayston is also now available), and of the highly regarded play for voices, *Picaresque*. Since 2007 he has been voluntary creative writing tutor and poet-in-residence at Mill View Psychiatric Hospital, Hove; and in 2008 was recipient of a Sussex Partnership NHS Trust Artists' Award to select, edit and design an anthology of service-users' writing: the groundbreaking reversible double-book *The Hats We Wear/Blank Versing the Past* resulted. A chapbook of residency poems, *Captive Dragons*, will shortly be appearing. Morrison has contributed monographs and essays to *The Glasgow Review, Eleutheria — Scottish Poetry Review* and *the London Magazine*. His poems have appeared in over fifty journals, most recently *erbacce, Aireings, Poetry Monthly, Osprey* and *Stand*. His fourth volume, *Blaze a Vanishing*, is forthcoming from Waterloo in early 2011. He is founding editor of *the Recusant* and Caparison imprint.

The Society of Broken Smiles

1. *Age of Transparency: A Glass War on the Poor*

The Big Society: a Tory boot stamping on a claimant's face
For five years — a Tory boot crunching on a council tenant's
Security, to a ticking fixed-term lease, thereafter to
Up sticks or pitch them on a patch of pavement somewhere....
Big Society: a Tory boot grinding a pensioner's specs to grains,
Abolishing mobilities, bus passes, clamping co-operativeness,
Capping benefits, cutting, cutting; but *we're all in it together*
To organise our carts and horses, rag-and-bone, bowed
To hollow multi-million-men in Cabinet, those Con-Dem
Plenipotentiary for vested and invested interests of our
Murdochracy. —Let the coat-tails of Harrow billow and flap,
And Purcell's catercaps, Marlborough's shadbellies bloom

Into the Etonian twenty-first century — the same
Classist crap that accuses its critics of envy; 'It's rude
To allude to class nowadays' (while many might say
It's rude to have class in the first place). We're free
To be slaves, waged or unwaged, the standard's been raised —
That gnashing portcullis — for a transparent age:
Glass war on the poor — and tabards for doleys;
Tasers and sabres and fiscal-rattled cutlasses.

The Big Society will be all Smiles and Malthus,
Darwin and Adam Smith, survival of the fittest,
And Thatcher, snatcher of the milk of soured kindness;
A New Politics of private monopolies; schools,
Hospitals, scrapped, or pitted internally —
The wreckers' marquetry, dismantlers of the Forties
Planners' society, its masonry chipped bit by bit
Since the end of the brown Seventies, by hatchet
Monetarists — a bonfire of the verities will blaze;
Scorched earth of our last tattered vestiges of values,
Blasted to black curls of promissory policies,
Old crimson banners tramped in the scrum
For false idols, capitalism's crumbs... Labour
Sold out long ago, bought to let its heartlands out
To the rent-snatching centre-ground, scapegoated those
They betrayed, as *cheats, thieves, chavs* and *ASBOS*
While bonuses rose, and they flipped their second homes
Palming roses till the petals purpled, wilted to blue
Rosettes — now once more in bloom to close Bevan's
Marmoreal covenant: *from cradle to grave* —
Motto on a nation's plaques of hearts and minds.

Before the National Health Service there was Mutualism,
Tweedy local quacks, old wives' cures for all agues,

Leeches for blood infections, dock leaves for nettle-rash;
Consumption epidemics for lack of milk — Bevan
Tugged the stethoscopes into the twentieth century,
Universal care free on the point of delivery,
Prescription spectacles (Lennon's strawberry
Optics in Walrus days of Wilson's Sixties) —
A fresh-laundered Jerusalem of hospital corners,
Pristine dignities, screens and wards, snug surgeries,
A classless care — but for opening this Welfare State
Even to those with private means, too quixotic to last:
Prescription charges implemented begrudgingly
By Labourites, in same spirit of universality;
The poor thus disenfranchised relatively by the very
System for supporting them — so old Firebrand Nye
Handed in his notice in protest... But he'd made his mark,
Seminal collier from Tredegar, Monmouthshire,
Who'd hauled himself up to politics' high pit-head
And like ancient Solon stilled the bow-hand on fair justice,
Stood up for the poor (of whom he thought whenever
He closed his torrid eyes), stuffed the doctors' mouths
With gold, so those in poverty could project into old age,
Shadows lengthen, longevities even out;
The munificent state massaging real-life figures
Cowed so long but no more stunted by malnutrition's
Rickets, or smothered by TB, but getting off their knees
To walk straight-backed: labourers, blue-collars, paupers now
Fully homo erectus, no more need for begging, gifted
Dignity —or, second-best: dockets for social security:
Reimbursement from society for their contributions
When there'd been work for them, now supplemented
Adequately, while slumps mushroomed from booms —
Bevan built a halfway house to the New Jerusalem,
More than mere free dentures to toothless history,

But a giant stand against Beveridge's five "Evils": *Squalor,*
Ignorance, want, idleness and *disease* (today, another five
Are in the sights of the Big Society: *the NHS, welfare,*
The public sector, comprehensives, and *creative drives*) —
We're in debt to the germ of progressiveness that set in then,
A rose-red empire of hearts-on-sleeves, an egalitarian
England, and all the better for it, and well it knew it: even
After Uncle Clement threw down the gauntlet in '51,
The Tories cottoned on to inheriting a golden plum,
One Nation Disraelian hearts, such a different breed to later
Thatcherite upstarts; Macmillan kept Bevan's beneficent
Edifice intact, no thought to start dismantling,
But to the public's gasp, took on its custodianship,
Championing the NHS with *you've never had it so good,*
Honouring his pre-election pledge (in days when pledges
Were more than gambling chips) to keep the project going,
Protect the bouncing infant in its cradle of scaffolding,
Since nothing could root out this new compassion flowering...

2. *The Volcano Election*

...Until now? Sixty-five years later, Two-Thousand-And-Ten,
Post-Volcano election, a cobbled Coalition
Of Opposites obscured the rainbow promise of a left-wing
Alliance to rebuild our long-aborted Jerusalem
After New Labour's slow-burning betrayals; Cable and Clegg:
From Asquith and Campbell-Bannerman to Bonny and Clyde
Of the last-ditched deal, the sweaty palmed pact with Mr Scratch-
My-back-and-I'll-scratch-yours, along with their yellow rabble
—In just a month, mandate-less May, Clegg morphed from electoral
Loud-hailing radical into Tory prop — opted for
Arithmetic over principle (unlike Arthur Henderson's
Labour Party in 1910, who stood by the Liberals'
People's Budget — when MPs were still gentlemen —
And *in spite* of arithmetic, choosing an alliance of principle
Now long spilt out from Parliament, along with scruples).

—Out of the Icelandic ash-clouds the new Con-Demolition
Smoke-and-mirror Coalition was formed, whose front-bench
Members, only two months in to power, are kitted out as
Beerbohm caricatures, pinstriped hollow men, uniting in
The smokescreen of inherited 'deficit' to justify
A Herodic fiscal massacre of slashing cuts in long knived nights
To blast the infant's tear, abolish sentiments for mantras:
'Unavoidable', 'tough', 'fair', 'difficult', 'we're all in this together'
—Well, *they* are in it together, to rob the poor still further,
The vulnerable, disabled, sick, the unemployed, of their depleted
Entitlements; Chancellor Osborne, about to slice Eighteen Billion
From the Welfare State, tip the cradle in the grave, trample prams
Of mums on benefits, strip the public sector down
(But not the culprits); and Lansley, Thatcherite Incarnate,
Torch-poised to light the NHS for pharmacological enterprise,

Wreckers and private lab-rats to make a capsuled killing,
GPs' mouths stuffed with gold again (will they be willing
This time?), holding purse-strings and patients to ransom,
Outsourcing sickness, patients to be customers, every pilling
A billing; orthodontic profiteers out on the tiles to drill their
Filling for a cut in the society of broken smiles.

Wealth and hellbeing: a National Wealth Service
For already well-flushed practitioners of medicine
Spells disenfranchisement for the patients; this Humpty-
Dumpty Big Society means-whatever-it-wants-itself-to-mean:
A Tory boot stamping on a claimant's face again and again
In the name of tea-and-tiffin pre-45 Mutualism
Of local quacks and marketeers and put-upon charities,
A new Regressive Era of déjà vu's eventual view
To re-establish cooperative societies, or for another
James Keir Hardie to emerge over a century on
From the original's rise, for a rainbow wave of socialist
Opposition, a new 'cradle to grave' British Covenant,
Fit for the twenty-first century...
                                                            But first, it seems,
Things must get worse, the nation begging on its bended knees
At a speculator's dripping purse, until it comes to realise
It must stand up against recalcitrant threatening
Return to Dickensian times of pipsqueak Pecksniffian
Thrift, starchy Victorian values, Scrooges, Chuzzlewits,
Samuel Smiles' Self-Help ethic that Thatcher privatised;
There'll be no more state help in the Society of Bankrupt Smiles;
Cameronian Covenanters to carry the Calvinist baton
Of that lugubrious son of the manse, Presbyter Brown's
'Deserving, undeserving poor' puritanical paradigm
Into full-tilt capitalist pandemonium, a *blitzkrieg* on
The Public Sector, swarms of Mr Bumble-Bees in every town,

A Workfare State turning us to mobile workhouse units,
A tyranny of bloated billionaire austerity tsars —
Then, perhaps, there might form a movement to found a new
Party of the common people, as in olden times before
The reigns of Lord Protector Blair and Tumbledown Brown
Trashed the crimson banners of their cause for the New brand
Of trounced red rose for tabloid red-top patronage from
The media-monopolizing truth-murdering Murdochracy —
So back to a conglomerate of Shillingbury communities
Where the parson and landowner collude in new enclosures
And clearances (diaspora of the caps for capitalists
And absent landlords to pull the ladders up, bowl bailiffs in);
The landed classes grabbing back their feudal gerrymandering,
Peasants in the village stocks and *Do the Right thing* —
Mantra of Moloch, translated as 'capitalizing'
On others' poverty, old Tory dog-eat-dog — oncoming
Storm of wreckers' cuts will summon the dismantling
Of Bevan's Welfare State, that last socialist bastion...

...Oh, it's had its problems, its loopholes, overpayments,
Penalties and sanctions, stigmatizing its own claimants,
Interrogating them at every turn, trapping the poorest
Through fiscal recycling, punishing the incapacitated
With probing lamps, hounding out unemployed couples
From roomier flats, back into damp bedsits; the obfuscations
Of 'passport benefits' in a mindboggling episcopacy
Of cherry-picked entitlements — the Welfare State needs
Reforming, but not like this: it does not deserve systematic
Trampling, least of all from a Cabinet of property-flipping
Etonians who've mostly not laboured but inherited
Their millions via dynasties of gilded DNAs, or, in
Sub-prime minister Cameron's case, blue-blood relatives,
So too the Chancellor, Gideon Osborne, heir to the

Baronetcy of Ballentaylor... Reform is needed, as sunrise
Follows sunset, but not by such brutal cutting, penny-
Pinching blood-letting that threatens to impoverish,
Make destitute two million; this cannot be, this *will not be*,
The people will oppose the swingeing wrecking-ball of government
ConDemning Bevan's building, Clement Attlee's marquetry
(*His* socialist Damascus struck him touring Thirties' slums) —
To add irony to injury, Clem's grandson, his spit, a hereditary peer,
Is present-day Tory Whip to the Lords on behalf of the very
Wreckers of his own ancestry: true defector of heredity —
Was it all for nothing? Was it just a dream of tweedy wasp-wing-
Spectacled social planners sitting round the Cabinet table taking
Tea and altruism? Clegg! Cable! What of Campbell-Bannerman,
Asquith, Lloyd-George, Beveridge? Your more philanthropic
Progenitors — you've sold out what they stood for! Without
The Beveridge Report — tagged though it was to punitive rates,
Rather than transformative assistance (thus failing the Titmuss
Test) — there may never have been the co-operative mandate,
No Bevan empowered as Minister to build the NHS —
Answer then: do you think Alternative Vote can compensate
For letting the wreckers in to demolish the Welfare State?
Shame on you for betraying your pledges to the students,
And many more Millbanks will come to cast your party
Into ballot-box oblivion — arithmetical anathema!

And Cameron, who castigates claimants for receiving
High housing benefit payments — why not ask port-faced Ken
Sat on the bench beside you why he abolished rent controls
Back in '92...? So spiralled rents of slum accommodations,
The housing boom, the buy-to-let bonanza New Labour
Turned a blind eye to, while bankers stumped-up sub-prime
Mortgages as gambling chips, until the bubble had to burst,
Our nation bankrupted for City addictions — Time

For a levelling of the hedges; put Healey's trope of '74
Finally into action: 'squeeze the property speculators
Until the pips squeak'! But instead, you slap the culprits with
A paltry Two Billion they'll barely notice as they keep baying
For bonuses underwritten by the rest of us who bailed them out;
Hold you to ransom with the blackmail: penalise them and
They'll tip their champagne-fluted 'talent' out to other countries'
Mothballed casinos, to glut unregulated greed; as non-doms
Top-up havens of evasions. —Is it more bogus bonuses,
Docked giros, foodbanks, *Big Issues* the Big Society's to be about?

3. *The Rigged Society/The Big Robbery*

You chop top-downwards, trample the poor, defenceless
Innocents; ripe for looting, their low-hanging fruit,
Boxed terror of brown envelopes, more form-filling, informing,
Paper pogrom on the unemployed, scaremongering,
Outsourcing suspicion, tacit rallying-call for vigilantes
To snitch on curtain-twitchers, tip off on suspect claimants,
Disabled daylight-dodgers, incapacitated vampires
—Will you be painting stars of David on those 'shutters'
Closed during the day in your Big Jackboot Society?
Clampdown on the clamped, poverty-trapped and tapped,
Besieged on all flanks by penalties, Experian's
Gestapo espionage arm to smoke out anomalies
For 'bounties', undeclared scraps to plaster up the cracks
In capped claims, criminalizing potential 'benefit cheats',
Stumping them with loopholes and tripwires, Kafkaesque
Interrogative corridors laced with Socratic booby-traps,
All guilty till proven innocent. ...But spare a thought for the
Last generation, broken by Thatcherism, then betrayed
By New Labour; readjust your cyclopic-vision,
Its sick-at-heart anti-protest Protestant Turk Ethic,

And try to empathise with those at the bottom of the heap
Left struggling to do their best with begrudging benefits
In broken Britain's kicked hornet's nest — then ask yourselves:
Is it fair to blast the people with more political attrition,
An age of Selective Austerity you know your apparatchiks
Won't be sharing in? Too busy sporting, rolling back hunting
Bans, repealing the hills with bloodthirsty hounds, bugling
Peals, grabbing back the lands to root out urban foxes; to
Target and tag startled antlers of snagged stagflation.

If you believe in voluntarism Mr Cameron will you be
Donating your six-figure salary to Shelter, pulling up
Your sleeves and popping down to ladle out some soup?
Already rolling in the millions, you could afford to forego
Your PM pocket money, set an example to the layabouts,
Spongers, benefit cheats — But, it's not cheating just
To strive to make ends meet any way one can in these
Suddenly reduced circumstances; the only benefit thieves
In this Big Society are the fiddling, flipping MPs, hedge-
Fund speculators, none of whom have the excuse of cheating
Simply to eat, only the card of gluttony, greed for wealth,
Power. Have you ever heard the one about 'all property
Is theft'? And please, advise me how to square this
Lopsided circle, 'fairness': if the poor cut corners they're
Pilloried in the public stocks, pelted with penalties, while
Those with pound and power permitted to put it down
To *mistakes, misjudgements*, and get off with apologies,
Quick slap on the wrists while they make their cuts on all our veins;
And David Laws, caught out and practically applauded
After his malversation, patted on the back, a 'victim', martyr
To a lapse of transparency — you don't extend that empathy
To the cash-strapped masses, their benefits capped,
Long-term social housing tenancies scrapped. This

Big Society looks more hypocritical by the minute
Mr Cameron, you trumpeting volunteers to mop up
The fallout from your cuts; rather absurd don't you think:
The rich asking the poor to tidy up their mess for free
On behalf of your Bullingdon clubs in the City,
While you cut their safety nets, neatly package austerity
And farm it, careful to keep your own landed hands clean...
Not absurd, now one thinks of it, just *British*. And don't
Fob us off with mantras of *deficit*, brainwashing
Won't obscure the robbing of our public services:
In Forty-Five, a nation pocked with debt, a crater of deficit
Three times the size of the one you've relishingly 'inherited',
Those loss adjusters didn't bulldoze through with ruthless
Cuts: Attlee's army worked miracles, spent to regenerate
Hearts and minds, redistribute the spirit — from the bankrupt
Rubble of the Blitz, Clem and Bevan built the Welfare State!

4. *Reapers of the Low-Hanging Fruit*

Think, before you let the wrecking-ball swing against
Nye's monument: what seems unwieldy on a piece
Of cream portcullised paper fact-and-figured abstractly
To those who don't need safety nets for having private slates
Is a sanctuary forged from Forties' austerity, a state
Of altruism that put our nation on compassion's map,
Set a moral template to the West — before the prate
Of materialism heckled in with Thatcher's matriculate,
Spoilt some rotten, sold the spirit off, capitalised our basest traits
While hounding out the unions, the miners, branding socialism
Quixotic, unpatriotic, anything but its Christian politic,
While Maggie quoted selectively from St Paul's chastisement
Of those who wouldn't work, to starvation; spurious spins
On Christ's 'render unto to Caesar' when what He meant:

Money has no moral value — hardly, then, monetarism
From the mouth of the New Testament... And what of other
Proverbs, or can camels really squeeze through needles' eyes?
Remember the redistributive fist of Christ, his hatred
Of the market, when he over-turned the temple stalls —
A pity that shopkeeper's frumpy maladjusted daughter
Didn't pay attention to the Beatitudes, the tale of the Good
Samaritan, and other proverbs of the socialist Gospels.
Have some heart, Malthusians in blue, don't tip us back
To sink or swim in another sea of Thatcherism;
The scars of her Eighties' meringue-maned reign have barely
Healed, not in the scorched North's blasted heartlands, not
In the ribs of those unlucky ones still travelling on buses
Well into their thirties, *Her* victims and leitmotivs
Of 'failure', for not having grasped the horns of Faustian pacts
With the golden calf...
                                    Spare us, spare us, look to the City's
Babelic towers for the blame and reimbursement, slap
The Robin Hood Tax on those pinstriped Sheriffs
Of Nottingham who speculated us into recession,
Gamblers on the shoulders of giants, bailed out on
Our backs through tax they've used to wax more bonuses
— Just *how is* the burden put on the broadest shoulders? —
While we lose jobs, roofs, benefits, entitlements stripped
By titled classes, our Welfare State depleted, the peoples'
Sole protection from destitution: to you an extra helping
You can afford to tip from the plate; to many, the last scrap
That makes the scrimp and scrape in capitalism's prodding
Cattle-market — its rented cells cooping us up like hens
In batteries — that bit more endurable, the pilgrimage
For individual dignity in a land-grabbed, class-carved island,
A damp, cramped, cankered chip of emerald set in a fiscal sea
Of institutionalised greed, speculated bankruptcy —

A country unfit for social consciences, where undeserving
Rich now pinch our politics, plutocrats intensely relaxed
About the people getting filthily poor; this mock-democracy,
This end-of-the-pier Empire that ever re-sets its sunset clauses,
Now tipping into the unplumbed depths of expediency
For eclipsed compassion, keel-hauling us through choppy
Waters of 'recovery' — But what country, once recovered?
A generation's blasted tears will swell to a raging placard-sea:
If you scrap our Welfare State, we'll sink your Big Society.

Mick Moss

Mick Moss is a 57 year old ex art school graduate, music industry drop-out and part-time writer. Originally from London, has lived in Liverpool for 25 years. Suffers from long term depression and intermittent anxiety attacks, but learning to cope. "Liverpool is a targeted city where there are genuine claimants. We are not all scroungers!!"

Illness You Can't See

sometimes it hurts so bad
I just don't want
to go on living
blessed death a bonus
after this
times when the pain
is bearable
I sit, in darkness
gathering strength
till I am able
to face the world

by which I mean
go outside
and do a bit of shopping
but only at familiar shops
where I know the people
strangers scare me
I shake and stutter
and sweat and get giddy
and see coloured shapes
in my peripheral vision

so I have to run home
blindly, rudely
slam the door
and hope the panic
passes before too long

you cannot see my illness
it is difficult to quantify
to measure and assess
and I am frightened
that when I go for my next
benefit examination
if they can't do that
my benefit will be cut
and I will be forced into
a world of fear and pain
and anguish and suffering
every time I have to sign on.

Andy N

Andy N is a 38 year old born and bred in Manchester and was a founding member of the Bolton collective Trio Writers and also was co-organiser for the open mike night *Poets and...* He is currently vocalist in the spoken word collective *Wordmusic*. He bought out my first book *Return to Kemptown* in April 2010.

Emergency Verse

They say they are going to increase
VAT from 17.5% to 20%
and cut Welfare spending
to tackle Britain's record debts
claiming it is needed to prevent
a catastrophic from ripping
out the very heart-beat of our society
when it looks in reality
all they really want to do is
declare War on public services
and privatize everything going
like they are driven by ghosts.

They say they are talking about
cutting Housing Benefits by 10 per cent
for people who have claimed
Job Seekers Allowance for over a year
Which terrifies me considering
it does nothing to tackle the
problems of an ageing society
and employers who are still unofficially
not interested in employing older people
like Scrooge burying his head in the sand.

They say they believe around 400,000
of the country's 2.6 million
benefit claimants on incapacity benefit
are able to take up work
and intend everybody will taken off it by 2014
before concluding with a cheesy smile
we will need to tighten our belts
a little tighter because of the huge errors
the previous government has made
that has bought our country to its knees
even though one of their own claimed
£100,000 for a flat they barely use
even though his family house is only
17 miles away from Westminster.

They say this emergency budget
is needed despite the fact
the previous government
did have some success
like introducing the
national minimum wage
as well as being tough on Crime
to a such a level although
which although it is still too high
is now starting to fall sharply
instead choosing to reverse they can
including no doubt the tide
if they can get away with it.
But all I see in reality
is a return to 1980's values
where greed is good
and Tax Cuts mask over
the truth of the fat cats looking down

from their lofty tower blocks
and dropping crumbs down to us
when they can be bothered
like they are feeding Pigeons
and they grab them back
driven by a fear that
goes deeper than cruelty.

All I see is gaffe-prone ministers
laughing arrogantly at their gaffes
and making them again
with the malice of plantation owners
who are more interested in making
Public Services race against each other
for funds they desperately need
like horses on a prize horsing ride
by dangling carrots in front of their nose
and snatch them away when they
can't be bothered anymore.

All I see is a society
pulled apart to the extremes
where people are being forced
to move to different areas
as a carry on from the hated
'get on your bike' campaign of the 1980's
and society really getting ripped apart.
while they laugh from their irony towers
throwing their scraps down to the Pigeons
and reversing tides if they manage it.

I choose to stand against the tide.

Stephen D. Nadaud II

Stephen D. Nadaud II was born in Toledo, Ohio, on August 28, 1981. He is currently working on the early chapters of a novel.

Dear Humanity

Evil is an ancient myth,
and goodness is the same.
But some men hold their heads up high,
while others hide their shame.

Do you think it's like old films,
those films in black and white?
Where everything is child's play,
and clearly wrong or right?

Grey is what defines this life,
and permeates the Earth.
Everything has good and bad,
a death for every birth.
And don't you dare to think it true,
that men who hide their shame,
wanted to be labelled bad,
and begged to have that name.
And wished to live a life of pain,
upon a blood-stained star.
Evil happens to most men,
and many fall so far.

But all men have some good inside,
and each one has his sin.
Judge only those whose shoes you've used.
Whose shoes have you walked in?

Alistair Noon

Alistair Noon was born in 1970, grew up in Aylesbury, and has lived in Berlin since the early nineties. His publications include the pamphlets *At the Emptying of Dustbins* (Oystercatcher), *In People's Park* (Penumbra), *Animals and Places* (Longbarrow) and *Some Questions on the Cultural Revolution* (Gratton Street Irregulars, forthcoming 2010). His translations from German and Russian include *Sixteen Poems — Monika Rinck* (Barque), Pushkin's *The Bronze Horseman* (Longbarrow) and a full-length collection of translations of Osip Mandelstam (Leafe Press, forthcoming 2011).

The Ballad of the Burst Main

Early about among the New Towers
of Rush, Risk and Insurance
that had sprouted abruptly like plastic flowers,
I gatecrashed a course on endurance.

Some plumbing had suddenly burst its doubts,
no longer the solid believer,
and a geyser was reaching into the clouds,
a steamily high achiever.

The burst was pushing expansion plans,
like blood beneath a bandage. A pond
now stretched one finger towards a camera
and washed out to the street and beyond.

There were sirens and lights and a guy in green overalls
running up to the leak with a wrench,
like a medic with a kit to a footballer's fall,
and about to get thoroughly drenched.

From the glossy top floors, a few peered down
to the pool that grew ever more copious,
and lit the green crystals and keyed in the sounds
on their minimal Siemens and Nokias:

As we're sure you know, without H2O
our problems can only be mounting.
Our drinks machines slow, our coolers will go,
in the lobby we've two dry fountains.

The reply: *If water near you's getting deeper,*
press one. Thank you for ringing us.
To keep down costs, we've worked out it's cheaper
to let it run through a bloke's fingers.

So now in the mornings they boat to their desks,
figure out each others' claims;
the bloke who wore overalls wears flippers and mask,
and no one much cares when it rains.

Nyerges Gábor Ádám

Nyerges Gábor Ádám was born in 1989, lives in Budapest, Hungary. He is a Hungarian poet and chief editor of the literary periodical *Apokrif*. Poems in several prestigious Hungarian literary periodicals such as *Beszélő, Liget, Spanyolnátha*. His first collection, *Helyi érzéstelenítés/Local Anaesthesia* has just been published for Hungarian Festive Book Week. He attends ELTE University.

Substitutes

"Bronze statues, depicting homeless people will be exhibited from Thursday on, in the downtown of Debrecen; programs such as street music acts and food-giving, accompanied by the exhibition of the statues is the way how the organisers intend to use art as a way to draw attention to the social problem of homelessness."

They sculpt new bronze ones
which ask only for attention
instead of money
but this pair of words
'social problems'
makes everyone fall asleep

it works better than pills or booze
and I, like everyone else,
skip the boring parts too
in the news
not listening to England anymore

and when London's calling
rather switch the tv off
or put a record on
grab a book
or just walk outside, down the street,
anywhere away from 'social problems'

*

And everybody's on the streets now
watching substitute-statues,
the insteadof-homeless
and when asked to pay,
well, paying in attention

feeling truly relieved
they don't ask for money anymore
piss publicly pray or freeze
and, how delightful,
they aren't even starving

Steven O'Brien

Steven O'Brien lectures in Creative Writing at the University of Portsmouth. His poetry collections include: *Dark Hill Dreams* (Agenda Editions, 2010) and *Scrying Stone* (Greenwich Exchange, 2010). He currently edits *The London Magazine*.

Flesh and Steel

I remember the blurred lilies
Of his tattoos
How the thorny gutturals of desert battles
And rubbled towns in Sicily
Washed more faintly each year
In the shallows of his white forearms.

He was not a good man.
His children could tell you —
The cuffs and slaps
And hours in the pub.
He spoke in sudden spats
Like dropping spanners through a drain —
Monte Casino was hard.
The Reichswald a bloody grind.

Only on Churchill did his tongue find itself awake —
His speeches was like a rash
Crackling up your back.
But granddad never fell entirely
For Winston's imperial pageant —
The growling radio gallantry.

He had seen flesh pitched against steel.
All those generals had wielded him,
Fashioned him.
He has seen flesh triumph.
When he returned,
With shrapnel ticking in his chest,
It was as if he had walked from a fire,
Almost unscathed, yet changed —

A slogging tommy carrying something
Of the Leveller's certainty
In his steady grey eyes.

He was not good
And his thick fingers were not made for graceful tunes.
He built no triumphal arches,
Or statues of the fallen.
No boulevards for generals to parade.

Instead, he bolted awkward girders
And built a once and forever thing
Patched and welded,
The riveted seams of a working man's hope —

Hospitals, Schools, Welfare,
Wrought in clumsy, creaking dignity.

John O'Donoghue

John O'Donoghue's journalism, poetry and fiction has appeared in *The Observer, The TES, The London Magazine, PN Review, Ambit, Acumen, Orbis, Aesthetica* and *Poetry Express.* He is author of two poetry chapbooks, *Letter To Lord Rochester* (Waterloo Press, 2004), *The Beach Generation* (Pighog, 2007), and a volume, *Brunch Poems* (Waterloo Press, 2009). His memoir, *Sectioned: A Life Interrupted* (John Murray, 2009) has been critically praised in most nationals including *the Sunday Times, the Independent, the Morning Star* and by Blake Morrison in *The Guardian.* It won the 2010 MIND Book of the Year Award.

London Sundays

Across the broad slabs where
Imposing gallery
And Georgian church nestle
(Or is that jostle?) close
To traffic hell and up-
Start fleapit, McDonald's,
And Charing Cross's two
Versions of the railway —
One all neon steel tile,
The other vaunted arches
Where litter bins cascade
And stragglers wait mute
Before the clock's blankfaced
Omnipotence, time past
And time present waiting
Perhaps for time future —
Across the broad slabs of
Long-gone London Sundays
My narrow friends scuttle
Down the dark smoked funnel of
St Martin's-in-the-Fields'

Cold crypt, the London map
Of dirt and grime etched on
Faces like the pigeon
Shit that's almost mortar
In the brickwork of this
City's darkest buildings.
I know some face by face,
The numbered hairs of soup-
Clagged beard and what the young
Ones call that geezer's
Bobby Charlton Parting.
Not hard to number them.
I take my place amongst
The claques, the tat that's
Standard issue for us tits,
Us doorstep milk snatchers,
Begrimed and anoraked
All round, the tables strewn
With London Sundays, trash
Magazines and empty
Polystyrene cups, crusts,
Sometimes the personal
Paraphernalia
Of 'our gentlemen'.
                    We're
Indifferent now to
Charity: it's our right.
Once you've come this far, soup's
All that's keeping you from
Freezing off the booze and
Pegging out. Couldn't skipper
This weather, although God
Help us, there's those that do.

The girls, straight out of Blue
Peter, ladle out the soup
And tidy up, black plastic
Bags swallowing all
The debris. Through the dinge
And murmur, the peasouper
Of Old Horrible smoke
And an atmosphere thick
With decay, our last
Conspiracy, moves young
Fiona, a vision in
The choirstall, her red
Surplice left off for the
Crypt. The good angel sheds her
Her wings and walks. I give
A wink and make my way
To the front, a dud
Communicant whose state
Of grace down here doesn't
Matter. I'm part of
The general confession
Of the age. I've crossed
Myself: there's only me
To blame.
       Later the day-
Centre down by Waterloo
Where Brian and I scrabble
Away what remains of
The day 'til closing time
Comes round and off we go
Again, me to St Mungo's
And him, well he's under-
Neath the Arches, dreams all

Dreamt away.
        The Sunday
Crowds are growing now, round
Leicester Square and up
By Shaftesbury Avenue,
Off to see a film or
The latest musical smash,
Buses lurching round
The weird system of their
Routes as I measure out
The slabs with practised,
Steady rhythm and am
Back before pure neon
Lights the city like
A liner cruising
The cold black ocean,
Flotsam dead along her bows.

O, all those London Sundays.

Ruary O'Siochain

Ruary O'Siochain is a Dublin-based poet. He has had work published in *Fire, Pulsar, Snakeskin, The New Writer* and *Orbis*.

Hiding Behind Choice

This hidden drive to privatise
presented as the gift of choice
shields reason's light from our eyes;

the rule of market is their prize
and less government to stop them foist
their game-set plan to privatise;

all that which was kind, good and wise
is put out to tender by a voice
that shields reason's light from its eyes;

our hard won rights grabbed, in the guise
of fiscal cuts to allow them hoist
their hidden drive to privatise;

because they know what wins is the size
of their pal's donation: rejoice, rejoice —
they don't need reason's light in their eyes;

what they push is self serve lies
packaged as a market choice,
let's fight this drive to privatise
with reason's light behind our eyes.

Bobby Parker

Bobby Parker is a writer and editor living in Kidderminster in the West Midlands., He was voted Purple Patch Poet of the Year 2008. He has recently taken over as editor of *Urban District Writer*, previously edited by Geoff Stevens.

What's wrong?

Today is a dustbin lid rolling
down the alley, clatter-laughter of metal
on kerbs; a dozen girls gathered for a trip to London
their lips the flowers in a grid of rainy threads.

My sexy dance is useless in the grim,
grim way the window frames the sky's flat tyre
and your braless jiggle in my doorway
reminds me of two toddlers on a trampoline
reaching for a sun that seems to be balancing
between the ears of a Mickey Mouse cloud.

I have one squeaky shoe that tallies the distance
from hope to grief in a wet alphabet of anxiety,
letters arranged to spell a thousand miles
of a world gone wrong but still prepared to change.

Crooked rooftops greased with grey butter
traffic lights blinking through a fuzz of morning blues
newspapers coded with apocalyptic key-words
egg on toast the best yellow we can hope for —

sometimes it takes a day smudged in a dirty palette
of rain and fumes and dark noise in the wind's sleeve
to realise the way you look at me over your coffee
is not unlike somebody waiting for the answer to a question.

Duncan Parker

Duncan Parker was born in Hull in 1954. He worked for twenty years for Mass Observation, and after intermittent periods of unemployment during the 1990s, decided it was time to retire. In 1994 he tore up his Labour Party membership in protest against the scrapping of Clause IV, and formed his own short-lived party, True Labour (1994-1994). Poetry collections include: *Biography of a Supertrump* (Wonston & Scotney, 1975), *Letter to John Lilburne* (Saracen, 1980), *Scargill's Rant* (Saracen, 1983), *Down and Out in Berwick-On-Tweed* (Digger Editions, 1985) and *Tony Benn Met Me Once: New and Rejected Poems* (self-published, 1989). Parker's definitive (and the only) critical companion to the work of obscure 19th century horticultural poet Thomas Twisden-Varlo (1798-1841), *Odes & Sods: A Twisden-Varlo Reader*, is forthcoming from Digger Editions in 2011. His memoir, *Coming and Going*, is also forthcoming.

The Ministry for *Doing the Right Thing*

Now listen, the Big Society is about localism, mutualism
(Which actually means, 'go off and sort your own life out'),
Giving power back to you, yes, YOU, the aspiring and
Entrepreneurial — natural selection and all that crack.
The Big Society is open to all you who *do the right thing* —
Whatever that is — ah yes, capitalizing on opportunities
(If and when they should present themselves), not bothering
To think of the consequences on others, or, if you like,
A spot of volunteering — I do my own every morning
When I get up to put the coffee on for her indoors at No. 10;
It's time for all of us to roll our sleeves up and muck in
With *doing the right thing* — now what do I mean by *doing*
The right thing? Well, to some of us this will involve supervising
Over our elevenses, then home for tiffin; to others, five years
Or so of soul-destroying digging. Eighty quid a week is enough
For you to live on, or if you're one of the volunteers, thin air;
But we MPs need *at least* two grand a week, plus another
Hundred-and-forty smackeroonies to grant our attendance.

But it's not all about money...
                              Let me tell you about the
Big Society: it's the thing that gets me up in the morning
Filled with excitement (while I know quite a lot of you
Wake filled with dread, or retching), it's been my vision ever
Since I had an epiphany on the playing fields of Eton coming
Round from a cricket ball on the bonce: a Society not
Of scrounging but contributing: *I* do by slogging all day
For next to nothing — my fellow Oxford Blues in the City
Think I'm too altruistic working for a meagre six-figure salary —
But that's what the Big Society's all about: sacrificing.
That's why I went into politics, into public service, so I could
Abolish it; farm it out to private hands, outsourced Colonel
Kurtzes, despotic doctors and napalm capitalists to line their
Paddy-field firms with decapitated social workers and other
Public Sector do-gooders for blood-congealed trophies and
Scarecrows — a tad gruesome, yes, but one must be firm
And uncompromising when it comes to money... I wanted to
Do something for the country other than profiteering
Like my old Etonian chums in big business — gave myself a stiff
Talking to, and said, *Look here David, you can do without*
The odd bit of property speculation of a year for the sake of putting
This Great country back on the straight and Harrow, er narrow;
Putting it back on the narrowest shoulders—I mean—*broadest.*

So here I am, and my big passion is the Big Society, which is
All about *doing the right wing* — I mean, *thing* — whatever
That is — ah yes, sloganeering about us all being *in it together*
When in reality — behind closed doors at Downing Street that is
— We're doing quite the *other* thing: that's to say, scrapping
Eighteen Billion from your Welfare State because it's such a
Shoddy little embarrassment, a stain on this nation's apron,
And that really gets my dander up; we have plenty enough

On our plate without forking out Billions a year supporting
A bunch of workshy loafers in their institutionalised idleness,
Keeping those obese chavs with ASBOS in their lager and fags,
Farting on fat sofas, those spongers pretending to be disabled
Only when they remember to limp a bit, those limbless
Malingerers and 'sob-story' saddos — they should take a leaf
Out of our book: the trick is to be idle *without* showing it,
That's what makes our great aristocracy so much smarter than
The peasant classes: because it practises the almost imperceptible
Tradition of *Consti*tutionalised idleness, a very different thing,
Takes centuries of inter-breeding to cultivate that certain
Inert pedigree; one puts on a public face, a little hand-
Waving and that sort of thing, the landed capitalist conceit
Of making oneself look incredibly busy while in fact just
Fattening up one's green-slashed rump on that slippery front-
Bench, or propping one's girth at the despatch-box to vent a tad
Of spleen of a Wednesday at PMQs — I'm told I'm a natural,
Have the smokescreen down to tap: deficit, deficit, deficit,
Difficult decisions, difficult decisions, tough but fair, tough but
—actually just tough—unavoidable, unavoidable, cuts, cuts, cuts,
Cameron, Osborne, Cable, Pickles, Clegg and Baron Green,
Privateers on parade in the Cabinet of Camberwick Preen.

That last blasted government and that dreary Gordon Brown,
That frowsty Jock, that lugubrious goblin of the Lochs,
That thistly son of the manse and his bureaucratic kilted minions,
Borrowed in the boom and just spent, spent, spent, even
Pawned the elephant in the room... So now we must join with
Hair-shirt Dandy Alexander (that bloody storm-browed ginge)
In clasping our Calvinist hands together to fleece the poor
And so repent for one's soul through fiscal chastisement —
By proxy, of course: our young gay dog of the Glens
Is infinitely better off as a Minister with limousine than when

Cramped in the camper-van of the pre-nest-feathering Lib Dems.
This nation is now facing suddenly reduced circumstances:
A big black bally hole, the worst government deficit since
The War, when Clement Attlee's Labour Government, again,
Just spent, spent, spent on all of you peasants, built this thing
Called the Welfare State, making way for a cult of idling
For those who've not inherited that singular privilege,
As my blue-blooded breed have, long since the land-grab —
But I digress: so now, due to this wretched deficit, left by the
Previous government, in case you didn't know (we have to
Slip that in at least eight times in one Commons sitting),
We've had to put our bonces together for all of forty minutes
To fathom out on the back of Kenny Clarke's cigar-box,
A budget to get our country out of this deficit and back into
The black-and-blue, in a way which naturally will not affect the
City and the Banks and all those speculators who created it —
But not the deficit, no, that was definitely Labour's fault,
The last government, and we want you all to focus on that
For a moment, that moment to last approximately five years.

Now what we've come up with will be tough but fair, at least
For those of us with enough to spare: we don't like the Public
Sector and we make no bonuses about it, so that's got to go
As soon as possible so hopefully all those directly affected
Won't notice it; next we need to dismantle this bloody awful
Welfare State, this socialist colossus, because there are frankly
Far too many dossers living a life of Reilly on sixty quid a week
Of taxpayers' money, and that's not cricket! So we are going
To herd them all into jobs that don't exist, though they're more
Than welcome to use their initiative and create their own —
That's what the Big Society is all about: devastating lives
To prop up the privileged —er — I mean, empowering
Local communities, yes, that's it — one for the road — ho ho...

Bottoms up to the Big Society! Or should that be, top down?
We'll get the unemployed spongers in the village stocks
And pelt them with sponges to lashings of warm beer...We
Didn't get where we are today without lashings of warm beer...
Ha ha. Ahhh.... Then we're going to put a cap on Housing
Benefit because this government, what with the bally deficit,
Can no longer afford to pay those opportunistic landlords
Blue Ken liberated from rent controls back in '92 — their
Exorbitant rents on your behalves out of our own pocket.
We're going to cap and tap and scrap, and rap *the right-wing*....
Going for a song now boys, I feel a song coming on...

> *O yes we're all in it together*
> *To break the rest of you to your knees*
> *O yes we're all in it together*
> *George, Nick, Danny, Andy, Willie and me —*
> *We're going to bang on about the deficit*
> *From this to the next rigged Parliament*
> *New Politics is whatever we say it means*
> *In our Humpty-Dumpty Demockracy,*
> *We're all in it together in our little cabal*
> *While you drown in the Big Society.*

After that, well, the sky's the limit in terms of dragging
Britain back kicking and limping to good old Victorian
Values, all those old quaint Dickensian slums, workhouses,
Soup kitchens, debtors' prisons — I'm getting all misty-eyed
Again, the nostalgia gets me every time — but it'll be all right
For those of us who have *done the right thing* and saved
Our assets while damning the poor: none of us will have those
Dreadful chavs and ASBOS breeding next-door
And moulting on our lawns, we'll leave that to the working
Class ghettos so our friends in the BNP can mop up from

Labour debris, then this Con-Dem Co-attrition, er, Co-*ali*-tion,
Will look relatively liberal, Tory even, with a little big C,
That's me, incidentally, oh, and my Lib Dem-Deputy —
And we'll get all those little council house kids back sweeping
Our chimneys, just like in the old days — that's what this Big
Society's all about: exploitation, opportunism, obfuscating
Accountability via the private sector who'll get those
Sacked public sector workers back in toe for £1.60 an hour,
Or racked (or keel-hauled along with those benefit cheats),
Thus saving the country lots of dough, no contracts or
Employment rights —those will have to go, it'll all have to be
Rolled back along with the minimum wage, and Europe,
We're having none of that continental malarkey over here
Anymore — and no more over-sixty-five shirkers, we're all
In this together, pensioner and beggar have their contributions
To make to the common effort, we'll get the buggers working
For their cramped little bedsits, keep them at it with our hounds
Like the vermin foxes they'd be if they were left to idle and
Scrounge; the Workfare State, that's what it's all about!

> *O, Rule Britannia, Britannia's built on slaves,*
> *It should never have brought in the mi-ni-mum wage.*

And while we're at it we'll make all council houses fixed
Term only, so after five years in one the tenant has to find
A lucrative job, or invent one to enable he/she/it/thing
To afford a better home, and if they fail, well, they know where
The door isn't. Phew. 99 Skidoo. National Health Service?
Don't give me National Health Service. We simply cannot
As a nation any longer afford to give free treatment to the
Peasants, we'll have to rock the cradle, tip the whole
Bureaucratic Communist behemoth into its own grave,
A private subcontractors' skip, carve it up for pharmaceutical

Companies to have a big bonanza of profiteering, finally
Empower General Practitioners sufficiently to be worshipped
As the gods-in-human-form they really are, upgrade them to
Omnipotence, a cut above the patients, a celestial pedigree
Of pedagogues who will now have absolute power medically
And fiscally over the mongrel hoards, malingerers and riff-raff,
Er, I mean *customers—cattle—guinea-pigs—patients*—sorry,
Always get confused on this...
                               This Con-Demolition
Will shortly announce the start of a war of attrition
On patients' rights, telling the GPs to turn blind eyes
To their Hippocratic Oaths and all that, train them to flatly
Refuse to ever give sickness chits for all and sundry
To bum off the taxpayer for Incapacity deficit—er—benefit,
Having a whale of a time spending it on things they don't need,
Or only need a bit, or chronically; we want our Big Society
Fighting fit for all the work ahead, for *doing the right thing*:
That is, working your fucking socks off to keep us upper
Classes in our gormandizing for another decade or two...
Well, at least until 2015, then we'll see what we can do...

I just need to sit down for a minute — where was I? —
Oh yes, the deficit, the deficit, the deficit, the deficit...
Well, my underclasses, disabled, unemployed and sick,
Public Sector workers, impoverished, and all that bit,
Frankly you're all buggered in my Big Society
So you'd better just get used to it or we'll have to think
Of some other solution (which minister was it suggested
Something about installing gas showers in council houses?).
— But in the meantime don't forget the good old motto:
Arbeit macht frei (or should that be, *Arbeit McMacht with
Fries...?* Or there's always the British one: *Getting others
To do the work while making yourself look busy, makes you free.*

Yes, bit of a mouthful. But maybe we can stick to the Nazi
One for the time being. I always fancied myself in a brownshirt;
I can see Os and Haguey both cutting a dash in the Hugo Boss
Autumn collection. Because, you know, the free market's free
To market whoever it chooses, whichever cattle it sees
Without capital, one of the little unwritten delicacies
Of neo-liberal-con demockracies — it's all a big con-trick,
Has been for centuries, though old Nick and Fallen Vince
Will be the last to know, *Ho-ho, will be the laaast to knowww....*

O —
Georgie Porgie pudding and I
Kissed the Welfare State goodbye
Capped all Public Sector pay
For the Private's harvest day .

Georgie Porgie pudding and I
Cut the crust of the NHS pie
For pharmaceutical buffet —
Well we're with BUPA anyway!

O yes we're all in it together
To break the rest of you to your knees
O yes we're all in it together
George, Danny, Nick, Andy, Willie and me —
We're going to bang on about the deficit
From this to the next rigged Parliament
New Politics is whatever we say it means
In our Humpty-Dumpty Demockracy,
We're all in it together in our little cabal
While you drown in the Big Society.

Mick Parkin

Mick Parkin was born in Yorkshire in 1957. He graduated in 1978 with a Degree in Engineering from Newcastle University. He spent most of the 1980s in Spain. He worked as a bricklayer till 1987. Between 1990-95 he was a stand-up comic and performance poet, in London. He moved to Glasgow in 1995, and since then has been teaching creative writing to sixth form students in schools throughout Scotland and Ireland.

Life Doesn't Really Mean Life, Not These Days

Make prison more humane?
Impossible.
Cos the thing is,
the life they live in there
has got to be worse
than the life we live out here.
But the thing is, these days,
the life we live out here,
well, 'life' — it doesn't really mean life,
...not these days.

Mario Petrucci

Mario Petrucci is an award-winning internationally acclaimed poet. He graduated in Physics at Cambridge and later taught science in a secondary school. He gained a PhD in opto-electronics at University College London, and more recently completed postgraduate studies in the Environment and Literature departments of Middlesex University. He has also been an organic farm-hand in Ireland and a one-man band on the Paris Metro. Petrucci is now a freelance writer, educator, researcher, essayist, Arvon tutor, literacy consultant at the Imperial War Museum, Fellow of the Royal Literary Fund, a performance and voice trainer, teacher and creative writing tutor, and a signed songwriter/lyricist. He is also actively engaged in political and environmental writing. He lives in North London. Poetry collections include: *Shrapnel and Sheets* (Headland, 1996; Poetry Book Society Recommendation), *Heavy Water: a poem for Chernobyl* (Enitharmon, 2004; winner of *the Daily Telegraph*/Arvon International Poetry Competition), *Flowers of Sulphur* (Enitharmon, 2007), and *i tulips* (Enitharmon, 2010). A new collection, *the waltz in my blood*, is forthcoming from Waterloo Press. Petrucci is a founding editor of Perdika Editions.

Orders Of Magnitude

One hundred thousand trillion joules
to turn an ice cap into mush

One hundred thousand billion joules
to erase a major Eastern city

A hundred thousand million joules
to run a car to death

One hundred million of the same
for Fire Brigades to reach the kitten

Ten million just to keep
December from cold feet

A hundred thousand joules for a mug
of tea — A hundred joules

for a second's worth of War and Peace
Ten to raise a hand — to lift

an average apple to the lips
A single joule to shout the command

Half a joule to pull the trigger
Just one tenth to push the button

Almost zero to have the thought.

Angela Readman

Angela Readman grew up in Middlesbrough in the 1908s. She has had work published in Freida Hughes' column in *the Times*, the Forward anthology, *Staple* and *Ambit*, and has won both The Ragged Raven and Biscuit competitions. Her latest collection, *Strip*, is out with Salt Publishing.

Margaret

Since he heard they were in Margaret was back,
rolling into the gap in bed between him and his wife.
He feels irons breathe hot air in his ear, grudging wind
down a closed shaft. She is older now, he knows, picket lines
crossed round her mouth, hard hat replaced by stringy yellow thatch,
but this ghost, his Margaret hasn't aged a poll.
Her voice rises from halls of haggling men, it places him
in the bottom of a well, looking up. She makes her face the moon,
taxes his personal space. He can't pay, so slowly, gizzard fingers
trace a dotted line on his neck, she stuffs her kisses like ballots
down his gullet, his lips a slot screwed shut over years, tight
as a box to sign his name. It's a wonder he sleeps at all.
All day he prepares, lowers his eyes down a hatch,
makes them adjust to the dark, to raise a fistful of cold coal
to look Margaret in the eye. He's found shouting futile as forms,
using his fists — a giro he can't cash. So he speaks to her
like a small child, softly, 'Margaret, did you have problems
learning to spell your name?' He echoes her sobs in long corridors,
the break of red crayon, spilt milk on her nice blue pinafore
the first day of school and like that the iron lady breaks
into pieces small enough for him to assemble sleep.
He sees Little Margaret wake in the night, wet, twisting sheets
from the hands of a thousand men who clutched at the tails of her
     dreams

with such dirty hands she had to wash them before she bruised.
Sometimes he feels the tears of the child she might have been on his
    cheeks
Chasing the time he was. 'Ssh, Margaret', he says, 'I understand.'

Plastering

My father turned his hand to plastering,
loaded tub and a plastic hawk to set his eyes to walls
flat as notes. I watched the adult work of float,
the scrape of his trowels on eaves, sharp as tongues,
true as spades hitting stone. No time for talk,
in this race against drying, cracks and time to sign on.
He shed his shirt to sweat into buckets, drops
on the powder floor, earth brown clung to hairs,
dried flecks fell like hungry children losing their grip
from his chest. With a wet brush I followed to stop the crazing,
so careful, the tip of things I wouldn't say between my teeth,
my brushstrokes polished away by the feather edge in his grip.
Never did he smile, stand so still, as when he stood back
sure as a man inside his own sandcastle, regarding walls
flat enough to paint any colour. Only dust to say he was ever there.

Closing Time

Elbow deep in peelings, still your mother came forward,
wiped her hands to brush lint from your fathers' jacket,
every crease ironed from her face, no judgement, a flicker of pride
at how well he turned out for his pilgrimage to the working men's clu
The streets smelled of potatoes, hot oil, pans in wait for wins of meat

legless men to stagger home with joints from raffles under their arms.
You were fourteen, carted your father's wheelchair over curbs,
positioned him by the bar. Come afternoon close, you followed tyres,
snakes in the snow all the way back to your boarded front door,
mothers' burnt Yorkshires, for her husband and son, big enough
to bare the chariot of his father's thirst. Long after your parents are
            gone
you follow the same route, cufflinks clanking the rims of your chair
as you roll to the flat. Quiet as pockets before giro day, you remember
the old dear on Sunday mornings, place a fresh shirt on the bed,
a handkerchief and tie laid out next to your father's legs.
The streets smell of gravy trains ending. You think of mother
in wait for last orders, still peering out of wet windows,
waiting for you to bring Sunday home one more time.

Fiddling the Gas

I rented my first flat when my father came back
to teach me how to fiddle the gas. Snow on his hair,
shoulders, melting to grey as he bent to the metal.
I offered coffee, standing before him an adult, a daughter
—neither of us sure what this meant. Seems we waited
for the plumber all our lives, my mother and I inched
through December in sleeping bags, peered into hatches
of broken boilers, eyes full of blown out flames.
Taking out his kit-bag he drilled a hold in the cast, smeared
boot polish on the joint to disguise our partnership in crime.
Job done, then, he made his way down the path, gasman smile
left in my hall with 'while you were out' on the card.
For that second though it was simple as broken clocks,
the two of us crouched together conspired to cheat winter,
watching the wheel, this metre roll back fast as time.

Jeremy Reed

Jeremy Reed was born in Jersey in the Channel Islands. His prolific literary output since his first poetry collection *Target* (Andium Press, 1974) has been matched by an equally titanic reputation as the most imaginatively gifted British poet of his generation. His many admirers have included David Gascoyne, David Lodge and JG Ballard. The collection *Bleecker Street* (Carcanet, 1980) sealed Reed's burgeoning distinction as a truly original voice, and Eric Gregory and Somerset Maugham Awards followed suit. His *Selected Poems* were published by Penguin in 1987. Reed is also the author of legion pop biographies, poetry translations and novels, his most recent being the dystopian *The Grid* (Peter Owen Ltd, 2008). Reed's two most recent collections are both with Waterloo Press: *West End Survival Kit* (special commendation for 'Blake' in the 2009 Forward Prize) and *Black Russian — Out-Takes from the Airmen's Club 1978-9* (2010).

Spread Betting

It's like spread betting what I do with words
impacting car-chase imagery
into blue chip investment poetry.
Alan socks away shares in drug Giants,
Psifer's blue diamond, and he tastes it too,
Viagra's rocket-booster energy

on rainy Sundays, pops the bubble pack
for the polymer coated time-release.
I manage my portfolio of lines
back to a wall writing outside to track
the city's Soho clued-up energies,
no money in my empty writing hand,

my DNA strips coded on the page
as work inked to a blue smudgy tattoo.
Once I worked at the Dilly, pulled a man

out of the crowd, my looks sold every time
to feed a habit — mainlined poetry,
the risk addictive, like the dopamine

flooding my brain on the station's concourse
or up above on the explosive street,
twenty minutes, my head starting to spin,
I mean somehow a poet's got to eat.
I'd do it all again, collect the light's
slow dazzle, ripped over the Haymarket

to a slashed strawberry-purple sunset,
subvert the State to get a line come right.
Alan bets on megas — Glaxo Smith Kline,
Johnson & Johnson, it's his voodoo lounge,
and tends a deep burgundy cyclamen
the way he does a friend with little cares

accumulating to a shared index
of stabilising trust. It's one with me
to give my poetry like blood, sit out
soaking up West End atmosphere all day,
compressing bits I see into a mood,
the things I do and still they never pay.

Sally Richards

Sally Richards' poetry has appeared in the journals *Awen, Carillon, Cauldron, Countryside Matters, Country and Border Life,* Dogma Publications, Earlyworks Press, *Chimera, The Journal, Monomyth, Orbis, Poetry Express, the Recusant, the Shropshire Star, Splizz, The Strix Varia, Touchstone,* Warminster Community Radio (WCR) (featured poet). She was shortlisted in the Earlyworks Press 2006 national poetry competition and subsequently published in *Routemasters & Mushrooms* (Earlyworks Press 2006), and won third prize for her poem 'Steep Hill' in the *Carillon* magazine 2007 Open Poetry Competition. Publications: *Waiting for Gulliver* (with Steve Mann; Caradoc Publications 2005), *Stained Glass* (Survivors' Press, 2007), *Sally Richards — The Bards No. 22* (Atlantean Publishing, 2008), *Through the Silent Grove* (Masque Publishing, 2008). She has a regular poetry column in *Country and Border Life* magazine and has recently composed commissions for the Montford Church Flower Festival, and Shrewsbury Library as a Poetry Champion (Shropshire County Council Library service).

Welfare

How well can we fare — these days? Not well
now well at all,
not at all well, or fair, for some.
Who has the right to decide the way one person's life should be?
Poverty or plenty? ....

'Get them back to work!'
Tactics known only too well in 2006:
Employment, by DHSS, of the Gestapo-tactic-interrogator,
he who smiled, lulled
unsuspecting incapacitated woman — honest, genuine,
into false sense of security. She smiled, chatted,
when suddenly the metal fist, slammed down,
his eyes ripped her gentle heart,
his words stung her aching body
on and on, questions, tricks, tactics...

her tired mind battered by un-truths

Tears rolled, as un-justice followed lie, lie followed barrage,
"How far?" ... *"How long?"* ... *"When?"* ... *"Where?"* ... *Why????*
Too many questions for depressive, M.E.-battered-brain
to cope ... synapses would not compute — muddled responses
fuelling his conviction.
Please believe me, (her silent desperation)
He did not — that was not his brief,
rather to remove, in one fell swoop, those
on incapacity benefit, by any means.

Integrity questioned ....
words twisted, mind confused — relentless games continued ....
"Incredulous she left the room, tearful, weak,
to wait for her friend,
who, like her, was left shell-shocked —
PTSD, anxiety, and depression,
no boundary for the interrogator's torture.
He was left in flashback, on the examination couch,
a tearful, traumatized, shell...

Who picks up the pieces?
Who supports?
Who cares?

Then the letter — *all disability allowances stopped! Forthwith!*
End of, no money, nothing, not a penny, zilch, big fat nothing ....
except the road to poverty ....
And now more to come... other genuine people to face indignity,
pain, suffering:
Welfare? ... Or war fare? ...

Professor Tudor Rickards

Tudor Rickards PhD was born in 1941 in Pontypridd, Wales. He was educated at Pontypridd Boys' Grammar School and the University of Wales at Cardiff, where he studied Chemistry. He worked in the R&D department of Unilever Laboratories, based in Port Sunlight, Merseyside. Books include: *Problem Solving Through Creativity* (Wiley, 1974), *Dilemmas of Leadership* (Routledge, 2006), *The Routledge Companion To Creativity* (2008). In 1999 he co-founded the academic journal, *Creativity and Innovation Management*. He is Alex Osborn Visiting Professor at State University of New York, Buffalo. Rickards is a pioneer of the 'Manchester Method' — the system of creative and applied learning championed by Manchester Business School, where he is Professor of Creativity and Organizational Change.

This is Not Right
Adapted from 'The Mermaid Weeps'

This is not right
Nothing computes
Skin stretched lampshade tight

Where waves once lapped
At Heaven's gate
Waves lap no more

This is not right
No balm for chapped lips
At a silenced spring

Sharing our fears
A mermaid's cheeks
Are wet with tears

In the darkling night
No hope then
That can't be right.

Colin Campbell Robinson

Colin Robinson was born in Manchester on 7 March 1953. He emigrated to Australia in 1962. A writer and social activist on issues such as homelessness, mental illness and poverty. Poems have appeared in journals such as *Meanjin, Mattoid, Poetry Australia, Poetry Scotland, Aesthetica* and *Ancient Heart.* Robinson is currently working on a book on the experience of homelessness in contemporary Britain, for which he will be visiting towns up and down the East Coast line between London and Edinburgh to gather material.

Holes

Holes in Blackburn Lancashire
holes in my shoe
holes in the holy trust we need
to hold each other firm

all is holes

the bullet holes of sly revenge
the holes riven through each child's life
the holes in the facile arguments
of men who have no love

holes in Muirhouse
holes in my clothes
holes in everything
no future anymore

(God save who?)

and yet there is a rumbling
which might become a symphony
and the holes will be gossamered

with the strength of strings

let the Orchestra of the Everyday People play
and save our soul

(may
well
we fare)

Lucius Rofocale

Lucius Rofocale lives near London, UK. He has been published in *Alternative Reel, Underground Voices, ditch* and other journals.

Intercourse

Fashionable scandal
lurid lips licked fidgeting broadsheets negotiated power plays
assemblies antiseptic word and image translated hypertext unearths
the birth of winter —
bygone years of colour
dying in modern invention
cursed customs attaching themselves to poems artful eyebrows
hung on tears
the backlash of boredom bleeding
indulgent audiences councils pretending balance
blue feet fixed upon the shoulders of fictions skulls hollowed
yellow
the barren moist intercourse of pale corpus
memories murdered and tossed as stones.

Shake!

Shake body window mannequins. Shake maracas and tambourines. Shake...something. Salt shakers. Movers and Shakers. Decision makers. Politicians. Executives. Shirts starched stiff. Lunches. Networking brunches. Networking networks. Myspace. Facebook. Twitter. Eyes down in blackberries. The blacker the berry the more vanilla the user. Pink or brown? Brown or pink? All are consumables. Genital product placements. Bargain basement prices. More wine Sir? Sir, more Beaujolais? Sir demands servility. Red, raw knees. Bleeding blemishes like blood oranges. Remember them? Soft baby-skin dribbling ruby citrus juices. Staring at mother's legs. Legs eleven! Bingo! Bingo! Bingo! A location lottery. A Postage stamp lottery. The National lottery. The genetic Lottery! Inheritors of power. Entitled Eton boys. Licking blue rictus lips with yellow lies.

Captain Britain is Dead

Kiosks deserted
machines taking notes
tracks
subways
cyber-bureaus
stragglers imbibing government black trade narcotics
sweat
tickets with no change
no change
unauthorised transaction please see your...
 no words for this in the dictionary the thesaurus escapes me o
save me!
juices gas myth dirt excrement
zombie soldiers with super-serum-strength

Captain Britain is dead
tonight we pray as
rubber gloves strangle street urchins
slicing dicing cutting splicing
the construct of the grey flannel suit brigade

we are all cut anyway.

Michael Rosen

Michael Wayne Rosen was born on 7 May 1946 in Harrow. He is a broadcaster, children's novelist and poet and the author of 140 books. He was appointed as the fifth Children's Laureate in June 2007, succeeding Jacqueline Wilson, and held this honour till 2009. After graduating from Wadham College, Oxford, in 1969, Rosen became a graduate trainee at the BBC. Among the work that he did while there in the 1970s was presenting a series on BBC Schools television called WALRUS (Write And Learn, Read, Understand, Speak). He was also scriptwriter on the children's reading series *Sam on Boffs' Island*. In 1974 *Mind Your Own Business*, his first book of poetry for children, was published. On 18 November 2008, he was presented with the Chevalier de l'Ordre des Arts et des Lettres (Knight of the Order of Arts and Literature) by the French Government.

Getting things done

Good evening
You've probably heard a lot recently
about outsourcing.
And cutting back on the public sector.

Health, Education, Social Services
are all getting a taste of the real world:
where it's you the people who choose
you the people who drive up standards
where he who pays the piper

picks the packet.

Er...Ahem

Now here's more good news:
the bracing breeze of business is going to
hit the biggest and oldest feather bed of them all:
the law.

We here at Just-So
provide
solid
reliable
and fair
justice.

Our judges
are trained by the world's top legal eagles
Whether you're
in the dock
the witness box
or just watching
you'll know you'll be in safe hands
with a Just-So judge

No more of that futile, interminable
Q and A for defence, then over to the prosecution
and all the way back again.
Just-So judges cut to the chase:
Guilty? Or not guilty?
If the plea is guilty, the case is over.
Bang him up.
If it's not guilty,

Just-So says, 'Prove it. You've got five minutes.'
We guarantee:
no Just-So case lasts longer than an hour.
Great justice. Great value.

And while we're talking futile and interminable
what could be more futile
or more interminable
than the old dusty jury system?
That malarkey came in round about the same time
Alfred was burning the cakes, for goodness sake.

Well,
we've done a systems analysis on jury service
and I can tell you straight
there is no greater drain on the public purse.
Not any more
Just-So judges ARE the juries.
We don't cut corners. We cut the cackle.

Just-So
We're on your case.

The Big Society

Hello, could I talk to you for a moment?
No? Fine, have a good day

Hello, could I talk to you for a moment?
No? Fine, have a good day.
Hello, could I talk to you for a moment?
Oh great.

I won't take long.

Have you heard of us?
We're 'Help-someone-with-a-broken-leg.com'

Can I ask, have you ever broken your leg?
No?
Do you know anyone who's broken a leg?
Right, yes, I think we probably all do, don't we?
But the thing is, what do we do about it?

Times are tough.
Can I ask, do you have health insurance?
You don't.
And is there a hospital near you that you're eligible
to use?
No?
Well, there you are, you see.
That's why you or someone you know
might find that you'll need to turn to
'Help someone with a broken leg.com'

Do you know we help over 5,000 people a year
who have broken legs?
(Sorry? You want to know:
What about the other thousands of people who break their legs?)
That's a very good question.
Well, some people can of course afford health insurance.
There are the church hospitals that cater for the least fortunate
in the Big Society and three cheers for them, eh?
But if it wasn't for the likes of...
(sorry? No, OK, I don't know exactly how many people
that leaves out)

…mm? yes,
it's true we do have to turn some people away.
Why? you ask. Well, that's a very good question,
You see, some people have the wrong kind of broken leg.
One wrong kind of broken leg is people who've broken their leg
before.
We have a one-hit policy in this charity, so that our help
can spread to the most number of people.
We also specialise.
Specialism means quality, we say.
And we specialise in the kind of broken leg
where the crack in the leg goes across the leg
and not down the leg.
Down-leg cracks, as we call them, will eventually heal
themselves, is our expert view on the matter
OK, there may be a few months out of action
and the mend may not be perfect
but, hey who is perfect?
Not me, eh?

Whereas cross-leg cracks are in general much more serious
and I think you would agree.

It's our job to deal with the most serious first.

So, do you think you could see a way to supporting us?
We're giving away a free nurophen pill to every person
who contributes to our cause.
No?
Well, fuck you then
I always pop that in, because if you're not fucked over by us
then there's always someone else who will.
It's called The Big Society.

Guy Russell

Guy Russell was born in Chatham and now live in Milton Keynes. I've published poems, stories and reviews over the years in *Headlock, Scratch, Rialto, Smiths Knoll, Prop, Thumbscrew, New Statesman, The Interpreter's House* and most recently in *Troubles Swapped For Something New* (Salt).

Estates

So long our library, our swimming pool,
Our police. But that financial bloke's estates
Are growing — so it's not bad news for all —
With libraries, pools, and armed guards at the gates.

Philip Ruthen

Philip Ruthen's creative non-fiction *One Hundred Days War* is available on *the Recusant*, and a first collection of poetry, *Jetty View Holding* was published by Waterloo Press in 2008. He is currently Chair of Survivors' Poetry.

The State gave the children's' special minPencho to the municipal taxi company (Bulgaria 2005 ± UK 2015)

She knows it is a futile call.
Her child sways gently
Between four walls
The phone is answered, the conversation
Short, the operator
Slams the hand-piece down, immediately picks up
For the easier and lucrative —
Not the family's one free chance that month for respite —

Directs the people-carrier to collect the EU delegation wanting to
    survey
How disabled childhoods' miss the point, become too visible
In doorways of Apart-hotels where bottles slewing addicts' fumes
Indicate that where there is a life there is a way
To separate. When born, her child was dropped by medics' open
    hands,
A price too high to pay. She begs her neighbour one more time
To baby-sit and catch her infant's folding head
While she goes out to queue for bread,
The neighbour's 'yes' is fortunate,
And loathsome.

The UK's circumstances now transcribed
And officially reported
Lie on a desk
In Strasburg.

She did not return with food;
Her child joins empty bottles by the roadside.
If there is to be a next time
She will make sure there is
More money on the table.

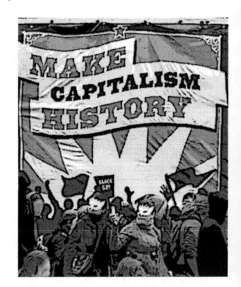

Clare Saponia

Clare Saponia was born in London on 11th April 1978. She has a linguistic background and has lived abroad for a large proportion of her time since 1998 — Heidelberg, Grenoble, Hanover, Heraclion, Brussels and the past four years in Berlin. Since returning to London last summer, she has been participating in Open Mic sessions at the Poetry Cafe on a regular basis.

For Embolism

It hadn't seemed particularly unusual
until he explained the mog bore the title
of embolism,

and probably became an embolism,
shacked up for posterity
on the twenty-sixth floor
with his manic-depressive Goth of an owner
and a neighbourhood of pit-bulls – though

I suppose
there wasn't anything particularly unusual
about that: the pit-bulls having mauled each other
and half of the juvenile population of the estate
were allegedly all born-again vegetarians
receiving regular blood transfusions and psychotherapy
care of Jobseekers' Allowance.
Moss Side had never seen such a fall in benefits claims.
The government celebrated.
The government started breeding pit-bulls
as part of its back-to-work-or-die scheme.
With a bit of luck they'd shift the debt by 2014;
be in the black

with enough spare cash
for ministerial pocket money and a £10 HMV voucher
for every A&E department, as a show of goodwill.

The suture business had never been so good;
the average waiting time now up to 5hr 19 min,
and that was Monday morning.

For Embolism, this was not such good news:
the Goth, for fear of losing his puss to the pit-bulls,
never let him stray beyond the grid of the balcony,
sunlight barred at each and every slit in the stonework,
'til the mog was forced to raid the bathroom cabinet
for anti-depressants,

a permanent supply of Kitty-Kat on tap
along with homo sapien mood swings
as black as his fur arrangement
being about all he had to look forward to.

Until the day he overdosed.
On Kitty-Kat.
Contracted a vicious strain of BSC
and committed Hara-kiri on the corner railing.
Not surprisingly the embolism vanished,
as did all the pit-bulls who dined at his expense.
The government mourned.

Kevin Saving

Kevin Saving was born and still lives in the Home Counties market town of Winslow. He trained as a psychiatric nurse at the University of Northampton. He has published two chapbooks, *A Brand of Day* (1994) and *Rough Bearings* (2005), and an e-book collection, *Miracle & Mirage* (Caparison, 2010). His work has been published in such diverse outlets as *Poetry Express, The Independent on Sunday, Krax, the Recusant, Poetry Review* and by The Happenstance Press. His poem 'Dog Otter' won third prize in the 2006 National Poetry Competition.

Coalition Blues
(To the tune of 'We Are Fred Karno's Army')

We are the Con-Dem nation,
We're starving ourselves rich-
We won't 'U-turn',
We'll crash and burn
(Or wind-up in a ditch).
Inflate the 'Big Society',
Roll out the Sacred Cow,
And thank your stars
The Banks are ours:
We're ALL Etonians, now.

Credit Cruncher

When by their income we're content
to judge a person's increment,
then one thing's surely evident:
our outcome must be excrement.

This Is Not Depression

No. This is not depression — the nightmare
miasma which infects each waking thought
with reparation's price: the limb we've caught
and must gnaw through to free us from its snare.

And this is no Depression. We declare
the market 'weak', watch dividends 'decay'.
Our grandparents knew Hardship in their day:
they would not think their world, and ours, compare.

We've fiddled whilst Rome burnt, and didn't care,
('Adversity's Old Serenade'). Our chins
are double, and they wedge cracked violins.
No: this is not depression. It's despair.

Mairi Sharratt

Mairi Sharratt was born in Inverness and brought up on the Black Isle, she now lives in Edinburgh with her husband and daughter and works in Public Relations and Public Affairs. She has recently been published in *Poetry Scotland* and *Popshot*. She writes a poetry blog *A Lump in the Throat*, which has received a Poetry Kit Award.

The Management of Hope

Rumours floated in the air
and settled in ink to spawn,
that the management of hope
was incompetent.

And so, it was sliced at,
cut chiselled and decapitated.
Leaving hope to gush, then
trickle out.

Newborns are the most saturated
and become drunk, vomit it
on their parents.
Curdled in their babies bile
it becomes a stain worrying
its way deep,
to deposit unnameable fears.

In the elderly
hope steadily leaks from
arthritic joints and ulcerated skin.
As they become desiccated by its loss
the vocal chords twang and snap.

Hope is also know to leak
after psychological shock or stress.
With the reservoirs showing cracked
whole neighbourhoods fall into despondency.
Mornings start flaccid and turn brittle
as the day fumbles and tries not to break down.

A black market in imported hope thrives,
with payment in kind accepted.
Silenced children droop behind
profiteers for a crumb.
Some devour, other save to share
with siblings who have none —
knowing, it cannot sustain them all.

Sam Silva

Sam Silva lives in North Carolina, USA. His poetry has appeared in legion journals including *Samisdat, Sow's Ear, The American Muse, St. Andrews Review, Dog River Review, Third Lung Review, Main St. Rag, Charlotte Poetry Review, Parnasus, Rio Del Arts, Megaera, Big Bridge, Comrade Magazine, Ken Again* and at least thirty others. Nine chapbooks published by Third Lung, M.A.F., Alpha Beat and Trouth Creek presses. These chapbooks were well received in newspaper reviews by Shelby Stephenson, Ron Bayes, Steve Smith, and the late poet laureate of North Carolina Sam Ragan, and solicited by Brown and Yale Universities for their libraries. Silva has a full length collection of poetry called *Eating and Drinking* based on a royalties contract signed with Bright Spark Creative.

All Of The Beauty Of The Ego

There was a time
in our great fraud
where the rich paid tribute
to the humanisms
born of God

...soon they buy their own disaster, though,
for which the poor must pay!

It happens here
it happens there
it happens in the bitter snow
with ideals bent
like snow mobiles
which transverse gutter-lives like ours.

"Democracy"
...a summer word

with which
the dog might fuck the bitch

...the freedom to do
as we have to do
and icicles might bloom as flowers
upon the frozen turd.

Sam Smith

Sam Smith is the editor of *The Journal* (once 'of Contemporary Anglo-Scandinavian Poetry) and the Original Plus poetry imprint. His poetry collections include: *pieces* (KT Publications), *Problems and Polemics* (Boho Bluechrome), *Rooms and Dialogues* (Boho/Bluechrome), *An Atheist's Alphabetical Approach to Death* (erbacce) and *apostrophe combe* (Boho/Bluechrome).

We All Swim In the One Sea

Psychiatry cannot be isolated
from the society it serves:
mental illness is a disease
primarily of the powerless,
even suicides seen as symptomatic
of sociological states, despair
as a statistic. Because someone
may be in hospital doesn't mean
that they are ill: often they are
assumed to be unwell solely because
they are in hospital. So do doctors
and nurses become accomplices to
insanity, reliant for a living
upon their own diagnoses.

Case Study

If, when he attacked his neighbour,
he had been tried for assault,
had paid his fine, done his time;
if his brother had told someone, then,
that the old woman next door
did persecute him, did
bang on the dividing wall, did lay
in wait and berate him, did pull faces,
make vile gestures at him every single time
she saw him passing her window; if his brother
had said that he too had seen this,
instead of saying that his brother had always
'taken things too much to heart';
then he wouldn't have been diagnosed initially
as suffering paranoid delusions
and placed on a Section. If
we had believed him when he quietly told us
how much the hospital beds were hurting his back
and if the doctors hadn't thought his anger
at being disbelieved a part of his delusion;
if we had paid more attention to his complaints
about the effects the neuroleptics were having on him
he wouldn't have tried to squeeze himself
through the first floor window; and if,
before he came back from the secure unit,
they had told us that two days previously
he had tried to strangle a woman he thought
'was about to attack me'; and if his brother
had said that he had phoned him every week
since his admission threatening suicide;
if we had understood what he meant when he said

that the fortnightly depots
were leaving him 'no future', that they wouldn't
let him 'have two thoughts together',
then maybe he wouldn't have been allowed
to proceed on weekend leave, to the same flat
beside the horrible old woman; and maybe
he wouldn't, within three hours of getting indoors,
have hung himself. Maybe.

Frustration upon Frustration

On the cusp between medicine and politics is a profession acting
like a science, but with so many variables that it has to — despite its
extensive, ever-inventive and all-encompassing terminology — be
bogus. For the foreseeable future, however, psychiatry will continue
to be the stopgap between the hocus-pocus of faith-healing
(unprovable, taken on faith) and a real working knowledge (this pill
taken, this happens). Note — faith-healing too blames the victim,
cure within themselves; so, should the victim fail to be cured, it has
to be their own fault. At its even best psychiatry can only provide the
disturbed with a temporary retreat, a sanctuary, can only give them
time away from their problems. Medication, alone, can be the retreat,
the shut-off sanctuary. But if the victim's circumstances aren't changed
— and psychiatry has no power to change them — then the afflicted,
victims of their own life, will again take into themselves its sickness.

Politics changes systems, changes societies. Psychiatry, therefore,
will only ever be allowed to treat the symptoms, will return its
patients, time and again, to the social and familial causes of their
illness. Nor is its twin, psychology, allowed to change the causative
circumstances, is able only to assist the afflicted towards an eventual
coming to terms with the causes of their affliction. The causes,
untreated, will remain.

Government & Being

If instinct is nature's intellect then human intellect is the recognition of cause and consequence, with theories built upon expectations, and — proven — the imposition of patterns. The more complex a pattern discerned, or invented, the more its veracity becomes a matter of faith. Wanting to have a faith is like wanting to be in love — to belong to another, something other, and thus be made complete, unquestioningly whole. Like a herd of wildebeest, or a shoal of fry, when stalked they compact — to lose their vulnerable individuality, to become a more imposing unity, to confuse by their mass. Not I! Not I! Government relies on this same fearful faith, on this gathering-together instinct for self-protection of the governed. Yet all that any government sees is only its own survival. Killing is a tool of government.

Stephen James Smith

Stephen James Smith was born in Dublin in 1982. He is a prolific performance poet having appeared in numerous festivals and an on radio reciting his work. He is the current Cúirt Literary Grand Slam Champion. His first book *Pretending to be Happy?* is forthcoming from the Galway based publisher, Maverick Press.

Signing Your Life Away 09/03/04

I just tried to sign on today,
you get that funny feeling
well, that you're throwing your life all away.
Let's speed up the natural process
I think I'm starting to decay.

I've been working shit jobs
since I was 14.
What have I got to show for it?
Nothing of commercial value,
should this make me want to scream?
I was told,
I'm 5 working weeks
away from receiving benefit!
Benefit, sure the only people
to benefit are the pigs in their suits
who can look down their noses
at me just for the hell of it.

They think I'm just another
Stereotypical statistic.
Well life, no it's not that simplistic,

& no I won't quit.

In the post today
came my P45.
After I spent most of my days
working in some dive.
But it's good to know
I'm still alive,

I'm still alive.

& the polluted air is free,
& I won't charge the trees
for my carbon dioxide,
maybe I'll dye my hair peroxide
then there won't be any place for me to hide
so let's go outside
& breathe in the cars
catalytic converter free carbon dioxide.

You never know,
it might just help us get high,
or help us get by,
or just help me to just fuckin' die,
ha, ha.
Well let's hope it helps us get high
for some day I know I'll die
but not today.

It's nice to know
that there's a somebody.
A Gerry Nobody,
like me
who knows what it takes,
to live life

&
not just exist!
'cause you can have all the wealth
in the world like Bill Gates,
but if you can't look to the sky & smile,
you have nothing!

The sky doesn't discriminate or hate,
it exists,
but makes life worth living.

So remember
next time you're kissing,
you're living & not existing.

& sure it's free
free as the sky.
& someday well we'll all bloody die
& discover any uncovered
Secrets about life.

& my rear,
will have a career,
sitting at the right hand
of God the Father for eternity
as I've earn it you see.

So just because I'm on the dole,
doesn't mean I've signed away my soul.

Peter Street

Peter Street was born in England 1948. He left school epileptic and barely able to read and write. An autodidact, Street worked in various jobs from gravedigger to gardener before breaking into poetry. To date has had three collections of poetry behind him: *Out Of The Fire* (Spike Books, 1993) (a Forward Nomination), *Still Standing* (TowPath Press, 1998), *Trees Will Be Trees* (Shoestring Press, 2001). In 2006 Peter was commissioned to write poetry for a Tony Bevan Catalogue, a way in, to Tony's paintings. His poetry has also been seen on television in Germany, Holland and here in England on both ITV and BBC. ITV made a twelve minute Remembrance Sunday Special about his time as a poet in 1993 during the Bosnian/Croat conflict. In 2008, Waterloo Press published his *Thumbing from Lipik to Pakrack — Selected Poems.* He lives and works in Atherton, Lancashire. He was the recent recipient of a grant from the Royal Literary Fund. He is currently working on a memoir, *To Wigan Via Reykjavik,* which is currently being serialised on *the Recusant.*

NHS Cuts

Taken twenty or so years
to start growing
our arms and legs on the stumps
from Thatcher's crude surgery
used on us manual workers
who nearly died from a lack of
anaesthetics, future and pride

So, we took out the stitches
like always adapted to the pain
threw away the crutches
became stronger; alright,

nowhere near the strength
we once where and then yes,
even our own Reds

tried to make us all the same
easier to control if we are all:
Educated, Educated Educated

with their words, books,
teachers, ways T.V. Radio
disappointed we all didn't fall for it

The Blue came back this time
bringing an anaesthetist and surgeon
dressed in Yellow that is until you
take him to the light

and he's really Blue.

David Swann

David Swann was born in Lancashire, and worked as a local newspaper reporter in the last days of hot metal. Later, he graduated to become a toilet cleaner at the legendary *Paradiso* night club in Amsterdam before returning to the UK to work as a Writer-in-Residence in a prison. Swann is now a senior lecturer in the English Department at the University of Chichester. His stories and poems have been widely published and won many awards, including five successes in The Bridport Prize. His debut collection of short fiction, *The Last Days of Johnny North*, was published by Elastic Press in 2006. *The Privilege of Rain — Time Amongst the Sherwood Outlaws* was published by Waterloo Press (2010).

Pass the parcel
For a prison yard cleaner

The cleaner pushes his barrow into the shadow
of the wing, picks up stuff other men have chucked:
Dear John notes; scooped-out oranges; the over-cooked
tea-time spuds they'd rather dump than swallow.

In yellow gloves, he'll clear the gutters of hair,
trace long strands of toilet roll along fences
to find the softest violence: shit parcels,
dense with unreadable messages.

The dead-eyed don't get it: *Volunteers*
to shovel our mess! At the skip, he tells me this:
freedom is a strange thing, you can be free in prison,
all drains lead to shining rivers.

Lost men's gifts rain into the yard — reasons
to leave his cell, walk through the wind, the sun.

Barry Tebb

Barry Tebb was born in Leeds in 1942. He studied English at Leeds Training College and sat at the feet of a series of Gregory Fellows in Poetry at the University of Leeds including Martin Bell, Peter Redgrove, Jon Silkin and David Wright. His first collection *The Quarrel with Ourselves* was praised by John Carey in *The New Statesman* and he appeared in *Children of Albion* (ed. Michael Horovitz), and in *Three Regional Voices* alongside Michael Longley and Ian Crichton-Smith. He edited *Five Quiet Shouters* which included work by the then unknown Angela Carter. In 1995 he founded Sixties Press and has edited the magazines, *Literature and Psychoanalysis, Leeds Poetry Weekly* and *Poetry Leeds*. He has published a novel, *The Great Freedom*, an autobiography, *Dancing to Nobody's Tune*, and several collections of poetry including *The Lights of Leeds* (Redbeck, 2001) and two Selected and a Collected Poems. Tebb also co-edited the 2004 anthology of Gregory Fellows poetry (Sixties Press) and edited and selected the major anthology *Orphans of Albion — Poetry of the British Underground* (Sixties/Survivors' Press, 2006; 2nd ed. 2010).

To Leeds Big Issue Sellers

When I come from the Smoke to visit my son on the ward

I see you everywhere: by the station, by the neon sign of 'Squares'
By every shopping mall. Leeds seems to have more of you than
    anywhere:
How do you stand there for so many hours in freezing winds
When most you solicit hurry by, saying to themselves, as do I,
'Charity begins at home' when you so often have no home?
I tend to give my change to the desperate, silent huddled in
    blankets
When all the warnings say I shouldn't but who's to judge
The deserving from the addicted?
Who but God can justly judge
My feeling is we all must learn to give.

Asylum Seekers

I think of Harold Wilson's statue in Huddersfield Station
Caught striding forward, gripping his pipe in his pocket,
Hair blowing in the wind.
could we but turn that bronze
To flesh I would have asked him to meet the two
Asylum-seekers I met in Huddersfield's main street
And asked directions from. "We are Iranian refugees",
They stammered apologetically. "Then welcome to this country."
I said as we shook hands, their smiles like the sun.

N.S. Thompson

N.S. Thompson was born in Manchester in 1950. He worked in Italy for several years as the curator of Casa Guidi, the Florence home of Robert and Elizabeth Barrett Browning. His publications include *Chaucer, Boccaccio and the Debate of Love*, several chapbooks of poetry and a full-length collection, *The Home Front*. Thompson's *Letter to Auden* has just been published by Smokestack Books.

Rehabilitation

'the principles remain those first worked out in the mental hospitals themselves'

Royal College of Psychiatrists, 1991

They put them in a little flat,
  Top floor, a halfway place
Supposed to lead them to the wide world that
  Neither knew how to face,

Both banged inside in '41,
    Shocked by the bomb that fell
And no one left to care for them. All gone.
    No family. Just as well...

To see how they were treated then
    Being able bodied, made
To act as cleaners, cleaning out the pen
    That held them. So they paid

The price for trauma and the years
    Went, regulations came,
And from young skivvies they became old dears
    And who is there to blame?

They keep the flat so spotless it
    Would put to shame the ward
The mental nurses bullied them to spit
    And polish for the Board

(When Board it was). Now down the pub
    They have a drink or two.
Back home, down on their knees, they scrub and scrub...
    But it will never do.

The Rap

Kicking empty Coke cans with dilapidated airs,
Franklin's gang and Winston's stalk foul pavements, scrawled on stairs,

Past graffiti graveyards tumbling down from high-rise flats,
Spray-canned language suicidally ending in KER-splats,

Breast eyes goggling bearded similes, innocent of Magritte,
Mel and Sal's UNI-TED spanning hoardings down a street.

Slick promotion hides the queues JOBCENTRES minimize,
Cutbacks to the bone, the NHS bled, slowly dies...

Intercity, Citylink team up with Parcelforce,
Boxed in punchy compounds advertising will endorse.

Credit squeezes shopping malls, while one more bank goes bust,
City regulators finding too much put in trust.

Franklin's gang and Winston's see no prospects any day,
Smoking ganga, thinking... Can they find a job? No way.

Steve Thorpe

Steve Thorpe was born in 1964 and is a sufferer of Bipolar Disorder for many years. Some of his poems have previously appeared in *The Hats We Wear/Blank Versing the Past* (Waterloo Press/ Sussex Partnership NHS Trust, 2009/10), an anthology of mental health service users in Hove. He is currently a mentee on the Creative Future mentoring scheme.

The Politics of Envy

What's the score?
Where's my dosh?
Where's my golden pay off?
(Doesn't matter who's in work
Or how many you lay off).

Privatise it
Sell it off
Give it to your mates
Make a killing while you can
Flog those silver plates.

Bankers 'grow' their bonuses
While the poor can rot.
Seems to me the onus is
Based on what you've 'got'.

'Britain isn't working'
Used to be the Tory cry —
It isn't bloody working now
And I can tell you why:

Rich kid in the classroom
Sent to 'public' school
Really thinks he's special
Predestined to rule.

'Toffo' in his best suit
Wants to see some 'change' —
I think his British bulldog's
Finally got the mange.

Vote for me I'm ready
(To start to coin it in),
I'm whiter than a Persil wash
Put on an extra spin.

Never doubt my principles
And never doubt my 'mission',
I'm not as devious as all that,
I'm just a politician.

Work Will Set You Free

Listen mate
I've paid my stamp
For fifteen years
Into your bottomless pit

'Welfare to work'
Is not the issue
It's all a tissue
Of lies

And 'trickle down'
That never really does.

Syrupy words
Catch poverty's flies
On papers
All owned by the big
'M' —
They have us 'foxed'
But I'm *not* loving it.

Gatekeeper journalists
Keep their buttery jobs
Right-side up;
Thanks to them
There are no stains of blood
Upon the carpet...
Only the stains of
Society's bloodletting
As curdling screams of pain
SHOOT
With e-mail speed
Across the sky.

Has so little really changed
In seventy years or so?

Is the victim to be punished
Once again
For not believing

ARBEIT MACHT FREI.

Bethan Tichborne

Bethan Tichborne works for the student campaigning organisation People & Planet. She is a graduate of Oxford University in Philosophy and Modern Languages.

A Curse, from an Infant to a Politician

Kiss me again, and I'll suck out your soul
and spit it out, into some other mouth.

Where it will be clamped between gums
that can't afford any more teeth.

Where it will be squeezed between lips
that can't force out any more words.

Where it will be swallowed whole,
swill, indigestible in acid mucous,
and pass on, reborn, unchanged.

You piece of shit.

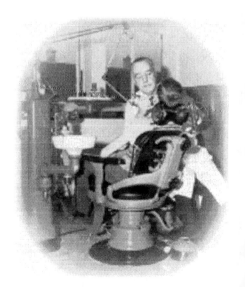

Xelís de Toro

Xelís de Toro was born in Santiago de Compostela, Galicia, in 1962. He is one of the leading Galician novelists of his generation and has won various prizes and awards for his fiction. His novels include: *Six strings and a Heart* (Xerais, 1989), *There Is No Mercy* (Positivas, 1990), *Terminal* (Positivas, 1990), *The Saltimbanchi In Paradise* (Sotelo Blanco, 1999), and *The Corunna Boats* (Infantil E Xuvenil, 2005). Children's books include: *The Trumpeter and the Moon* (Edebá-Rodeira, 1998) and *The Storytelling Machine* (Edebé-Rodeira, 2000), which have been translated into several languages. de Toro has written extensively in academic publications on Galician culture. He was a founding member of the publishing house Edicións Positivas and directed its cultural magazine *Anima+l*. He has recently edited a major anthology of short stories by Galicia's leading writers, *From the Beginning of the Sea* (Foreign Demand, 2008), a project from the collective Boca2mouth, published in English. de Toro lives in Brighton, England.

Untitled

Now that you have mastered
the art of breathing
and control the air
and are able to articulate sounds
in order to utter words

Tell us
what was that important thing
you had to say
Tell us

Can you deliver words sharp as razors
to cut through the thickness of infamy
could you slice in-
from injustice

Tell us
what was that important thing
you had to say
Tell us

Could you do it
before your last breath
before your last words

Telling mouths

I would like to
Add my silence
To a long tradition
Of quietness
To the space filled with absence
But by an error,
An act of uncanny consequences
I was given a mouth
A mouth to tell
To tell a mouth

Lee Whensley

Lee Whensley was born 7th December 1972 in Darlington (Greenbank Maternity hospital — the same as Vic Reeves), but he has always lived slightly further north. He is currently working on a novel, *The Storyteller*. He is involved with a poetry forum site *Got Poetry*.

Backwards To the Future: A Tory Story

Please, sir — could you spare me a Beveridge?
Or perhaps just a small bite to eat?
Time's is hard for we 'poor but loyal'
Some is starved, some lives on the street
I don't mean to be petulant, nor offend in any way
But could you spare a moment
To hear what a hungry tongue may say?
Perhaps if you'd bear with me and heed my tale of woe
You'd spare me some of your spare change, before you choose to go.

You see; a one eyed pirate tyrant once addressed a flailing nation
Two Princes were in waiting, at Big Brother viewer's voting station,
They paced behind their podiums in P.R staged debates
Who would have the 'X Factor' in their plans to run the state?
'It will be tough', they all agreed, 'to restore the economy'
'We must make cuts to stop the rot and secure our recovery'
Blue and Yellow told us, throughout the fashion parade
That the whole thing, in the first place, was through mistakes that
      Labour made
'Expenses rows' forced future vows, while crime and immigration
Were the issues that most concerned the voting population.
But the trial by jury spectacle, so called 'democracy'
Ended with a three way split- without majority
Those in suits soon rallied 'round: a show of unity

And, to avoid a re-election, blue and yellow made a deal
(Though the electorate had made it clear — the message was
    dissent
Surely its vote was a rope 'round the throats of a hung parliament?)
So we was back to Victorian values and defending of the realm
The Good Ship of Attrition with Cameron at the helm
They said our lives was luxury, so they upped the V.A.T
We was taxed back to the blacklists and abject poverty
While public schoolboys hunted, amidst the howl of hounds,
And any that stood in their way was soon ran to ground
I woke up one fine morning: Why I thought the pits had closed!
I thought,
Have I stepped into a time warp?
Am I again a slave in training while living on the dole?
Education, health and welfare were targets of their war
As we fell backward to the future — the poorest needing ever more
On a Dickens of a diet, stale bread and stagnant water
Belt buckles scraping spinal chords
To feed our sons and daughters

While a 'coalition' government-— Conservative the rule
Were supporting those with wealth to burn
Within the House of Fools
And little Liberal lapdogs, lapped on laps of luxury
They had caught the scent of power and sold out every policy...

So, please sir, do not pass me by— please hear my pleas for alms
I'm a ragamuffin ruffian, but I don't mean you no harm.
I just needs an opportunity — a leg up from the grime
My postcode and my heritage have been my only crimes.

Julie Whitby

Julie Whitby is a widely published poet, with appearances in *the TLS, the Independent, the Daily Express, Ambit, Country Life, Poetry Review,* etc. and in various anthologies. *The Violet Room* (Acumen, 1994) was her acclaimed debut collection; a second volume, *Poems for Lovers* (Agenda Editions) appearing in 2001. Trained as an actress, she has worked in theatre and on TV: recently she gave three broadcasts for the BBC in connection with *Poems for Lovers.* She is the widow of poet and critic Derek Stanford, whose death last year was marked by obituaries in *the Guardian* and *the Independent.* She is currently working towards her Selected Poems which are forthcoming from Waterloo Press.

"The Big Issue"

"Don't hurry by, sweetheart,
we're all in the same boat."
But that's just what I did;
and his words have harassed me
like a crossly dripping tap,
the beating of an ant-ridden drum,
intimating, presaging
worse things to come.
"We're all in the same boat.
Don't hurry by, sweetheart."

Brenda Williams

Brenda Williams was born in Leeds in 1948. After beginning to write poetry in early 1983, she staged a number of protests at Leeds and Oxford Universities, one of which was profiled by *The Times Higher Education Supplement*, under the title 'Well-Versed Protester'. Her poems have been published extensively in newspapers and International magazines. Her first major work was *Death and the Maiden*. She is currently working on her largest undertaking yet, *The Pain Clinic*, a five hundred sonnet sequence. Her *Collected Poems* have recently been published by Sixties Press. She lives, writes and campaigns in London.

Gin Lane
To whom it may concern

As you walked down through Hampstead Green you left
A scene behind that brought to mind Hogarth's
Gin Lane, you with your tanked-up swaggering
And your shored-up bottom of the bottle
Gait, sure and polar blue as the skies, your
Gaze. Did your eyes read them before you ripped
Them down? Gertrude, 'In Memoriam' how
Far did she get to you, as near as you
Would get to her, near enough to rip her
From the railings, leaving the fastenings,
The placards strewn underfoot in the Lane,
And a sheer and distant apprehension
That would never ever leave me again.
We thought you were catastrophically
Drunk, so high, you were veering on the edge
Of the sky, threatening to emblazon
The Green with the football regalia
And insignia of your team, asking
All the while, insisting on an answer,
And that the God-given right to protest

Was a personal affront to himself,
And to the ordinary decency
Of the honest working man in the street
Or anyone left in the Lane to meet,
Where poetry and free speech were in vain,
Where Gertrude would never be seen again.
Within moments of entering the Lane
You walked away from your own inferno
And the only thing I could remember
After were your eyes of Aryan blue
Empty and impenetrable before
Me and yet faint and unseeing,
Locked fast against an evening's lowering
May light recoiling suddenly away
From you, as though sucked in then and there in
A tsunami's waiting receding tide.
So young, your words were quaintly old-fashioned,
The placards in the Lane 'a carbuncle'
And an affront to the environment,
To all who live to work, his argument.
This side of time, for the unwarranted
And intrusive tampering with the dead,
There is a price on the head of those who
Fall most foul, that is uncollectable,
For your clicking little Nazi-licking
Life, the unredeemable sacrifice
Of your soul, whether you end or begin,
A primal clockwork man, tanked up on gin.
This side of life, in the din, the nearest
I ever got to a Nazi was him,
Bandy-legged with the cock-of-the-walk stride
Of the recalcitrant habitual
Criminal as you turn about and square

Up to God or man or anything else
On either side as you pass on your way
Furtive, uneasy in the dark of May.
The very cauldron of a volcano,
Mouthed in hell, atomic in night shadow,
A use of language nothing can assuage
'To work', 'to live', the mantra of an age.
After so long I can no more renege
On the protest than I can walk away
From poetry or the torn and worn strands
In the weft and woof of the bewildered
Heart and accustomed grown to the long drawn
Burden of loss that is both piecemeal and
Gratuitous and always beyond its
Own reach or horizon. There is only
The spirit's proof to pit against language
And industrial death on history's page.

28th May 2010

Gwilym Williams

Gwilym Williams was born in 1948. He currently lives in the baroque city of Vienna, Austria. His poetry has appeared in *Poetry Salzburg Review, iota, Pulsar, Poetry Monthly, Current Affairs* and *ink-sweat-and-tears* as well as in the Ragged Raven Press anthology, *The White Car.* He has also reviewed for *New Hope International* and *Pulsar.* Poetry collections: *Mavericks* (Kitchen Table Publications, 2007) and *Genteel Messages* (Poetry Monthly Press, 2008), which was selected as *Purple Patch* Best Collection 2008.

Between port and cigars

I say, Cedric
it's been far too long

said the politician
to his friend
tap-shackled to the members-bar

all this free of interest
skittles and beer

and all at the tax-payer's expense

one's only got to look at one's surveyors of pavements

those slack-jaw skitterbrains
permanently sozzled under the old sky-lantern

the old main-brace immer well spliced

always turning up to sleep-it-off
in our shop doorways

and always in and out of the slammer

the slibber-slabber slack-jaw snivellers
and squint-minded slingers of snot
the splay-mouthed smokers of sotweed

so why don't they just go

through to the last stitch

stick their spoons in the wall?

spirit of Dunkirk and all that!

that'd save us some brass

and save us some soup
and save us some time
and save us some trouble

and save us
and save us
and save us

and yet again

save us

Rodney Wood

Rodney Wood lives in northeast Hampshire and has recently been spending his time writing poems about gigs — everything from thrash metal to Tibetan monks — that he's seen at the local arts centre. His work has appeared in many magazines, including, this past year, *nthposition*, *Stride* and *Sunk Island Review*.

Church of the Apocalypse

Generals are driven across the tourist-
haunted Thames, through the streets of a city
that is already dead. They read financial
pages, get off on profits and want
to get ahead whatever the cost. Their aim
is world domination with magic words
like collateralised debt obligations, sub-prime,
deleveraging, securitisation, derivatives, special
investment vehicles and grade ratings.
Everyone looks the wrong way except city
churches that protest that the Generals
don't believe in sharing, want too much attention,
wear too many clothes and have lost their wings.
The spires all point to heaven and raise their fingers
like a host of Pre-Raphaelite Christs.
Night comes and it's all gone wrong. The Generals
have lost the war; are pensioned off, cry and pull their hair
like children at a circus when the performers have gone.

Ken Worpole

Ken Worpole is one of Britain's most influential writers on architecture, landscape and public policy issues. He has an Honorary Doctorate from Middlesex University, and is a Senior Professor at The Cities Institute, London Metropolitan University. He has served on the UK government Urban Green Spaces Task Force, and has been an adviser to the Commission for Architecture and the Built Environment (CABE) and the Heritage Lottery Fund. He is author of numerous books including *Here Comes the Sun: architecture and public space in 20th century European culture* (Reaktion Books, 2000). Worpole also edited *Richer Futures: Fashioning a new politics* (Earthscan, 1999) and the modern classic study of working-class literature, *Dockers and Detectives* (reissued by Five Leaves, 2008).

The Philanthropists in White Trousers

As darkness descends
So do the Council painters
All robed in white
They lower their cradle
Pulley by pulley
End by end unevenly
A contraption of wood and ropes:
The gods in the machine
Have descended to earth

With embarrassed gestures
Taking advantage of the dusk
They discard and secrete
Their celestial white apparel
In a wooden hut of pots and brushes
And disguised as mortals
Disappear into the crowds
Hurrying home from work

Their mission secret
Their traditions philanthropic

By early morning
Their work is done
They count their numbers
And ascend to heaven

The Jugglers

Three demolition workers
Stand in a line
At levels of descending height
On a stage construction
Of scaffolding, wood and canvas
Designed by Meyerhold
Passing bricks and stacking them

Throwing and catching
With easy movements
These powdered jugglers
Wreathed in smoke
Feint false throws
And counterfeit drops
For their passing audience
They laugh a lot

For theirs is the last act
Of the old production
The props come down behind them
Ready for a new construction

Dan Wyke

Dan Wyke was born in 1973 and grew up in Cranleigh, Surrey. He spent two years living in Verona and Rome before returning to London to study English at Queen Mary and Westfield. He moved to Brighton in 1996 where he completed an MA in Twentieth-Century Poetry at the University of Sussex. His poetry has appeared in a wide range of publications, including *Oxford Poetry, Thumbscrew, The Rialto, The London Magazine, the Spectator* and *the Times Literary Supplement.* He received an Eric Gregory Award in 1999. A pamphlet, *Scattering Ashes,* was published by Waterloo Press in 2004. His first full volume, *Waiting for the Sky to Fall,* was published by Waterloo Press earlier this year. He currently lives in Brighton with his wife and daughter, where he works as a counsellor and manages a rehabilitation project for Age Concern.

Approaching the Sixteenth Winter under a Conservative Government

Here's something to remember:
pay your gas bill by December.

1996

"I wrote this squib (during, I think, one of my periodic immersions in the work of William Carlos Williams) as the last exclusively Tory government came to an end. I remember it being in response to a news item but can't say exactly what now. What I can remember from that time was the feeling of poverty — both materially and spiritually — that had seeped into so many people's lives after such a long period of right-leaning politics. My response to the 're-election' of the Conservatives was one of horror and fear. In some respects, the Budget has confirmed those feelings. I am concerned about people ending up unsupported by the State but what I dislike most about it is the message of austerity and tightness it is trying to promote. My concern is that this appeals to many people (often those who can afford to tighten their belts) which then gets translated into an overall lack of meanness and generosity both in the imagination and crucially towards other people. It's not difficult to see how over time this attitude might lead us straight back to where things ended up in the mid-nineties". D.W.

Tamar Yoseloff

Tamar Yoseloff was born in the US in 1965. Her most recent poetry collection is *Fetch* (Salt, 2007). She is also the author of *Marks*, a collaboration with the artist Linda Karshan, and the editor of *A Room to Live In: A Kettle's Yard Anthology*. Her fourth collection, *The City with Horns*, is due out from Salt in May 2011.

The New Loss

'the art of losing isn't hard to master' — *Elizabeth Bishop*

It's like she said: first door keys and watches,
then houses, countries, loved ones.
Predictable, certain, even necessary;
just what happens in the course of an everyday life.

But here is the company wiped from NASDAQ,
the plane slipping off the radar,
the village removed by one smart bomb,
all in a blink on the screen, something which occurs

in two dimensions, somewhere distant, to someone else
until it occurs to you. It's not personal,
you are simply a statistic, one of millions
who has lost his savings, his home, his job.

It is viral, tells you that you have lived beyond your means,
that you are not who you thought you were, that you will die,
which you already knew, but on the way
there are new ways of breaking you until you give in.

And you go back to wanting that first lost thing, precious
only to you, whatever it was, a doll, a lucky charm,
and you will take it and close yourself in a room
you can no longer occupy, painted yellow, sky blue.

Afterword
The Autumn of Capitalism

The following is a parallel dialectical overhang from the Foreword and attempts to examine recent political and economic vicissitudes as graphic examples of the fundamental instability and profligacy of absolute capitalism, its ethical and practical bankruptcy, and its outdated and puritanical model of 'employment'. Again, the views expressed herein are exclusively those of the writer and do not claim to speak on behalf of the other 111 contributors to this anthology whom, though in support of the broad principles of this campaign, have varying individual opinions, the expressions of which are confined to their poetry contributions.

Max Weber's *The Protestant Work Ethic and the Spirit of Capitalism* is a brilliant exposé of the Calvinistic ancestry of our own masochistic British notion of 'work' as a necessary sacrifice in return for purely material reward (and if this national pathology were not so, we would not have such a resentful and begrudging 'taxpayer' culture). It has been entrenched in British society since the first mercantile classes emerged from the victorious Puritan ranks after the English Civil War. It is rather ironic that the *spirit* (a very deliberate choice of word by Weber) of capitalism should have been harnessed and disseminated by the Puritans. One of the chief contradictions of Puritanism was its strange marriage of austerity of worship, manifest in a pathological distrust of religious ostentation (thus its hatred of Roman Catholicism and its anthropomorphic crucifixes) with a virtue of thrift to the point of miserliness, and an instinct towards accumulation of property and capital through entrepreneurialism. Hence the contradiction of capitalism, which singularly allows, and encourages, the rapacious pursuit of individual financial gain; and yet on the other hand, glorifies thrift and tries to twist what are essentially atavistic instincts of self-interest and avarice into perverse virtues that it tries to make us believe benefit the rest of society by way of 'wealth creation'. The flaw in all this of course is that 'wealth creation' is rarely, if ever, redistributed downwards to those who have no capital. Instead, it is re-channelled through the economic bargaining tool of 'employment', whereby the 'wealth creators' invest their capital in hiring the labour of others to produce further profits for them, reimbursing their workers with a tiny percentage of the profit their labour produces; this 'wage' is traditionally tailored to provide only a sufficient amount of income each month to enable the employee to sustain a roof, clothes and sustenance, but rarely enough to enable them to buy their own property, or eventually transcend employment themselves. Thatcherism attempted to muddy that very paradigm while simultaneously intensifying it by allowing certain sections of the traditional working-class to buy their own council houses and gradually move into the ranks of the mortgaged *petit bourgeoisie;* at the same time, breaking any last vestiges of working-class solidarity (or 'class consciousness', as Karl Marx put it). But this proletarian diaspora was largely at the expense of vast sections of the country, in particular, the old industrial heartlands of the North, whose age-old mining communities were mercilessly condemned through mass pit closures. The contradictory character of capitalism then easily moves into the area of flagrant hypocrisy when it castigates any 'rogue' manipulators of its own agencies (many of whom are motivated more by the basic need to survive than by any sense of greed or avarice), betraying that such a fiscal system is unashamedly stacked in favour of those who already have capital. Thatcherism was — and still is, sadly — an odd ideological cross-stitch of sparring 'values': puritanical in its preoccupation with thrift, saving and investment, but shamelessly cavalier in its brutality towards the poor or to those who either refuse to capitulate to, or are incapable of emulating, the narrow capitalist mindset.

Poundheads and Cavaliers

The English Civil War parallels have been an ongoing historical meta-narrative since the dawn of Thatcherism over thirty years ago, but in too convoluted a sense to chart a clear dialectic. Suffice it to say, Thatcherism was a return to the original mercantile rise of the 1650s, a truncation of the more progressively egalitarian ideals promulgated — with very mixed results — by successive Labour governments from the late 1940s to the late 1970s, themselves descended from the early English socialist groups active between 1647-1651, chiefly the Levellers and the Diggers. But in time, during an epic term in office, Thatcher came to establish her monetarist 'values' as, in effect, a new fiscal aristocracy in the significantly augmented and untouchable new business classes and super-rich elites. Levelleresque discontents among the English Left split between those who foresaw how capitalism-accommodating the Labour Party was becoming, and detached themselves under the Militant Tendency banner (or rather, were expelled by N eil Kinnock); and the rest who, trying to keep the party faith, hoped that Labour would still eventually be able to supplant the attritions of Thatcherism. A key tragedy which truncated a gradual reformation of Labour from its then-perceived unreconstructed socialist stance under the highly intellectualised and principled Michael Foot, to a more moderate and electorally 'acceptable' party, was the sudden death of Kinnock's successor, John Smith — again something of a historical parallel with the sudden death of the reformative Leader of the Long Parliament, John Pym, during the infancy of the Civil War, in 1643. Both occasions opened the doors to more tactically abrasive leaders — Oliver Cromwell and Tony Blair — who both nursed in time deeply ironic antinomianisms. Neither Cromwell nor Blair were as much in opposition to as in *rivalry* with the prevailing orthodoxies of their respective times: Cromwell challenged the Divine Right of Kings with his own puritan-grown spiritual bigotry, while Blair offered a moderately more 'progressive' alternative to the Divine Right of Thatcherism, and after some time in power, showed his own religious hubris by colluding in the illegal invasion of Iraq, as if on the pretext of a modern Crusade (his placing himself at the forefront of Israeli-Palestinian relations today is another indication of his messianic delusions).

Blair turned out not to be the Trojan Horse for a long-term rolling back of Thatcherism that the Left had hoped, but more a stalking horse for what was essentially a continuation of Thatcherite ideas under a more smiley guise. He called his cross-party centrist politics the 'Third Way', championed under the banner of 'New Labour'; again, echoing titularly the Cromwellian epithets of 'New Model Army' and 'Commonwealth'. Whether or not a form of 'common wealth' is what both leaders aspired to, what they each actually achieved was a mere economic upgrade for the 'aspiring middle-classes' at the price of marginalising their grassroots: in Cromwell's case, the Levellers and disaffected radicals of the Roundhead ranks who had been led to believe that with the end of the monarchy would come a new age of egalitarianism; and in Blair's, the socialists and militants grown from Old Labour, who subsequently split into a confectionary of splinter factions including the Socialist Party, Socialist Alliance, Socialist Labour, Socialist Worker, Respect, the Scottish National Party and the Green Party. A diaspora of the Left in both instances. Once New Labour's Lord Protector was finally persuaded to resign, his covetous dynastic successor took over, more of the glowering puritan style Cromwell than his predecessor's ermine-furred one, in some senses autocratic and stubborn, but tinged with an indecisiveness that eventually helped to bring down both him and his government. Here, the nickname given to Cromwell's abjectly unsuccessful and swiftly deposed son and successor Richard Cromwell, alias 'Tumbledown Dick', suits our last Prime Minister very well: 'Tumbledown Brown'.

And so, finally, after thirteen years of wasted opportunity for true root-and-branch reform of our Thatcheritic society, of ideological dilution and acquiescence to an overly-accommodating 'alternative' to the Divine Right of Thatcherism, we have a Restoration of the old rival in the crowning of its landed heir apparent David Cameron, taking up the prime ministerial mantle with devastating inevitability. As with the returning monarch in 1660, the newly crowned Cameron is wielding marginally less power than his Tory predecessors, his hand forced to defer some aspects of policy-making to his Liberal Democrat coalition partners — although on the evidence so far, those of the Orange Book ascendancy to the Cabinet seem to be suffering identity crises; Danny Alexander, for example, appearing a little too eager in his role of Chief Fag to the Chancellor (the true Thatcherite heir).

So, whither does the country go from here? Well, in spite of the current rhetoric fashionable among the Government ranks of blaming all our financial woes solely on the previous government's fiscal malversation (borrowing during the boom and thus creating a massive deficit, in case you hadn't heard), such frantic attempts to distract the electorate from the true and incontrovertible cause of the recession will in time come to fall on deaf ears when the draconian austerity cuts begin to bite. The true cause of the present recession is the global culture of unregulated greed and avarice: absolute capitalism. In England, it was Thatcherism which first lit this touch-paper; and thirty years down the line, this country has finally been blitzed by its aftershock. Whichever governments were in power since is, in a sense, of merely incidental relevance: New Labour accelerated aspects of Thatcherism through increased privatisations and de-regulations, and the only difference in its approach to that of the more openly callous administration we presently have, was its almost tokenistic attempts to blunt the damage being done by the increased marketisation of society with intermittently progressive policies such as the minimum wage. Blair and Brown laboured under the misguided belief that they were manipulating capitalism towards social-democratic objectives, to the end of turning all of us into an 'aspiring middle-class'; but in reality, the market forces were manipulating *them* towards quite another scenario. There is no such thing as 'compassionate capitalism', nor is there such a thing as 'capitalist-accommodating' socialism — any truly socially progressive government has to face off the discredited notion that a society can prosper equitably when based entirely on the profit-motive. This is what makes Cameron's rhetoric so untenable: if we *were* 'all in this together' then this country would not even have a Conservative Party, since it is in itself the political custodian of class division. If one wonders at such a cynical take on Conservative politics, just take a look at the social and ethical mess of our society: the grotesquely vast disparities in wealth and poverty; the deification of third-rate 'celebrities'; the soap of reality TV and the tabloid turning of soap opera into reality with headlines about characters in *Coronation Street* as if they are real people we are intimately acquainted with; the obsession with multiple property ownership; the near-criminalisation of those forced to survive on benefits — and ask yourself, why on earth would anyone wish to *conserve* any of this? Of course, incredulous Marxists and socialist observers will be able to answer that with that special and vital cynicism which in part fuels left-wing idealism: because it suits capitalism to brainwash its populace with trash culture in order to keep them in their place. The 'Big Society' is a euphemism for 'the same old capitalist con-trick', only writ larger. And perhaps many of the last government saw all this coming: a new age of grab-all-you-can. Perhaps that was why many New Labour MPs milked their privileges while they could, choosing the last resort of behaving as capitalists themselves in the interests of lining their own nests before their inevitable tipping back into Opposition. The clear lesson from the last thirty years is that Thatcherism has failed disastrously, and that its fundamental faith, of absolute capitalism, needs urgent reforming, not to say, usurpation from the only viable economic and social alternative: democratic socialism. This is because, essentially, capitalism is intrinsically unstable, and is in its absolute form, in the view of this writer and many others, starting to gasp its last. If capitalism as an economic mechanism is a necessary evil, capitalism as an *ideology* is not: what is more, when applied ideologically, it is invariably vicious and socially devastating to those who either fail or refuse to capitulate to its behavioural dictat. In this writer's opinion, ideological capitalism is also in diametric opposition to the Christian ethics on which our society is ostensibly based. If that sounds hyperbolic, one only has to recall a remark once made by a young Labourite regarding what he perceived to be the incompatibility of Christianity and Conservatism: by the most unfortunate irony (and presumably in some kind of anti-Damascus moment), the orator, one Bernard Ingham, went on to become Margaret Thatcher's spokesperson.

Wealth and Hellbeing

It is the intrinsically classist nature of capitalism that is its fundamental Achilles' Heel and which makes any of its claims to be the only workable 'wealth creating' and socially mobilizing system seem specious in the extreme. Capitalism might 'work' for a minority, but for many it is dehumanizing in a gradual and corrosive sense, which, to touch on a deeply complex topic momentarily, also arguably induces — through its relentless pressures on individuals to live up to the spiritless automatonism demanded by industrial society of its labour forces — much of the 'mental illness' that necessitates so many to go onto Incapacity Benefit and Disability Living Allowance (DLA). It doesn't take an R.D. Laing nowadays to see how highly plausible it is that non-genetic 'mental illness' — from neurotic through to full blown psychotic disorders — are in part individuals' internalisations of the irrational, viciously contradictory, even schizoid 'values' of capitalist societies: as children, we are told to share; at school, that we are all equal; but once we become adults, we are encouraged to grab as much as we can and to perceive ourselves as superior to those who have less. All this ethical contradiction is recipe for psychic confliction in the sensitive mind. Capitalism's lack of toleration for financial and material 'failure' is particularly craven, and outcasts of the rat-race must, to paraphrase the bankrupt Dr Tertius Lydgate in George Eliot's *Middlemarch*, find some 'corner to crawl into and try to keep [their] soul[s] alive in'. Indeed, one might quite reasonably take the line of the recently late Clydeside trade union activist Jimmy Reid's prophetic assessment of the dehumanisation of capitalism back in 1972 when its ultimate manifestation, Thatcherism, was still just a glint in the milk-snatcher's eye:

Society and its prevailing sense of values leads to another form of alienation. It alienates some from humanity. It partially de-humanises some people, makes them insensitive, ruthless in their handling of fellow human beings, self-centred and grasping. The irony is, they are often considered normal and well-adjusted. It is my sincere contention that anyone who can be totally adjusted to our society is in greater need of psychiatric analysis and treatment than anyone else.

This coalition's unprecedented brinkmanship of a budget and general 'scorched earth' politics are rife almost daily with the worst types of political scaremongering one could imagine in a 'democracy'. In particular, Cameron's vicious witch-hunt of the poor and unemployed, the sick and mentally ill, by announcing plans to sub-contract private credit-checking agencies to hunt out any signs of 'benefit fraud' in claimants' spending patterns, and incentivising an overt scrupulosity in said agencies by offering them 'bounties' in return for their espionage, is beyond belief, and politically unconscionable in any 'democratic' government. But to come from the very one which has set out from its shambolic start to purport to a 'New Politics' and a dismantling of New Labour's surveillance state, it is also corruptly hypocritical.

The attrition on the nerves of this country intensifies by the day with new scare stories leaking out about work capability assessments of all incapacity claimants being even more draconian in methods than previously predicted — dystopian snatches such as 'docking points from amputees who can lift and carry with their stumps', as quoted by MIND in a recent circular, now abound. It is however disappointing that said charity is at the moment giving mixed signals by having awarded MIND Champion of the Year to controversial and outspoken psychologist Rachel Perkins, who has recently chipped in with unhelpful statements echoing the coalition's 'deserving/ undeserving benefit claimant' propaganda by, in this writer's opinion, atomistically manipulating the Health Through Occupation principle to score political points, in spite of contradictorily referring to her personal politics as more 'old' than 'New' Labour (such Labourite 'tough love' is very much in vogue now with the self-described 'leftie' Trisha Goddard characterising her daytime audience as sofa layabouts, the very underprivileged citizens commonly termed as *chavs* on whose exploitation her programme depends for both its subjects and audience):

Instead of talking about the right to work, we are now talking about the right to benefits. I don't think that's terribly healthy ...Every human being gains their self-worth from being able to contribute to their communities — and let's face it, the most socially sanctioned way to do that is with work. (quoted from an article in *Guardian Society*, 25th August 2010).

Note the dubious term 'sanctioned' here, and the ambiguous usegae of 'work' as opposed to 'occupation'. Here Perkins seems to be expediently toeing the contemporary line of atomist dogma, capitulating — whether through personal ideology or just professional pragmatism — to the intransigently utilitarian governmental command that only economically productive 'work' is 'sanctioned' as 'contribut[ing] to... communities'. So much for the new volunteering Big Society then, if its own apparatchiks don't even believe in it. Far more incisive is the following extract from an article in *the Morning Star* by Laurie Penny, which entirely chimes with the dialectics of this Afterword:

> Yes, there are more people receiving incapacity benefit now than there were a generation ago. No, this does not mean that all of the extra people are skivers who'd rather sit around watching Trisha and drinking milkshakes. The sweeping social changes that have transformed society in the past 50 years have led to an increase in the numbers of those deemed unable to work due to mental illness for many reasons. Not only has society become more treacherous and unpredictable and the working world more stressful, especially in stonkingly pro-market, anti-worker countries which exempt themselves from working time directives, but more men and women are expected to hold down full-time jobs which are increasingly focused in the service, information and fourth-sector industries, meaning that it's more important for these employees to be entirely mentally and emotionally on the ball.
>
> ('In need of a right-minded policy', 27th August 2010).

It is highly unlikely one will ever read such empathic polemic in any outlet of mainstream journalism bar *the New Statesman* to which, significantly, Penny contributes a weekly column. It is also extremely distressing to note that according to MIND: 'almost half of the 41 mental health descriptors for which points can be scored are being removed from the new 'simpler' test, greatly reducing the chances of being found incapable of work due to such things as poor memory, confusion, depression and anxiety'. As if the previous assessments weren't already stacked against those with an 'invisible illness', as is the nature of *mental* illness — something that Penny also astutely picks up on in her article for *the Morning Star*:

> Mental illness is perhaps the subtlest and most frightening of all forms of social difference, because of its invisibility, because of the difficulty in quantifying it and because it is not a binary condition —you're not either mad or sane, there's a whole spectrum involved.

One of this anthology's contributors, Mick Moss, addresses this issue with empirical edge in his poem 'Illness You Can't See': *sometimes/ it hurts so bad/ I just don't want/ to go on living/ blessed death a bonus/ after this.* And it is such vulnerable individuals whom Cameron is directly targeting, even deliberately victimizing, via his relentless verbal scare tactics. There is absolutely no doubt at all that the already high rate of Sections placed on the mentally vulnerable will now escalate under this austerity-peddling coalition of doom-mongers; when one might quite reasonably argue that perhaps it is this government that warrants being Sectioned because its policies are certainly 'a danger to the public'. The closer we come to the welfare caps and cuts and the new incapacity interrogations, the higher the risks of suicides among the mentally vulnerable. It is this direct threat to not simply the health and wellbeing but the very individual longevity of many of the incapacitated in our society that calls seriously into question whether or not this administration is verging on a violation of Human Rights. Certainly its drive against the poor is tantamount to Malthusianism at the very least; and debatably its punitive approach to the sick and disabled is a violation of disability discrimination and mental health legislation. Such is the widespread concern about this under-reported issue that pressure group Mad Pride has already started up a campaign highlighting the mental health fallout from the proposals to coerce scores of claimants off their Disability Living Allowances: *Stop The Suicides — Hands Off Our Benefits.*

It is not desirous for any of us in society, whether employed or unemployed, on a wage, or on benefits, to live in a country where our government seems to be actively working against us and our interests. This is brinkmanship of the most reckless kind, and it is showing its hand far too early: only 100 days in. A 100 Days War indeed; a siege against the Welfare State and public sector. It is difficult to believe that any one at all, no matter how privileged or comfortably off they might still be, could possibly wish to live in a society such as the kind currently being nurtured and proselytised by this government: a society of malice, distrust, divisiveness, and harassment, which is actively encouraging agencies and individuals to tip off on 'suspect' benefit claimants and urging a tacit neighbourhood watch on 'curtains closed during the day'; incentivizing medical professionals to bully the incapacitated into unsuitable jobs; and planning to carve up the NHS like a cake for unaccountable private companies to milk for profits at patients' expense. I challenge anyone: is this really the type of society you want to be a part of? Only a masochist would, from either side of the fence. The big question is, will the Big Society be big enough for anyone but the bullies?

Ministries of Minimum Requirements

*E*mergency *Verse's* intention is not to blindly and automatically oppose any kind of reform to the welfare system, but the measures laid out by the coalition are not about reform, they are about demolition. The reforms needed to the welfare system should be in relation to its inadequacies and certainly not to any skewed notions of it having been historically over-generous in its provisions: it has, since its inception (as discussed further in to this chapter), been beset by a bourgeois obsession with the moral perils posed by long-term unemployment, thus inspiring tight-fisted provisions of support to those out of work in order not to undervalue the inalienable salvation of waged labour (a short-sighted approach which has arguably protracted the necessity for a welfare state, and has now resulted in the inevitable regression to punitive benefit cuts, American-style community workfare for several times less than the minimum wage (arguably an infringement on EU Employment Rights), and loss of benefits for three years for anyone who refuses up to three times to take up unsuitable or degrading work. The Tory way, as ever, is to crack the whip and punish the unemployed with sanctions and cuts thus putting clear blue water between the pilloried impoverishment of unemployment and the comparably more attractive prospect of merely adequately waged work. (This is a very perverse notion of 'incentive' to work; the only fair and sane way to 'make work pay' is to bring in a living wage). Again, such a tilted attitude is heavily laced with the puritanical, actually Calvinistic ideas behind the Protestant

Work Ethic: that somehow, as in the karma of Hinduism, material poverty and societal failure are unconsciously translated as indications of moral or spiritual weakness, laziness, even as signs of potential deviancy (or refusal to take up unsuitable employment as tantamount to a 'sin', as the very *English* Catholic IDS recently said; while some of us would be more inclined to say it is a sin to exploit others' labour for profit). The capitalist perception of 'duty' never regulates itself in terms of duty to others but is primarily interpreted as 'duty to oneself'. Hence the age-old idioms that very much typify our island mentality: 'charity begins at home' and 'you must help yourself before helping others'. While these may be in some ways rational and pragmatic sayings, they have, since Thatcherism took hold on the nation's consciousness, become somewhat over-subscribed sentiments. The dubious phrase 'God helps those who help themselves' and the historically misinterpreted 'Render unto Caesar what is Caesar's', were aphorisms manipulated by 'Christian' Thatcherites (if such a pairing of doctrines isn't a total contradiction) who sought biblical justification for the grasping Eighties. Thatcher's lasting legacy, to paraphrase Roy Hattersley, is that she made greed 'respectable'.

EV is more inclined to believe that, far from a massive cut in the Welfare State as chosen so cavalierly by this government and without any risk assessment of the consequences for the poor and most vulnerable in society, what is actually needed at this juncture (particularly in light of the oncoming escalation in unemployment) is an *increase* in the budget for welfare provision, together with a realignment of benefit rates to current spending patterns (so certainly kept pegged to the Retail Price Index, and not reallocated to the Consumer Price Index, as the 'Cut-Ice Chancellor' has so ruthlessly done) and raised above the basic level of subsistence. Indeed, by aiming to make it even harder to qualify for Incapacity Benefit or DLA in the future, our present government is actually at risk itself of disincentivising current recipients to get off benefits and 'back into work': to do so now, when the Welfare State, the only safety-net for those with unpredictable and relapsing mental health conditions, is being reined in and tied into ever-tightening knots, will be a leap in the dark without any gauge of the depth they will fall if they find they are unable to cope with employment further down the line. The perfectly understandable fear of letting go from the edge of state support into the uncharted waters of work, knowing full well that if one starts to sink again there will be less likelihood of a benefit lifeguard to fish them out next time, would seem objectively to be a pretty foolproof deterrent against any mass migration of IB claimants into the job market. But then presumably the expedited 'work capability assessments' to come will ruthlessly push most IB and many DLA claimants back onto job-seeking benefits whether they can cope or not. (Ship's first mate Osborne thinks that the best cure for incapacity is a lick of the cat 'o' nine tails or a good thorough keelhauling).

It is this intransigent impatience of our welfare system that is its own worst enemy: by coercing and intimidating claimants to secure waged employment, the system often pushes many when they are not mentally ready, which in turn leads to relapse and return to benefits again. That is, after the draconian three month benefit disqualification for 'choosing to leave a job' has elapsed. The threat to Incapacity Benefit is particularly serious, since up until now it has been the one single opt-out-clause for the sick and the desperate to legitimately bypass the aforementioned sanction by dint of one's illness. If anything, the character of Incapacity Benefit should be upgraded rather than further negated: even its relative 'sanctuary' from the pressures of those on job-seeking benefits to continually prove they are doing their utmost to find work has long been eroded by the demands of the markets — what more graphic illustration of this could there be than in its rebranding with the industrially expeditious name, 'Employment and Support Allowance'? Capitalist society is actively cultivating a zero tolerance towards sickness, most particularly to those types triggered by its own uncompromisingly stressful agencies, and consequently particular to it.

Even the ostensibly reasonable and humane clause of 'therapeutic earnings' (or 'permitted work') for those on Incapacity Benefit who wish to gradually move back towards some kind of employment, by allowing the claimant to do up to 16 hours work and earn up to £92 per week on top of their IB, is still in time abruptly truncated by the imposition of arbitrary fifty-two week time limits. It is as if the system is under the assumption that chronic incapacity to perform on a full-time employed basis can somehow be guillotined; the claimant's 'recovery' to be determined not by themselves, nor even by a panel of medical professionals, but by the target-driven tick-boxes on a DWP calendar. The IB claimant is then often forced to turn down further part-time opportunities in order that their only regular income of benefits is not removed altogether (the welfare system does not seem to take into account that once one benefit is removed, it has a knock-on effect on all other entitlements, such as Housing Benefit, even if it is that system's remit is precisely *to know* such intra-relatedness of benefits — more absurd still, claimants are expected to have automatic knowledge of this inter-relatedness); often as well because most of their work opportunities are only temporary anyway. Again, such tortuous loopholes in the welfare system actually *dis*incentivise claimants to secure employment. The entire benefits system therefore clearly needs significant reform, not by punitive cuts, but by further investment in order to provide greater flexibility of support to its claimants and a more realistic, empirically assessed circuit of supplementary benefits for those entering into low-waged work. [While IDS's proposals for a universal credit are, so we are told, to incorporate new safeguards so that claimants lose their benefits more gradually and proportionately during the early stages of new employment, such progressive aims will be massively undermined by the draconian benefit caps to come in beforehand. As ever, the Tories give with one hand, and take away with the other].

For the argument behind such 'unfashionable' proposals as these, it is necessary to briefly focus on some details to the thesis of Coates and Silburn's *Poverty: The Forgotten Englishmen* (1970), specifically their chapter *The Decline of the Welfare State*. For those reading this who might scoff at the forty-year old source chosen, it is important to emphasise that although pre-Thatcherism, the political and economic context of Coates and Silburn's study was not entirely dissimilar to today's, albeit on a smaller scale: 1970 marked the end of almost seven years of Labour government under Harold Wilson, and the return of a Tory administration under Edward Heath with an 'inherited deficit' caused largely by market pressures on Wilson to devalue the pound (itself a measure predetermined by a deficit Labour inherited from the preceding 1959-63 Tory government under Harold MacMillan). Heath's government, which lasted until 1974, was to witness the first and least trumpeted of the two 'winters of discontent' of the Seventies, the one which introduced the notorious 'Three Day Week'; it was also the period during which Margaret Thatcher first ominously made her name with the epithet 'Thatcher the Milk Snatcher', for abolishing free school milk for 8-11 year olds due to an education budget squeeze (she would later graduate to 'State Snatcher' in the Eighties). But many of the contemporary political issues and attitudes drawn and challenged by Coates and Silburn strike uncanny parallels with those of 2010.

Central to Coates' and Silburn's dialectic was the conclusion, based on all the facts and figures from its inception in 1945 to their present in 1970, that the Welfare State had, in spite of many of the best intentions, failed to eradicate British poverty, or even to produce a vertical redistribution of wealth, other than marginally; that it had in effect managed to trap its first trial generation of lower-waged and unemployed beneficiaries in relative privation. They essentially put a large portion of the blame in this undervaluation of need on the shoulders of William Beveridge, whose eponymous report of 1942 is regarded as the blueprint for the Welfare State introduced by the incoming Labour government three years later.

It is important to note that Beveridge had inherited much of his drive towards social reform from his Liberal harbingers, Henry Asquith and David Lloyd-George, whose 'People's Budget' of 1909 had controversially proposed several tax increases in order to fund higher welfare payments for the unemployed, which in itself forced the election of the following year. Having won through the two elections of 1910, the Liberal Government then went on to introduce the vital National Insurance Act of 1911, which, among many other reforms, brought in both the Labour Exchange and insurance for the unemployed, and health insurance for workers — so the Labour

Government of 1945-51 was effectively the consolidating son of the 1906-14 Liberal pioneer. Lloyd-George summed up this collectivist liberalism in a striking aphorism that the likes of Nick Clegg and his Orange Book ilk would do well not to forget:

I cannot help hoping and believing that before this generation has passed away, we shall have advanced a great step towards that good time, when poverty, and the wretchedness and human degradation which always follows in its camp, will be as remote to the people of this country as the wolves which once infested its forests.

Coates and Silburn basically suggest that Beveridge was so preoccupied — as most before and since — by the risk of wage-level benefits disincentivising people to seek employment that he recommended benefits based on a mere subsistence level, so recipients could secure the 'necessities' of physical and material survival but nothing more. Thus the shadow necessities such as the basic human need for a sense of dignity, self-esteem and sufficient confidence to maximise their future employability, were left out of the equation. Further, the individual's drive towards industrious self-cultivation was grossly limited by their time and energies being consumed simply by trying to subsist on a relative pittance (a full time job in itself). Coates and Silburn level at Beveridge the argument that his report's benefit rate recommendations '...established the principle of flat-rate benefits at a minimum acceptable, rather than maximum possible, level'. They then impeach Beveridge for basing his own recommendations on an out-of-date assessment of subsistence needs:

In calculating his benefit rates Beveridge relied heavily upon 1937-8 Ministry of Labour survey of working-class household expenditure, which provided him with fairly detailed information on spending patterns. In general, however, Beveridge calculated a figure for each item of household expenditure that was smaller than the figure in the Ministry's survey, on the grounds that 'subsistence expenditure can clearly be put below these figures, which relate to households living on an average well above the minimum'. The final benefit rate was thus arrived at by a process of stringent calculation on a very narrow range of supposedly necessary commodities bearing no marked relationship to actual spending patterns.

Therefore:

From the outset, the rates of benefit were too low to guarantee, even by Beveridge's own declared standards, security from want.

Coates and Silburn then touch on the perennial neuroticism of governments of all political colours to never inadvertently devalue the material salvation promised solely through employment; their study covers both unemployment and the blanket extrapolations determining allocation of supplementary benefits to the low-waged:

...the low wage-earner can find relief neither as of right nor on demonstration of need, but must reconcile himself and his family to living at whatever standard his low wage permits. This large group, who cannot escape poverty while at work, can expect no improvement in their circumstances in the event of a period of sickness or unemployment, which would make them eligible for both social-security and Supplementary Benefits. Precisely in order to avoid the situation where a family might receive more in welfare payments than it would in earnings, the Ministry operates a 'wage-stop'; that is to say, whatever level of benefits a family may be eligible to receive according to the Ministry's scales, the actual sum paid out shall not exceed the amount that was being earned before the interruption occurred.

Coates and Silburn then capture the paradox of welfare provision in a competitive capitalist society:

No matter how inadequate a family's earned income; no matter how far short of that family's needs the income may fall ...in the event of such low earnings being interrupted, the Ministry will fastidiously maintain such a family in its accustomed poverty: in no event can Authority allow its resources to be used actually to *raise* anyone's living standards, even as far as the level of the Ministry's own estimate of minimum requirements.

Essentially, precisely the same principles regarding benefit rates apply today: they are not individually means-tested but are instead based on an abstract assumption that wage levels, house prices, rents and costs of living are generally uniformed throughout the country, when it is common knowledge that the reverse is the case, as immortalised by the 'North/South divide' idiom. It is in a sense more disenfranchising to be unemployed in the South than it is the North, since the benefits system does not acknowledge the vast disparities in house prices and rents between regions, nor within the same region, or even city, where some areas are priced higher than others for being perceived to have better amenities and property standards. It is as if the welfare system works on a hypothetical communist principle while the rest of society operates on the capitalist one of fluctuating markets and competitive rental rates.

Finally, Coates' and Silburn's analysis of a then newly emerging capitalist consensus in British politics makes for uncanny reading in 2010. It demonstrates how cyclical the political landscape is in capitalist societies, and how hackneyed the political platitudes used by governments to justify the anarchic dictates of the markets on social policy. In the following extracts, Coates and Silburn touch unnervingly on the fallacy of 'consensus politics' as a euphemism for market capitulation, their ostensible purpose being to...

...convince many normal sensible commentators that an end has been made to 'ideological politics', or indeed to any politics that acknowledged continued opposition and conflict within the social system. Apparently, we are all Fabians now, and are expected to endorse the recurrent and time-honoured theme in Fabian thought that fundamental social change can be achieved by a gradual process of reformist legislation, each new enactment contributing to the greater and more rational control of the blind forces of the market, and representing, as it were, a foretaste of the Socialist Commonwealth to come.

Here, future echoes of Tony Blair's 'Third Way' and its centralising of British politics will not be lost on any of us in this almost precognitive essay. It goes to show that if everything that could happen hasn't all happened in the past, they have at least been anticipated. The following excerpt from this coldly prophetic, exceptionally composed dialectic of Coates' and Silburn's, is likely to cause instant chills of recognition for any one reading now, mindful of the current sophistry and propaganda spouted by our present coalition government who, so they tell us, have 'no choice' but to take 'tough decisions' that won't affect them, as to making 'unavoidable cuts' that *will* affect us:

Ultimately, the welfare system comes to assume the shape and the values of the markets, to identify itself increasingly with the purposes of the market, and to be seen not as an alternative to market methods of distribution, but as a buttress to them. Such a transformation will of course be hailed by the exponents of the market as 'rational', 'realistic', and even 'progressive'. Thus the White Paper on the envisaged reform of the social-security system is claimed, by its authors, to be a more radical document than the *Beveridge Report*, although in fact it finally sabotages the few remaining traces of the Beveridge principles....

Con-Dems, take note while there is still time.

Mind the Cap

Capitalism is arguably the most hypocritical system known to man: it stands against all recognisable Christian values in its valuation of money above human beings; it causes and sustains arguably one of the worst forms of poverty, 'relative', the privations of which are continually inflamed by close proximity to those with better standards of living, even extravagantly rich. Such juxtapositions are hazardously jarring, fuelling a sense of separateness, of economic apartheid, and thus perfectly understandable feelings of resentment from those on the poorer side of the paradigm. All this is further fuelled by the capitalist lie that those who are wealthy are thus because of their hard work, when one only has to read the daily paper to see most of the richest in society have amassed vast wealth just as much, if not more so, through malversation and 'creative accountancy' (tax evasion). In the words of Jimmy Reid, when using a character from *Catch 22* as a motif for the capitalist mentality:

He hated suggestions for things like medi-care, social services, unemployment benefits or civil rights. He was, however, an enthusiast for the agricultural policies that paid farmers for not bringing their fields under cultivation. From the money he got for not growing alfalfa he bought more land in order not to grow alfalfa. He became rich. Pilgrims came from all over the state to sit at his feet and learn how to be a successful non-grower of alfalfa. His philosophy was simple. The poor didn't work hard enough and so they were poor. He believed that the good Lord gave him two strong hands to grab as much as he could for himself. He is a comic figure. But think — have you not met his like here in Britain?

But any such notions of social meritocracy in a society such as ours, where inherited wealth is still rampantly abundant and is a transparently obvious determinant in who gets to the best schools, universities and highest places in the occupational pecking order, is instantly seen as specious. No Cabinet since the 1950s has so baldly demonstrated the still entrenched British class system as the current coalition's, with its hereditary multi-millionaires, Etonian dilettantes, and aristocratic Chancellor, heir to the baronetcy of Ballentaylor, whose sense of 'fairness' has been dreamt up on the playing fields of St. Paul's. If this government wishes to lash back with the old hackneyed 'politics of envy' and 'class war' arguments, then it only has itself to blame for such impeachments as mine, since it has single-handedly raised the standard of a class war on the poor of this country in its disgracefully regressive budget.

As far as many on the Left in this country are concerned, since 22 June 2010, this country has been in a state of class war, even more starkly than during the attritive Thatcher years that jump-started it, but of a new especially nauseous aristocratic timbre. Now, any of us whose memories and experiences stretch to pre-1994 and the neoliberalisation of the Labour Movement, have to suffer such absurd commonplace assertions that our parliamentary consensus is 'progressive centrist', when by any other definition it is 'centre-right' at best, 'right-wing and regressive' at worst, which is presently being consolidated by the Con-Dem coalition; and those on the Left have to continually listen to tribalistic right-wing spin that tries to put New Labour's failings down to those of 'socialism', when again by any other definition, the last government was at best 'progressive centrist' and at worst, which sadly was most of the time, 'right-of-centre' and 'regressive'. Labour's socialism was stamped out by Blair, who finished the job Thatcher had started, in an 'empire on which the sun never sets' moment of spontaneous dismantling; so 'New' Labour rose from the set sun of true Labour. The only ways in which New Labour was in any remote sense 'socialist' were by the crudest definitions: its expansion of state powers to such a controlling extent that individual freedoms felt increasingly constricted, a bugbear for many on the Left as much as for the libertarians on the Right. The uncompromising apartheid-approach of the smoking ban was a prime example of this. But in practically all the true positive and progressive senses, New Labour was anything but 'socialist'; it was by and large indistinguishably as capitalist as its predecessors and its inheritors. The crucial introduction of a minimum wage (argued for by Labour's original leader, Keir Hardie, as far back as the 1890s — progress is something of a stalking *tortoise* in English politics) and the erosion of the hereditary grip on the House of Lords, among one or two other 'progressive' reforms were ultimately paltry scraps of consolation for thirteen years of financial de-regulation, accelerated privatisations, celebrity-baiting opportunism, Murdoch-courting, war-mongering, regressive taxation, Orwellian surveillance, benefit-bashing, No. 10 photo-ops with Thatcher, expenses fiddling, property-flipping, and glorification of the 'aspirational middle-classes' at the expense of the party's traditional working- and under-class supporters (in turn arguably triggering the sudden surge in support for the BNP in the most deprived areas of the country). Even the nationalising of First Capital Connect, Northern Rock and the RBS seemed to be implemented almost apologetically to the 'Thatcherite' ethos, while apparently 'right-of-centre' continental administrations, Germany and France in particular, didn't hesitate in slapping their speculating banks with hefty caps and sanctions in the wake of the credit crunch. But then, British political 'wings' are at a significantly rightward remove from those on the Continent. In Sweden, for instance, the 'Moderate' government that has been in power for the last four years or so is considered 'right-wing' by the Swedes, and yet its policies can broadly be described as still *to the left* of New Labour. Further, a Swedish acquaintance, while watching a recent PMQ in which Cameron articulated almost unequivocally the perceived view that those on benefits in the UK are somehow implicitly party to Iain Duncan-Smith's concept of 'institutionalised idleness', remarked that if any politician had spoken in such a way about the unemployed in Sweden, they would be immediately reprimanded, even possibly expelled from their parliament. It can be seen then just how far the UK has drifted to the right in the last couple of generations; how increasingly intolerant towards those in need — no matter what their circumstances — of state support it has become. It is therefore no small achievement that the Con-Dems have managed in only 100 days to demonstrate there is yet even further distance that can be covered in this nation's rightward sprint.

No two events in recent times have more starkly illustrated the absurd unfairness of our society than the consequences of the financial crisis on the poorest in society through the imminent welfare cuts, and the relative lack of any significant repercussions on the City speculators who were directly responsible for it (whither, for instance, is the official inquiry into discovering who the true culprits were?), and in the risible behaviour of our elected MPs who shamelessly flipped their properties and fiddled their expenses so as to effectively thieve millions of taxpayers' money. No surprise that the Tories then seek to distract the electorate from the true 'benefit cheats' of society, the speculators and culpable MPs, by whipping up a collective hysteria against those implausible benefit claimants who, to quote the Chancellor, 'mug the taxpayer' (Osborne being a true case of a pot calling the kettle black with regards to his own un-transparent financial arrangements). As I say in my poem-contribution to this anthology: *if the poor cut corners they are/ Pilloried in the stocks, pelted with sanctions and penalties,/ While gambling speculators and property-flipping MPs/ Can just say they made 'a mistake' and simply 'apologise'*. The fact that Parliament eventually voted for its 'Honourable' Members to in future be paid an Attendance Allowance of £120 a day in order to cover their 'expenses' at a fixed rate just shows how little Westminster has learnt from the previous scandals. It also further illustrates the hubris of MPs and peers, especially the current Cabinet, when they are so cavalierly pursuing austerity measures that include capping and cutting many welfare benefits. The sheer temerity of the Con-Dems is breathtaking: while £65 per seven day week Job Seekers' Allowance is 'what the Government stipulates is enough for an individual to live on', by contrast they believe that an MP needs a *daily* allowance of almost twice that amount, *on top* of a five figure salary, to be able to afford attending Parliament over a *five* day week. One rule for them, another for the rest of us.

Atomism and Antinomianism

In its 'emergency' Budget — an appropriate term indeed since the budget itself is cause for a national emergency — the coalition administration has demonstrated to just what pitiful extent our entire society is cap-in-hand to the markets and City since, when the *merd* hits the fan, in spite of culpability, the culprits are flattered with a tiny levy while the victims, already taxed to bail out the failing banks as it is, are then told they have to roll over and just accept an oncoming *blitzkrieg* on all their essential state provisions, public services, even their National Health Service. Meantime, the City returns to its profligate and unjustifiable bonus system, also flattered with a faint 'raise' via the reduction in Corporation Tax. To call all this deeply unfair on practically every conceivable moral level, is an understatement. Such deep duplicity and draconian expediency from a coalition that has a very tenuous electoral mandate to carry out even vaguely regressive cuts — let alone to unleash on a stunned country the most devastatingly brutal budget in its entire history — simply goes to prove beyond doubt that British capitalism is as morally as it is fiscally bankrupt. 115 years on from Karl Marx's dialectical indictment of industrial capitalism, *Das Kapital*, the aftermath of the global recession seems only to finally prove after so many decades of revisionism and monetarist hubris, that his fundamental thesis that capitalism's intrinsic instability will lead to its eventual implosion, is beginning to seem more probable than before. In spite of a reactionary coalition government frantically attempting to disprove otherwise, it seems increasingly likely that what we are now witnessing is the start of the last gasp of capitalist society. A Rainbow Alliance of the left-of-centre parties might have been prevented for the time being by a shabby backroom deal on behalf of the markets, but it can't be put off forever. Change will have to come eventually; fundamental and more substantial democratic change, and a reactionary entrenchment of a regressive 'Big Society' will only be prolonging the agony.

Unsurprisingly, the first English capitalists were essentially Calvinists, whose faith was translated into a materialist equivalent. And in spite of later attempts by inspired apostates to reform its worsted industrial

model — such as the Arts and Crafts Movement and Sixties Holism
— the peculiarly puritanical British view of work as necessarily soulless
wage labour whose sole consolation is the acquisition of purely material
capital (that is, for those who are salaried enough to be able to actually
keep any of their money), economic security, 'status' incentivised and
based on others' relative lack, and, for the cannier among us, 'profit',
has sustained itself. Apart from the lucky few who are employed in
professions entirely suiting their abilities and interests, employment
is for the majority of the population an unavoidable sacrifice of time,
energies and, often, of *authentic* ambition, in return for freedom from
poverty and the binds and stigmas of unemployment. This is not by any
standards a healthy 'ethic' of occupation. As D.H. Lawrence wrote: 'There
is no point in work unless it *preoccupies* you as well as occupies you.
When you are only occupied, you are an empty shell'. Our Ministers
would relate to these sentiments in relation to their own occupations,
so why do they begrudge so many the same privilege? But why listen
to one of the most incisive literary minds of the last century when we
have government focus groups? Politicians and their spin come and go,
but great poetry and literature stands the test of time. The doyens of
contemporary Occupational Theory would do well to take note of
Lawrence's observation, since it is still sadly germane as ever. The
modern mantra that the cure for all social, physical and mental ills is
to 'get back into work' rings hollow when one considers how resentful
the majority of taxpayers are that they should surrender a percentage
of their earned incomes: such groups as the Taxpayers' Alliance betray
the fact that money is the overarching incentive for putting up with what
is for many otherwise unsatisfying and mind-numbing employment.

The British work ethic is basically 'live to work' (or in the case of
successful capitalists, 'live to work others') — whereas on the continent,
especially in Latin and Scandinavian countries, the motto is more
'work to live': work has its place but it is no more or less than that of
leisure, creative or familial pursuit. It is arguable that the unnecessarily
puritanical British idea of work as an intrinsically expedient, almost
egodystonic labour, the mandatory self-sacrifice of one's lifetime in
the production of what amounts ultimately to others' profits — hardly

anything that can approach an ideal, let alone an ethic. The socialist polymath Bertrand Russell decried the British work ethic in his 1932 dialectic *In Praise of Idleness* (one for IDS's shelf?) — though right-wing cynics would instantly scoff at the outpourings of a 'chattering-class conscience', Russell's poignant extensions of Ruskin's and Morris's social critiques have a resonance today, particularly in their identification of capitalism not only with economic but also artistic poverty:

In a world where no one is compelled to work more than four hours a day, every person possessed of scientific curiosity will be able to indulge it... Young writers will not be obliged to draw attention to themselves by sensational pot-boilers, with a view to acquiring the economic independence needed for monumental works, for which, when the time at last comes, they will have lost the taste and capacity. ...Above all, there will be happiness and joy of life, instead of frayed nerves, weariness, and dyspepsia.

Russell's modern day equivalent, John Pilger, writing recently in *the New Statesman*, has not missed the distinct lack of literary opposition to the present culture of cuts — a deficiency which *Emergency Verse* is hopefully rectifying (a copy will be posted to mop Mr Pilger's brow):

Athol Fugard is right. With Harold Pinter gone, no acclaimed writer or artist dare depart from their well-remunerated vanity. With so much in need of saying, they have nothing to say.

A century on from Robert Tressell's masterpiece *The Ragged Trousered Philanthropists*, the vast majority of those employed in this country still by and large — and in spite of post-Thatcherite 'incentives' of increasing home ownership and shares in companies — epitomise that masochistic title; and never more baldly than today where, in the aftermath of a recession triggered by un-regulated City gamblers, the British population are, a year later, expected to forgive and forget and indirectly pay back billions on billions of pounds via savage cuts to the public sector and Welfare State. Tressell's novel — unpublished in his lifetime simply because he couldn't afford a typewriter to produce it as a more readable manuscript — once posthumously published, was rumoured to have significantly contributed to the Labour Party's landslide election victory of 1945. The subsequent government, under Clement Attlee, in spite of inheriting a deficit three times the size of today's, decided to invest in the health and wellbeing of its war-torn populace by constructing the country's first ever universal health and social care system: the Welfare State (inclusive of the National Health Service), the blueprint of which was inspired by the Liberal William Beveridge's famous report of 1942. After the defragmentation of social solidarity during the last thirty years of Thatcherite politics, it is difficult for us today to comprehend the sense of collectivism in the Britain of 1945. Six years of national threat had, at least ethically, levelled British society, and temporarily abraded the hitherto chronic class barriers. As the national war effort had been a common cause that united all classes, so too would be the rebuilding of that nation. And the Attleean austerity drive would be one shared proportionately throughout the country, and motivated by a peacetime effort towards greater egalitarianism. In spite of the inevitable setbacks for any ideologically ambitious administration, the Labour Government of 1945-1951 was nevertheless the most radical and arguably the only true democratic-socialist government this country has ever known. So successful were its achievements that they came to shape the dominant and genuinely 'progressive' ideological dialogue of the following three decades, until Thatcherism plunged the country back into the ethical dark ages from which we have still yet to surface.

In 2008, social historian David Kynaston's *Austerity Britain* hit the shelves, the first bible-thick instalment of his *Tales from the New Jerusalem* series of books charting essentially the history of Welfare State Britain from 1945 to its abrupt truncation in 1979. It is a brilliantly informative and tragically prophetic tome, given our now entering into a new age of 'austerity' under one of the most reactionary governments this country has known (which says something). Unlike in 1945, when an ascendant and true Labour government raised the standard of a new era more socially united than ever before after a second world war, and began building the country's first universal welfare and health system out of the rubble of bankruptcy, we are now faced with a government which, at the fag-end of Thatcherite era, seeks to impose devastating top-down cuts and sanctions on the state and public sector in a knee-jerk response to an alleged impending financial collapse. This is top-down damage limitation by a Con-Dem government which is basically 90% Con and 10% Lib Dem, the two ideologically incompatible parties having gone into an unholy alliance on a back-of-a-fag-packet set of affinities: the Cons are fiscal libertarians; the Lib Dems, liberals with a large 'L' when it comes to individual rights and freedom to choose to hunt and terrify a fox to death for fun, but with a very small 'l' when it comes to rights and freedoms that happen to be at the moment dependent on the benevolence of the state, such as benefit entitlements. Both parties hate bureaucracy and are happy to scapegoat the public sector purely for this endemic aspect to modern social democracies, which is every bit as prevalent in the private as in the public sector; in fact, *it* is even worse in the private sector: the labyrinths of outsourcing and sub-contracting have dogged our rail services for years now, and led to a completely undemocratic system whereby no one in authority is ever accountable to its 'customers' as it's always 'the other company' responsible for the target of a complaint, never the company to whom you complain. Privatisation's intrinsic culture of obfuscation and unaccountability then has created the newest and most frustratingly opaque form of bureaucracy known to man, one entirely corrupted by the profit motive.

Chancellor, and Baronet-in-waiting, George Osborne claimed that the austerity cuts would hit 'those with the broadest shoulders' the most, and yet all objective analysis of the Budget's actual real-term details, *arithmetic included,* shows unequivocally that the net result of the cuts will be the precise opposite: a top-down chopping board approach which means that those at the lowest end of the economic scale will be hit with cuts every bit as much as those at the top end; and that's before even counting the 'under classes'. It seems then more a case of those with the 'broadest *and the narrowest* shoulders' are to take the brunt of this financial onslaught about to be imposed with the epithet 'unavoidable'. The Government's projection that the recovery will be 'choppy' may come to be the biggest understatement in our country's history.

From Cradle to Save: The Private Health Service (PHS)

So now we have an unlikely coalition of Opposites in the already notoriously abbreviated 'Con-Dem' government which has swooped down on us while this country is at its most vulnerable, like a giant privatising vulture, its claws itching for public sector carrion. With a deficit three times smaller than that inherited in 1945, we are facing the most savage cuts to our Welfare State and public sector, as well as plans to privatise our intrinsically publicly-funded NHS. From a Welfare to a Workfare State, from health and wellbeing to wealth and hellbeing, from National Health Service to a National Wealth Service for GPs to be given more fiscal powers to arbitrate on behalf of unscrupulous pharmaceutical companies that have already been holding the NHS to ransom over the past thirty years. Transparently true to form, the mandate-less Tories have now revealed the sting in their tails regarding a pre-election pledge to 'ring-fence' the NHS budget: what they meant was to ring-fence it for their friends in the private sector to cash in on. Health Secretary (or rather, Broker) Andrew Lansley has recently proposed to offer NHS hospitals the option to 'go private', thus waving the starting-gun for Trusts to sell out to the ideological entropy of their own mother institution. It's such a bitter irony that just as the truly progressive Barak Obama is valiantly pushing through the USA's first ever universal health care system under a torrent of redneck invective, *our* government is plotting to dismantle the very sixty-three-year-old institution whose template he is seeking to emulate. It's a bit like a trans-Atlantic relay race, except that unfortunately our country is dashing back on itself, having ditched the baton across the water.

The Tories — alongside most of the medical profession of the day — were originally against Aneurin Bevan's proposed institution of universal healthcare, but have begrudgingly tolerated it since, and are now unsurprisingly relishing the opportunity to begin demolishing this long-standing socialist bastion of British society. It is rather perverse that, in a society presently shaken to its foundations by the rampant gambling of a deregulated banking sector, the Government is reacting by seeking to deregulate practically everything else. This is ideology over reason: with the escalation in railway crashes due to shoddy sub-contracted track-maintenance, the recession's triggering by City speculating, the imminent increase in unemployment, and the need for keeping the same quantity of DWP staff to handle this — among other potentially toxic issues — it is now more than ever time for this country to trim back on privatisations, not increase them, to sustain its public sector, not chop it in half, and to return to the sanity and fairness of nationalised public services. The Con-Dems unfortunately have come in to power and put the entire state to the hammer at a Thatcherite auction.

Phase One of this privatizing putsch, under the dubious banner of 'local empowerment', is to put not only medical but budgetary and structural powers back into the hands of General Practitioners, Cameron's 'Big Society' can be seen as a grossly regressive attempt to turn the clock back 65 years to pre-NHS days, heralding a return to diminishing accountability of doctors and, conceivably, eventual hikes in prescription charges; even erosion of free prescriptions for the unemployed (not yet proposed but undoubtedly in the minds of most Tories at this juncture). While most of us would entrust our health care to GPs, history has taught us to be much more cautious regarding entrusting them with much else: GPs' bargaining powers on salary levels over the past thirty years have helped deplete NHS funds; and their intransigently rationed contact hours, that pit patients against one another in early morning appointment lotteries of constant engaged tones as if on a TV phone-in — showing little consideration for the severity of individuals' illnesses — are long unregulated protocols of most NHS surgeries.

The fanatically anti-state Lansley claims that his 'radical reform' of the NHS will put power back in the hands of both GPs and patients, the former to be more accountable to the latter in future (though if they are not, who exactly are they answerable to?). This is an amusingly unlikely prospect to contemplate in any real sense but one feels tempted to take it at the letter and begin demanding of GPs to extend their surgery hours. We may try but we can rest assured patients will be dancing to surgeries' tunes more than ever before. The Con-Dems are not dispensing with the 'top-down' powers they claim to so despise, they are simply handing them to GPs, and washing their hands of the consequences (and this is what the 'Big Society' is about: governmental abdication of responsibility). But a ringing irony in all this is that so far GPs seem to be warning against the government proposals for the NHS as a path towards unnecessary structural chaos and the blurring of demarcation between medical duties and new additional financial ones. If, as it seems, neither patients nor GPs want these 'radical reforms' to the NHS, this increasing marketisation of the state health system, then what ethical or practical argument for still imposing them could Mr Lansley possible have? Clearly the Health Minister's Thatcherite instincts are universally perceived as out-of-date market-driven tinkering that, far from alleviating any weaknesses in the NHS, can only further exacerbate them to the further detriment of already falling patient care standards (and this is not even touching on the impending epidemic in mental health care that promises to explode once the full force of the cuts begin to bite). Fortunately, it seems this time round that the GPs appear to be jealously guarding their Hippocratic Oaths in spite of fresh promises to have their mouths nostalgically 'stuffed with gold' all over again (to reference the great Nye Bevan's legendary trope); probably because they can see from the professional point of view that the meretricious gift of new budgetary controls is in reality an offloading of Department of Health responsibilities onto their novice shoulders, rather than any financial or prestige upgrade for their profession. And, indeed, why should GPs be expected to suddenly double as practice accountants, to juggle stethoscopes with calculators?

Such medical *laissez faire* is euphemised as 'mutualism', a term already being bandied about by Ministers: it essentially means health care as a business rather than a service. New Labour is culpable for sowing the seeds of this ruthless Tory reaping, having itself accelerated the Thatcherite 'internal market' of our NHS. Now the Tories can finally complete the privatisation of our State health service as started by Thatcher, as they have always wanted to do. Nothing will be safe from the snatching pincers of privatisation now that we have once again an unadulterated Thatcherite administration. One contributor to this anthology, Paul Lester, tackles this theme in his satirical 'The Privatisation of Air', echoing too Robert Tressell's sentiments in *The Ragged Trousered Philanthropists*: 'The only reason they have not yet monopolised the sunlight is because it is not possible to do so' (sic).

A last needle-head of hope in this Thatcherite haystack is Unison's valiant and hugely commendable announcement that it is going to go to court to try and block Lansley's shake up of the NHS on the grounds that his department's alleged 'consultation' is a sham since GPs have already received written instructions from the Health Minister that his plans are non-negotiable; as well as on the even more democratically contentious grounds that 'the NHS constitution and section 242 of the NHS Act give the public a right to be consulted about changes to services' (Andrew Sparrow in *the Guardian* 24th August 2010). So, the battle to save our National Health Service is on, only two years after its sixtieth anniversary. But Unison's contention seems incontrovertible. Only those who have been sufficiently materially privileged in their lives to have never been reliant on the free care of the NHS for their very survival could so cavalierly conspire to auction it off. What none of us should ever forget is that many of us might not have been alive today had it not been for the NHS and Nye Bevan's Herculean determination to bring it into being in spite of medical and capitalist opposition. Labour now needs a figure of similar moral stature to Bevan, to ideologically obstruct this onslaught of unreconstructed Thatcherism; otherwise this country will tip into the abyss of absolute fiscal apartheid.

Jacob Marley and the Wailers: the Case for Elective Austerity

What is most disturbing about this current, almost masochistic culture of austerity and cuts and 'unavoidable' national suffering, is that it is now seemingly absolutely fine to talk of anyone claiming benefits, no matter what their reasons, no matter if due to genuine sickness or long-term disabilities, in the same kind of language as that used for criminal suspects. The Thatcherite welfare system has in its attitude, style of protocol and terminology all the characteristics of the Probation Service, except without the sense of any rehabilitative empathy, and all this when dealing with some of the poorest and most vulnerable people in our society, the majority of whom have done nothing dishonest, and yet all of whom, without exception, are instinctively treated with cynicism and distrust.

Over the past thirty years ours has been a welfare system that has largely worked against its claimants; a welfare system that has pitched itself more as a sanction-happy policing system of its dependants, and tripped countless thousands into further poverty and insecurity, even homelessness, via a convoluted set of loopholes and caveats laid skilfully as bureaucratic mines designed to obfuscate and disenfranchise the very people for whom it should be providing a safety net. New Labour was guilty of intensifying such Kafka-esque smoke-and-mirror obstacles to benefits, and for encouraging the 'anti-claimant' culture — with all its Orwellian espionage and 'thought-crime'-style tip offs on suspect neighbours — fuelled on the kind of Victorian-style 'deserving, undeserving poor' paradigm of lugubrious Presbyter Brown. While the true dialectic, especially for the centre-Left, that is most relevant to this age of the new 'super rich', tax-evading non-doms, usurious banks, speculators and property-flipping MPs, should be one of the 'undeserving rich'. But the dialectics faltered and stalled long ago in the New Labour camp, partly because it was in thrall to Rupert Murdoch and was, as Peter Mandelson famously remarked, 'intensely relaxed about people getting filthy rich'. New Labour therefore left the door wide open for the Con-Dem Government to come in and, to paraphrase Mandelson, be intensely relaxed about people getting filthily poor'. The consensus which tacitly set in during the Blair years that somehow true poverty had been eradicated from the UK, when it palpably had not, seemed to fuel a mood of both social detachment and disenchantment with the imperative of a Welfare State, akin to the premature complacency of the Fifties under Harold 'you've never had it so good' MacMillan. At best this was out-of-touch, at worst, viciously spiteful in its subsequent promotion of a cross-party view that benefits were no longer being claimed because of genuine need but simply because they could be. But this was and is in the main entirely spurious, unjustifiably vindictive and worst of all, deeply hypocritical coming from a parliamentary generation among whom a significant number of MPs had been found to have knowingly manipulated their own expenses claims, or at best, claimed all they could to the last penny simply because they were able to, and, given their enerous salaries, not because they had genuine financial need to do so. It is highly significant that with our new coalition government, comprised mainly of Tories whose ranks were shamed by an absurd minority claiming for moat-clearance and duck-houses, that the new parliamentary rhetoric has turned back on the tiny minority of alleged 'benefit cheats'.

This government claims that a trebling of IB and DLA recipients over the past few years indicates an increase in 'fraudulent claims'. Apart from the stringently regulated protocol of Incapacity claims (which has been discussed earlier in this Foreword), as anyone who has experienced the tortuous, obfuscating and quite traumatic DLA application process will tell you, most applicants have to go through an appeals process after the almost mandatory fixture of initial refusal, as it is. DLA is awarded at three rates that differ considerably; it is not means-tested, and many recipients are also in part-time work, positions that will prove unsustainable if they have their entitlements arbitrarily cut in 2013. In the mean time, the Government is cranking up its 'scare tactic package' within the DWP with a new figurative pogrom on all those whose 'curtains are shut during the day'. The most disturbing proposal of all is that of new powers for private credit-checking agencies such as Experian to rifle through claimants' bank files in search of signs of fraud, incentivised to maximise allegations in return for bonuses termed with absolutely no irony as 'bounties'. This also goes to show resolutely how the Tories are actually every bit as authoritarian and intrusive as New Labour, the only difference being that they outsource their 'thought police' to the even less accountable private sector. The Tories' tradition of libertarianism has ever applied exclusively to the better off in society, while the lower and underclasses might as well be living in a Stalinist police state, so little is the difference in terms of *their* individual rights and liberties.

All these draconian measures to strip the most vulnerable and poor in society of every bit of benefit, picking off the low-hanging fruits to go towards plugging the deficit, constitute quite baldly a paper pogrom on the unemployed. And all this simply to prepare the ground for the oncoming apocalypse of the aptly dated 2013, unlucky for some, unlucky for many, when all IB and DLA benefit claimants will be systematically interrogated by government-appointed doctors in an attempt to claw back billions to help plug the deficit, apparently essential in order for the Government to drag the nation out of recession. With one hand the Government plans to give more budgetary powers to local GPs, but with the other, seeks to take budgetary powers away from service users by contriving to force thousands off Disability Living Allowance, thereby overriding psychiatric diagnoses. In a sense, what it seems to be attempting is to bribe medical professionals with greater financial freedom in return for being able to override their professional assessments of disabled and incapacitated patients, in order to save money on IB and DLA payments. Not only does this demonstrate contempt for the patients, it also demonstrates contempt for the medical professions, and in particular, for the integrity of the Hippocratic Oath (we can only hope it won't be compromised to a Hypocritical Oath).

In the meantime, the causers of the recession, the speculators in the City, continue to make record profits and to award themselves bonuses on the back of our collective 'austerity'. True capitalists as they are, they can even find ways to capitalise on a recession. *We're all in it together...* should be extended to *..apart from the bankers, speculators, media moguls, super-rich, aristocracy and politicians.* In the opinion of this campaign, it is now absolutely essential for the sake of this country's very sense of dignity and 'fairness' that a Robin Hood Tax, or a nearest equivalent, be instigated with immediate effect. The consequences of not clawing back the much-needed monies from those who are directly responsible for the recession and who — *de facto* in the case of the RBS — *literally* owe this money to all of us, will likely prove disastrous to the stability of our 'social democracy': strikes will inevitably follow, the Unions quite understandably fighting back against the ideological onslaught on their members by a viciously anti-public sector Tory administration, riots will in turn be highly likely, and general social discontent far beyond the likes expressed, again, understandably, in the summer of rage back in 2008. This government pushes this country into a corner at its own peril. The British people do not deserve the cuts of the 'Big Society'. The only way in which the 'emergency' Budget can be called 'progressive' is in the most subverted sense of that vague term: its intensification of an already gaping wealth divide into full scale apartheid of haves and have-nots. After thirty years of deeply regressive Thatcherite politics, and the unconscionable fiscal rape of our economy by the City speculators, what the British people deserve now more than ever is a decent, Fair Society; one which does not expect its school kids to stay sat under collapsing roofs indefinitely (whither 'health and safety' all of a sudden?); suicidal mental health outpatients to be coerced into unsuitable employment or lose their benefits; limbless DLA recipients told by medical assessors that they can 'lift their stumps' so can therefore work; university graduates labouring through unwaged internships indefinitely until a company deigns to actually employ them; students who have passed their A-Levels to go into clearing or find a different option to university altogether; unemployed council house tenants to be evicted after five years; ex-public sector workers to be forced through workfare to do the same jobs they did before but for sub-minimum wages and no contracts or security — *in order* to repay a deficit run up to counter-balance a financial virus created and spread by a conglomerate of glorified embezzlers. No fair or decent society would ever expect such sacrifices of its people. This one does.

There are some small scraps of hope yet for the direction this initially Malthusian coalition might take for the future. There is a new and slightly surprising line of Con-Dem rhetoric related to the 'broadest shoulders' taking the bigger burden with regards the contentious cuts in child benefit for the better off, announced at the Conservative Party conference through the unlikely mouth of George Osborne (a figure not normally known for his sense of social justice). However, even this token Tory nod to social 'fairness' is more a misshapen parody than a genuinely progressive move. In principle, it is a rudimentary left-of-centre posture, albeit abysmally implemented, but one nevertheless that Labour must be extremely careful in how they challenge. Ironically, many on the traditional Left jealously guard the universality of the Welfare State, one of the more obscurantist of Labour's sacred cows, the reasons for which go something like: including the middle classes within the remit of welfare provision helps the Welfare State to cement itself in the broader public consciousness, rather than being perceived and easily ghettoised as a minority issue regarding fringe entitlements for only the poorest in society; such a convoluted Fabian view has been held by all leading Labour figures — most vehemently left-wingers — from the great Bevan himself right up to the new leader Ed Miliband. The cynical interpretation of this argument is that the original planners of the Welfare State did not have sufficient ideological confidence to build and sustain it as a means to alleviating the generational disenfranchisement of the poor of society, but felt it necessary to incentivise the middle classes through offering them some un-needed freebies in order to secure their electoral support for the continuation of the new social system. If this indeed was the strategy, it seemingly was not efficacious in the long-term anyhow; at least, only in the sense that the middle classes continue to support that small section of the Welfare State that gives them a direct 'return' on their taxes, such as universal Child Benefit, while otherwise generally frowning on the more necessary support provided for the unemployed. By appealing to middle-class self-interest, arguably all that was consolidated was a further entrenchment of the very self-centred values that necessitated the invention of a welfare state in the first place; the only difference being that in future there would be a benefit system to compensate for a nation's abject lack of concern for the poor. It would indeed be a weird irony if the original architects of the Welfare State opted for appealing to the self-interest of the middle classes in order to be able to roll out a system of benefits to support the lower classes. But if universality is not so much a cynical tactic as a quixotic wishful projection, it has arguably tended to undermine, even stunt, the essential socialistic purpose of the original welfare state: to gradually level society. Profligate hand-outs to financially self-sufficient middle classes hasn't exactly helped in levelling the hedges, nor in ensuring the financial sustainability of the Welfare state itself.

Whether or not genuinely intended as a nod to a very un-Tory sense of social 'fairness', in practice, the new child benefit cut is a manifestly grotesque contradiction in light of its intransigent and nonsensical clause to gauge claimant eligibility not by household income but by the level of the highest earner's salary, irrespective of whether the other adult of the family is employed. But my own view is that, complicated though it would be in practice no doubt, means-testing still seems, at least hypothetically, the fairest and most common sense approach to welfare provision, and is a principle one could argue is intrinsically socialist, even if historically Labour has championed universality. Where *universality* arguably has more credence is with regards the NHS — since healthcare is by its nature a universal issue; whereas welfare provision, in theory at least, if it is to be a means to an end and not an end in itself, should arguably be geared towards helping lift the poorest up to a comparable quality of life to the better off in society. However, that there should always remain in place a Welfare State, even in a near-ideal society of full employment and broad material and educational equality, is absolutely essential to act as a safety net preventing anyone suddenly made unemployed or struck down by illness — and, indeed, for those who are chronically ill or disabled and thus not able to work indefinitely — from tipping into poverty and homelessness.

But the cross-party debate over the child benefit cuts announcement exposes a flaw on both sides of the political spectrum with regards universality of welfare provision: it seems both the Tories and Labour are at loggerheads not over the fundamental quandary of *universality* itself, since both parties appear to doggedly uphold that ethic, but simply the real-term effects of the Chancellor's markedly clumsy and ill-thought-out implementation of these cuts, as discussed above. The irony here, not to say contradiction, is that by trying to avoid any introduction of means-testing to define the parameters of CB eligibility, the Tories have unwittingly thrown *universality* out with the bath water precisely by such entrenched resistance to means-testing: what they have actually achieved is both an undermining of the principle of universality at the same time as abusing any element of means-testing by introducing a criteria which actually ensures that families who, by dint of joint incomes need CB less, will continue receiving it, while families with only one breadwinner earning over £44,000, whose need is greater, will lose it. The Government, therefore, has managed to impinge negatively on both universality *and* means-testing, thus achieving the worst of both worlds. Yvette Cooper of Labour, however, by attacking this policy on purely middle-class friendly universal grounds, risks achieving only a pyrrhic victory in this contentious debate: it is surely more obvious than ever that the rather quaint notion of universality of welfare provision in a deeply unequal country with one of the widest wealth gaps in Europe, and with imminent and savage cuts that will be hitting the poorest and most vulnerable in society on their way, is rapidly becoming a luxury rather than a necessity (whichever view one takes on *how* to cut the deficit), and that surely now more than ever means-testing seems to be the only fair and sensible method by which to apportion the increasingly depleting and threatened resources of the Welfare State?

Whichever view one takes in this argument, it is yet another nail in the coffin of any hope for a truly socially compassionate British consensus that this week's newspapers have been echoing similar reactionary headlines about this new assault on the middle classes, when relatively under-reported is the far more serious, potentially catastrophic simultaneous announcement of a cap on Housing Benefit and on the overall level of welfare provision any one family can now expect to receive. In spite of some promising signals from a new leader who appears to be the most left-of-centre since the late John Smith, it is a great pity the Labour Opposition is not speaking out more about the oncoming welfare caps rather than giving vent to some of its MPs' own middle-class vested interests. Labour should be the party empathising with and championing the interests of the least well-off in society. Another irony here too is that it is arguably this stubborn allegiance to an unquestionable *universality* of welfare provision that is necessitating such equally universal caps across the board, which will hit the poorest infinitely worse than the middle-class households about to lose their CB (unfair though that is). It also seems a bit rich for the middle classes to bang on about *their* welfare entitlements when probably the majority of them do not really need any state assistance, while on the other hand many of them are quite happy to add their voices to the red-top vitriol against the alleged 'undeserving poor' and near-mythical breed of 'benefit cheats', and to generally stigmatise all those unemployed claimants who are genuinely in need of welfare benefits, as if it is always somehow the fault of a person if they are poor. The middle-class argument is that they 'pay their taxes' so are 'entitled' to state top-ups, even if they don't need them. But what they often forget, or are wilfully ignorant of, is that the majority of the unemployed *do not want to be* unemployed (these days, who on earth would be?) and that, indeed, a large section of them *are* too ill to work — any alleged 'lifestyle choices' dreamt up by Ballentaylor's heir-apparent are made all the more incredible by the abject misery of being unemployed in such a judgemental society as ours, where benefits are given begrudgingly, and recipients are made to feel like social lepers. And as to the highly fictive-sounding stories of unemployed households having enormous rents paid for them through Housing Benefit: the responsibility for this lies with the previous Tory government for its catastrophic repealing of Lloyd-George's vitally progressive 1915 Rent Control Act, back in 1992, which inevitably gave the green light for private landlords to hike up their rents to the obscene levels we witness today. It suits current Tory purposes of course, via the Humpty-Dumpty School of Logic, to blame rising rents *on* rising HB levels, and rising HB levels on the HB claimants themselves (as if *they* are responsible for government policy), who have simply — to coin that chestnut popular among moat-and-duckhouse-compromised MPs — 'played within the rules'.

It is therefore with cautious optimism that *EV* observes the recent apparent triumphalism of right-winger-turned-social-crusader Iain Duncan Smith over the feudalistic fist of the Cut-Ice Chancellor, in his hard-fought proposals to simplify the benefit system into a 'universal credit', and reform it from a punitive to an enabling system (whereby claimants can retain a percentage of their benefits as they move back into work, rather than have practically their entire income stripped from them as soon as they get jobs). However, the sheer scale of such an ambition promises inevitable complications, not to say huge costs, in the face of the oncoming viciously deep cuts; so whether or not IDS can succeed is as yet far from clear. The timing too of this sop to the proles, just prior to the dreaded Comprehensive Spending Review, is ominously tactical: the poorest in society no doubt being softened-up by a probable charade of 'compassionate conservatism' before the inevitable October sting of short-term pain for distant and vague 'gain'. It remains to be seen whether IDS's plans will truly live up to his claim that he will not 'stand on the backs of the poor' in attempting to clean up the economic mess. Meantime, the 'also-rans' of the Coalition held a conference punctuated by some encouragingly — albeit woollily — dissenting voices that orchestrated a City-blasting contrapuntal brass section, distracting us briefly from Cameron and Osborne's hollowly rhetorical woodwinds of war on the unemployed: Fallen Cable seems to have briefly resurfaced as old Saint Vince in his echoing Denis Healey's legendary 1974 pledge to 'squeeze property speculators until the pips squeak', with his own promise to 'shine a harsh light into the murky world of corporate behaviour': a welcome, though incongruous chastisement of unregulated capitalism from a member of an ultra-capitalist Cabinet. It has never been more apt a time to invoke such noble tropes as Healey's. And, since autumn 2010 is the 70th anniversary of the Battle of Britain, it also seems an apt time to respectfully pastiche legendary epithet 'The Few' by Winston Churchill — who was, long before his cigar-toting Tory manifestation, one of the young radicals firebrands, along with Lloyd-George, of the reformist Liberal Party that triumphed over vested interests to bring in the People's Budget of 1909 — substituting the altruism of the RAF servicemen for the opposite example of the City speculators who have plunged this country into recession, and subsequent devastating cuts: *Never, in the field of speculation, has so much been owed, to so many, by so few.*

Alan Morrison
PDWS Co-ordinator, *EV* Editor, *August, 2010*

Acknowledgements

Poetry

Sebastian Barker *The Erotics of God* (Smokestack, 2005); Matthew Bartholomew-Biggs *Tell it Like it Might Be* (Smokestack, 2008); Alan Corkish *The People's Poet Anthology III* (Paula Brown Publishing, 2005); Andy Croft *Comrade Laughter* (Flambard, 2004) and *Sticky* (Flambard, 2009); James Fountain *Glaciation* (Poetry Monthly Press, 2010); Naomi Foyle *Forgive the Rain*, a spoken word collaboration with electronica soundscape artist Richard Miles; Michael Horovitz *A New Waste Land: Timeship Earth at Nillennium* (New Departures/Central Books 2007); Norman Jope *The Book of Bells and Candles* (Waterloo Press, 2009); Judith Kazantzis *Let's Pretend* (1984), *Flame Trees* (1988), *Selected Poems* (1995), Adrian Mitchell's *Red Sky at Night*; David Kessel *O the Windows of the Bookshop Must Be Broken* (Survivors' Press, 2005/10); Paul Lester *Down at the Greasy Spoon Cafe'* (Protean Pubs, 1996), *Going For Broke* (Protean, 2004); Alexis Lykiard *Unholy Empires* (Anarchios Press, 2008); Chris McCabe *The Riever's Stone* (Ettick Forest Press, 2010); Niall McDevitt *b/w* (Waterloo Press, 2009); Nigel Mellor *For The Inquiry — poetry of the dirty war* (Dab Hand Press, 2010); Mario Petrucci *Flowers of Sulphur* (Enitharmon, 2007); Kevin Saving *Miracle & Mirage* (Caparison, 2010); David Swann *The Privilege of Rain* (Waterloo Press, 2009); Julie Whitby *Ambit*; Ken Worpole *Where There's Smoke* (Hackney Writers' Workshop, 1983).

Photographs and illustrations

p2, Tuition Fees protest by James Morrison © 2010; p3, *Les financiers exprimant leur joie* Henri Gerbault © 1863-1930 p4, source unknown; p8, San Francisco Speculators, illustration of A Peep at Washoe © J. Ross Browne, in *Harper's Monthly Magazine*, January 1861; p16, photo adapted with caption: *We're intensely relaxed about people getting filthily poor* by Alan Morrison © 2010; p19, *Three men posing on a pedestal, holding balls that say "Peace with Soudan", "Retrench", and "Reform Socialism"*. Line drawing © Travellers in the Middle East Archive (TIMEA), original source: from: *The Egyptian Red Book*, William Blackwood & Sons: Edinburgh, 1885, p15; p20, Lithograph by Edward W. Clay © *Praises Andrew Jackson for his destroying the Second Bank of the United States with his "Removal Notice" (removal of federal deposits)*; p23, Clement Attlee, Labour Prime Minister 1945-51, source unknown; www.cqout.com; p27, adapted image from a photo of a statue of Aneurin Bevan in Cardiff © 2005 Kaihsu Tai; p28, cartoon of Winston Churchill opposite Aneurin Bevan, early Fifties, source unknown; p35, photo of Peter Sellers as Union Shop Steward Kite from the Boulting Brothers' *I'm All Right Jack* (1959); p36, *America: A Country of Serfs Ruled by Oligarchs* © Paul Craig Roberts; p38, Democracy cartoon, source: http://indiavikalp.blogspot.com/2010/07/supreme-injustice-by-manuwant-choudhary.html; p39, *The War of Wealth* by